NOT WITHOUT A FIGHT

Ramla Ali is a Somali-born, London-raised professional boxer, with an undefeated record of four fights, model and activist. She took up the sport of boxing aged twelve, training and competing in secret from her family for over ten years. Ramla rose to early prominence as the two-time winner of the National Amateur Championships in England and winning the Great British Championships. With over seventy-five amateur fights under her belt, Ramla made history by becoming the first boxer to have won an international gold medal whilst representing the country of Somalia, the first male or female boxer to have competed at an Olympic Games for the country and the first female to turn professional. Ramla is an ambassador with Cartier, Dior, Pantene, Nike and a proud global ambassador for UNICEF.

NOT WITHOUT A FIGHT

10 STEPS TO BECOMING YOUR OWN CHAMPION

RAMLA ALI

with Shannon Mahanty

PENGUIN BOOKS

UK | USA | Canada | Ireland | Australia
India | New Zealand | South Africa

Penguin Books is part of the Penguin Random House group of companies
whose addresses can be found at global.penguinrandomhouse.com

Penguin
Random House
UK

First published by #Merky Books 2021
Published in Penguin Books 2022

001

Typeset by Jouve (UK), Milton Keynes
Printed and bound in Great Britain by Clays Ltd, Elcograf S.p.A.

The authorised representative in the EEA is Penguin Random House Ireland,
Morrison Chambers, 32 Nassau Street, Dublin D02 YH68

A CIP catalogue record for this book is available from the British Library

ISBN: 978-1-529-11877-3

www.greenpenguin.co.uk

Penguin Random House is committed to a sustainable
future for our business, our readers and our planet. This book
is made from Forest Stewardship Council® certified paper.

MIX
Paper from
responsible sources
FSC   FSC® C018179
www.fsc.org

For anyone who has ever felt like they don't fit in, this book is for you. The point is, you're not meant to fit in, you're meant to stand out and be great.

CONTENTS

PROLOGUE

Of all my childhood memories, one stands out the most. I was around eleven years old, walking home from my weekly Quran studies at the local mosque in East Ham, which is where I lived at the time. It was September – the cusp of autumn – but the sky was dark and heavy with rain. I remember walking past the local shops on the high street – the cash and carry and the chemist. The cars on the main road would race through the puddles, sending a gulf of brown water over my shoes and up my ankles. I had walked that route so many times that the previous journeys all seemed to bleed into one; but that day was different. My road, Sibley Grove, was behind East Ham station – and the last five hundred metres of my walk was always filled with commotion, people streaming out the station and passing me by, it was normal. I would work my way through the crowd before turning left onto my road. If someone followed me, I did not think anything of it. On that day, the second I turned onto Sibley Grove, two boys on mountain bikes mounted the pavement in front of me, they braked hard and positioned their bikes to block my path. They did not look that much older than I did; at most, they were in their early teens. They both wore dark and baggy clothing. One of them had the sharpest blue eyes, and slicked-back hair that was damp from the rain, or an excessive amount of hair gel. I was so close to home, I walked on despite them being in my path. When they got off their bikes, my life changed forever.

'Oi!' the boy with the slick hair shouted. 'What are you wearing *that* for?' He pointed at my head, covered by my hijab. I did not connect what he meant with what I was wearing. My hijab was a natural part of my attire when I was young; I wore it every day without really thinking about it. Both boys started laughing, which soon turned into an exaggerated cackling that I knew was aimed at me. Before I had time to respond or move out of his way, the boy with the piercing blue eyes marched right up to me. We locked eyes for what can only have been a few seconds – though in that brief moment, time seemed to stretch and we could have been staring at each other for minutes. His next action happened lightning fast: his hand rose up and he ripped my hijab off my head with one forceful grab. He threw it onto the ground and stamped all over it, laughing loudly, his dirty footprints turning my blue scarf black. I could not understand what was happening. My head was instantly cold and my hair was covering my face, but I was too scared to move it out the way. I was motionless as they walked back to their bikes and rode off, taking a left at Browning Road and cycling away. It was only then that I let myself burst into uncontrollable tears. In all that time, no one else had walked down the street and I consoled myself alone, bending down to pick up my wet hijab from the ground. As I brushed my hair out of my face, I realised I was bleeding. The pin that had been securing my scarf behind my ear had come undone, leaving a stinging pain and a thin trail of blood dripping down my neck. I rubbed at the wound, which only made it worse, and spread a sheer reddish tone across my neck like warpaint. I walked the last few metres home with my other hand covering my eyes – my family and I never talked about our emotions, and I didn't want to let them see me cry. I did not learn the importance of being able to discuss my feelings with others until much later. For a long time, I would bottle all of my problems up and try to face everything alone, and that is exactly what I did that day.

Back then, I was not old enough to understand what racism and Islamophobia were, but I knew I was not strong enough to face those boys on my own again. I gradually stopped wearing my hijab outside of my home. I did not talk to anyone about what happened, and while Mum would occasionally ask me why I was not wearing it, she never pushed me. I would tell her I took it off for a PE lesson and forgot to put it back on, until, eventually, she stopped asking. I realise now that my emotions from that day had slowly turned from shock to pain and a deep sense of otherness. I was young and I knew I came from a different country. Growing up, all I wanted to do was blend in alongside everybody else. That was the day I realised I could not. I was different, and try as I might I would never be able to fit in. While my hijab has always been a source of pride, in the eyes of those boys it was something they did not understand. A combination of fear and ignorance made them see me as an outcast, someone worthy of ridicule. I thought that if I never wore it, I would fit in, and then I wouldn't have been attacked; that they did it because I looked different. School confirmed my suspicions, as it was where I stuck out the most. For one, I was Somali – I did not look like the rest of my classmates who were predominantly South Asian. I was overweight – compared to the thin girls in my year, and I did not have long straight and shiny hair like them either. These popular girls always wore the latest clothes from Topshop and Miss Selfridge, and had boys lining up for them outside the school gates. My family were poor, and could not afford to buy me new clothes. Instead, I mostly wore hand-me-downs from my two older sisters. For a long time growing up, all these things combined to make me feel so sad, small and desperate to fit in. I did not know it then but that horrible day, one of the worst in my memory, would have a positive impact on my life. That moment inspired me to be a fighter.

It would be years before I'd be putting on a pair of boxing gloves and learning how to fight inside the ring. My first unofficial fights started far from the gym: in the many moments in my life where I had to learn to defend myself, be resilient, be patient, and use my silence to my advantage. To stand confidently face to face with an opponent and strategically think about my next move. To transform all the things that made me an outcast into my superpowers. My life has been full of obstacles, but I would not have it any other way, because each of these hurdles has taught me something valuable. In the deepest, darkest moments when I have felt the most scared and alone, those are the times that have shaped me more than anything. Through tears, setbacks and heartbreak, I have learned to keep going, and that is how I became the fighter I am today. It is not easy, but sometimes you have to face your fears and turn your vulnerabilities into your advantages; that is how you learn to be your own champion.

There is no other sport like boxing. It is as much about the mind as it is the body. You have to be as fast as a sprinter, as strong as a weightlifter and as rhythmic as a dancer. You need skill, strength and severe discipline, because if you mess up, your fate could be a lot worse than just losing a fight. You can lose your life in the ring. There is a constant undercurrent of danger; if you drop your focus for even a second, you can end up in a lot of trouble. I have broken my nose, suffered nerve damage in my neck and been concussed twice – but I am one of the lucky ones. You need the combination of both powerful shots and indefatigable mental strength. When you step inside a boxing ring, you have to believe you are enough, because inside the ropes you are truly on your own. There is no team or coach with you; it is just you and your opponent, and that opponent is hurtling towards you with a tightly clenched fist pointed squarely between your eyes. You have a fraction of a second to react. If you are smart and you pull it off, you have the upper hand. You have to be a real tactician. It is not all about aggression; maybe you slip out of her way at the last second and *then* you are ready to land a powerful blow in return, a strong left hook that she never saw coming. However, what happens if you do not react in time? She hits you with so much force you feel yourself stumbling backwards struggling to keep your balance and stay in the fight. She will already be coming back for more but your vision is blurry, your head is throbbing and you cannot think straight. You are vulnerable now. If she hits you again, she could knock you to the ground, or worse. During a fight, you have to understand how to read other people, so that you know exactly what they will bring to it. You can tell a lot about a boxer's personality just from watching them once in the ring. Do they come fully charged and full of anger, or are they strategic and clever? Do they hold back waiting for their opponent to get tired, or do they throw themselves in from the very first second? It is through boxing that I have learned how to understand others, but also how to understand who I am. It has made me both a fighter and a dreamer. I know how to stand up for myself and how to show compassion to others. Through my sport, I have made the kind of friends who lift you up so high you wonder how you ever existed without them, and I've found love too. I met my soulmate through boxing, a man who would become my husband, my coach and the other half of our very unconventional team.

A few years ago, my boxing career finally started to get serious. I had taken a huge risk and made the decision to compete for the country where I was born, Somalia. We had to do everything completely from scratch, but after many stops and starts, people began to pay attention to my career and my story enough to write about me. Suddenly, it was 'Ramla Ali, the Somali refugee who fled war and went on to become the first Muslim woman to win an English boxing title!', 'Ramla Ali: From refugee to Olympian boxer'. I have never shied away from sharing my background, but there is so much more to my story. Before my championship belts and trophies, my modelling career, my brand endorsements, my creation of Somalia's boxing federation, I was just a girl with a dream, one that I was willing to fight for. There have been many fights in my journey, and they have not all been physical. I have had to battle against my own self-doubt and the will of my family. I have been mocked, bullied, kicked out of gyms, and abandoned by coaches when I've had competitions just around the corner. Getting to where I am now has not been easy; every win has been accompanied by a handful of losses. There have been times when I have felt so crushed by an avalanche of doubt and depression that I have wanted to give it all up. There have been times when I *have* given it all up. I am human and I am not without flaws. My own version of my story is a lot darker and messier than what people might have read. I am not just a boxer; I am not just a model or an ex-refugee. I am the sum of so many different parts; I am all of these things. I am an activist, a humanitarian, a daughter of immigrants, a loyal sister and a loving wife. I am a strong woman, and though I am still learning, I am one who is dedicated to fighting injustice at every turn.

I often think about what I would do if I ever met the

boys who assaulted me again. I would love to face them now. I would stand taller, I would not be scared, and in my own way, my defiance and fearlessness would be my fight. On that day, I know those boys wanted me to go away quietly; instead they made me louder. Every person who has ever crossed me or doubted me has given me more power; they have fuelled my fight. I have competed all over the world, and whether I have won or lost, I have learned many lessons along the way. All of those lessons are in this book. This is the story of how I went from being a frightened little girl to a proud young woman over the course of ten of my most important fights. It is a story for the marginalised and the misfits. For anyone who has ever felt hurt, sad, broken or lonely: this book is for you. I am the first to admit that I am still learning, but what I do know for certain is that you can become your own champion.

FIND YOUR FIGHT

*'To be a champion you have to believe in yourself when
no one else will.'*
– Sugar Ray Robinson

My story begins in East Africa, in Mogadishu, the bustling capital of Somalia. I do not have many personal
memories of living there as a child. Any memory I have
has been built from the fleeting fragments of my imagination, and the small collection of family photographs we
still have of the beautiful three-storey house that we
lived in. It had this massive garden full of the brightest
of flowers, and apparently you only had to walk a few
minutes to be at the beach. My parents were merchants
who used to trade in gold and fabrics; they owned a shop
in Mogadishu but they travelled a lot for work too, buying and selling materials across the African continent.
I come from a big family. My sister Faiza, the eldest,
looked after us when our parents were away on business.
My second sister, Luul, is a few years younger than Faiza,
and then there are the boys, my older brothers T and
Abdulkadir, my younger brother Imran, and the youngest, Yahya, who was born after my family left Somalia.
Apart from Yahya, none of us knows our exact age or

when we were born. As a family, we have debated that I must have been born roughly thirty years ago, during the height of the civil war which completely ravaged the country. It's a conflict that's still ongoing now, and one that is thought to have claimed more than half a million lives, making Somalia one of the most dangerous places in the world. My parents had to watch the heartbreaking destruction of the place they loved and called home, the place they'd been raising their family for the majority of their adult lives.

In all the chaos of conflict, people often do not realise how difficult it is for 'simple' things to stay the same. When my siblings and I were born, noting down the exact day, month and year was not exactly a priority for my parents – it was a day-to-day quest just to stay safe. Even official hospital records were hard to come by to verify our ages, following the destruction. For my parents, the war had begun to define and dictate our lives. The air strikes destroyed many local businesses. Gradually, it was becoming more and more dangerous to leave the house. My older siblings had to stop going to school, and my parents had to close their shop. With no money coming in, and food and supplies becoming scarce across the city, it was a difficult time, but things were only about to get worse.

The air strikes in Mogadishu were constant. Whole towns and villages were reduced to rubble in minutes. Places that were full of vitality and life would fall silent, before it began all over again. The noise from the bombs dropping filled my family with fear. Each time they heard the distant rumble, they would gather us all up to take cover in the house. During one particular air strike, my older brother Abdulkadir was in the garden. My mum had told him not to go outside, but he was adamant he wanted to play, and that is exactly what he was doing when out of nowhere he was caught in the blast of a stray grenade. My dad and my uncle were inside the house, and as soon as they heard the blast, they ran outside to find Abdulkadir. He was badly hurt and barely conscious; he could not stand up, so they carried him back to the house. My mum went into shock as soon as she saw him, because his skin had turned a sickly green, a result of the chemicals in the bomb. My dad and my uncle knew they had to get him to the hospital immediately; but the roads were badly damaged following the strike so they placed him in a wheelbarrow and made the journey like that. Along the way, they came across destroyed roads that led to nowhere and blackened burnt-out shells, where tall buildings had once stood. Eventually they arrived at the hospital and handed my brother over. My mum made it to the hospital a little later, leaving Faiza at home to look after us. My mum desperately searched for my dad and uncle but could not find them. Instead, she raced in the direction of the operating theatre looking for Abdulkadir, and when she got there, she peered through the large glass window and saw a young boy being operated on. She called out through the glass to the limp body on the table. A nurse came out and broke the news to her that the boy lying in the operating theatre was not her son. Despite the doctors' and nurses' best efforts, Abdulkadir did not make it. It hurts me to know that at that moment there was nobody to comfort my mum; she must have unknowingly crossed paths with my dad and my uncle on her way in, because they were already halfway back home to give her the dreadful news.

It is strange to tell a story that shaped your family's life so much, but of which you have no direct recollection. It is through my family's will to preserve my brother's memory that I know these exact details, and because his death marked our departure from Somalia. The final days before we fled our home were an intensely traumatic time for my family, the memory of which still haunts them. My mother was laden with grief – she could not sleep, talk or eat – but both my parents knew what could be the fate of their children if they stayed. After some time, my parents made the impossible decision that our family had to leave to survive, and that we would start a new life in England. That was the plan; they had no idea if we would actually make it, but it was time to go.

Mass exodus was happening all over Somalia: families, individuals, everyone was making plans to leave. My parents arranged to get us on a boat headed to Mombasa in Kenya where another one of my uncles was staying. We would stay with him temporarily, until our main trip to England. We packed light, leaving almost everything we owned behind, taking only some clothes and some money. We travelled together as a whole family; my parents were not going to risk leaving anybody behind. A small passenger van took us to Kismayo, a coastal city over three hundred miles from Mogadishu.

Once we were there, we stayed in a coal yard with two other families. We were only meant to stay a few days; however, days soon turned into weeks while we waited for news of the boat that would take us to Kenya, our first stop. I can now see why the coal yard was meant to be a temporary place of rest. It was not at all safe for families, and one night a group of thieves broke in while we were sleeping and stole all our possessions, including all the money that my parents had saved to get us to England. My parents and older siblings were terrified the thieves would come back, and after that, we slept in the local mosque to be safer. My sister Faiza remembers seeing people walking around wearing our stolen clothes, and my brother T had terrible nightmares about the thieves, but we were powerless – there was nothing we could do about it.

When I think about these stories, I realise that fighting is in my family's DNA. The most basic human rights had been taken away from us; food, shelter, safety, things we can easily take for granted. My parents had to fight for our survival. I think a lot about what my mum has gone through. She is so strong; she would have done anything to keep us alive. In Somali culture, family is everything. We did not grow up talking about our emotions, but we have always been incredibly close. My siblings and I have all grown up and moved out now, but every Ramadan, my family and I make sure we break our fast together as one unit. There has always been a level of respect and hierarchy – particularly with the older members of the family. You always respect your elders,

5

even if you do not agree with them; you learn from very early on the importance of empathy.

We are a determined set. I have adopted many of my parents' traits, and I carry their instinct with me naturally, that drive to keep going and to stand up for what you deserve. I have also learned it over the course of my own life. When obstacles are in my way, I am forced to ask myself, is what I want worth fighting for? I've realised that fear and doubt don't always have to be negative emotions; instead, they can provide an opportunity, a chance to walk up to the cliff edge and say, I am choosing to fight for what I want – for myself or for the people I love, for the communities I care about, or simply for my own happiness. Whatever the challenge, the first step is confronting it; the second is choosing to fight.

We stayed over a month in Kismayo, and I do not know how, but my parents managed to borrow the money that would get us all on the boat to Kenya. We'd been promised a big fishing boat to take us across the Indian Ocean, but what came was a tiny sailboat without an engine. There were two hundred people packed onto a vessel made for fifty: we could barely move, and my mum distinctly remembers the size and strength of the waves rocking the boat. To this day, she has never stepped foot on a boat again. The journey lasted seven days. At one point, pirates almost attacked us, but thankfully, our boat managed to escape them. On board, there was nothing to eat and we drank water from dirty containers. My parents' survival mode kicked in again, and they made us all suck sugar cubes to keep up our energy levels and keep us alive. I look back at that time and think we were among the lucky ones. Around us, people were falling ill, and many did not survive the trip, but our family finally made it to Mombasa. We stayed there for a year while my parents worked endlessly to save enough money to get closer to our new home. We slipped into some sort of a routine. While Dad worked, Faiza looked after us and Mum would queue up for hours every day to get aid and food rations from organisations like Unicef. We relied on the generosity of others, and that has always stuck with me. In 2019, I became a Unicef ambassador myself. I visited Za'atari in Jordan, one of the world's biggest refugee camps, and met people queuing up for the same items we'd once queued for: nappies, sanitary towels, clean water. The young girls I spent time with were just like my sisters and me; they had not given up, they were fighters. They wanted an education and a career, they had hobbies and dreams and desires just as we did. Every day I strive to fight for them. It is easy to see traumatic images of people suffering and to feel helpless, but there's so much we can do, whether it is using our platforms to call out injustice, volunteering with organisations or donating to charities that do important work. Boxers come and go; I don't want to be remembered for what I did inside the ring, I want to be remembered for the good things I've done and the messages I've spread outside of the ring. Throughout my life I have depended on others; now I am in a position to be the one giving help, and that responsibility is one I take seriously.

We are lucky that we made it out of Kenya alive, and I am so thankful to everyone who helped us. Life at that time was challenging. My mum would still cry whenever she saw a young boy playing in the street. We lived in a small flat my uncle had found for us. Eventually my parents had enough money to get us all fake Kenyan passports. It was our only chance of moving on.

In November 1992 (I was aged roughly one or two) we landed at Heathrow airport. The second we walked down the airstairs the frigid temperatures shook us to our bones. We were used to winters that averaged twenty-seven degrees in Somalia. London was very different from that. It was freezing, and we arrived with little to nothing. We applied for asylum, citing the risk to life in our home country, and were driven from the airport straight to refugee housing in Paddington, where we stayed until our application was processed and the local council could find us a more permanent accommodation. A stray memory comes back to me from our temporary days in Paddington. Our first home was a basement flat at the bottom of a big grey concrete stairwell. Back in Somalia, we knew our neighbours very well, we all looked out for each other, and despite the political turmoil that seized the country it was otherwise a safe place, which is why my mum often left our front door open. She held on to that custom even in a new country. On the occasions when she would leave the door open, a little boy with platinum-blond hair would creep down the stairwell, push the door of our flat open, pull down his trousers and piss on our welcome mat.

Even if my mum remembered to lock the door, he would stand at the top of the stairwell and urinate directly down to our doorstep.

Luckily, we did not have to stay there for too long. Six months later, we were able to move to a council house in Manor Park, Newham. My family lived on a long street of terraced houses; each one identical to its neighbour, only ours had a cobalt-blue door and a little black gate that used to creak in the wind. The council gave us some money to start our lives and Mum filled the house with brown rugs and suede sofas from the local second-hand furniture shops. Living here was immediately vastly better; our GP, a kind middle-aged man, was at the end of the road, and we had a lovely next-door neighbour called Mr Raj. Mr Raj lived on his own, and every other weekend his three children who were around my age would come to visit him. I loved when they visited because Mr Raj would give all of us ice lollies while we played in the street and it felt like a real treat. We could just about afford to do a food shop to feed ourselves, as we relied solely on my dad's income. So when the time came for my older brothers and sisters to start primary school, Faiza added on a few extra years to my naturalisation papers, so that I could attend reception class and get free school meals along with them. I was excessively young to be in a classroom, and could not speak any English, but I was happy eating pizza and chips and playing with toys.

Slowly my family adjusted to our new life. Each day we would go to school, come home, eat dinner and then go to Quran studies at the local mosque. In all the steps of our journey to England, our family lost something at each turn, from my brother, to our home, to our possessions, but perhaps the most unspoken loss was the sacrifice our parents made to their own ambitions. My dad has always been a genius in my eyes. He is an expert in maths and physics, can speak fluent Italian and has numerous degrees. Like my mum, he instilled in all of us the need to work hard and succeed at school. He was qualified for any major role, however when we came to England, he accepted the first job he found as a construction worker on a building site. Dad just got on with it and never complained, even though I know he missed deeply the bargaining and the bartering that came with his former life as a business owner. He would work long hours and if we caught him after Quran studies, you could tell he was exhausted. My mum adjusted to her new role as a housewife too, ensuring the mechanics of our family life ran smoothly before we were old enough to help out – there were always delicious meals on the table, our school uniforms and hand-me-down clothes were always washed. She channelled her love for us into everything – she desperately wished us to have better futures, and a guaranteed way for this was our education. No matter the subject, getting below a B was a surefire way to annoy her, and she constantly drilled into us the need to excel at school. It is only now that I am older I realise that she pushed us so much because she could not bear the thought of me and my sisters becoming housewives like her. She transferred her fight for a better future for us through her strict approach to education. Growing up on a council estate, it can be hard to imagine anything beyond the concrete jungle that it presents to you. However, it can also be a magical place, full of beautiful and diverse people and families with a burning hope to move beyond their circumstances, parents who want to provide their children with a strong start and encourage them to envision their lives beyond where they are right now. Dreaming beyond our home was more than a dream; it was a path to reality. My parents' determination for us to get good grades, get good jobs and achieve a better life than they could propelled us all forward.

After four years living in Manor Park, we were told the lease on our house was ending and that we would have to move out. The council had found us a home not too far away, and any sadness that we had disappeared when we saw it had a garden. I used to spend hours there playing tag with my brother Imran, or digging around the earth with sticks looking for worms. My older sister Luul and I shared a room in the new home, which she hated and I loved; I would often have nightmares and I used to beg her to let me sleep in her bed. A lot of the time, she said no, but sometimes I could get around her particular brand of tough love, and on those nights when my big sister let me crawl under the duvet with her, I felt invincible. My sisters have always looked out for me, so it was no surprise that they both went on to become nurses: taking care of people is what they do best.

I often think being so young when we moved from

Somalia spared me from a lot of mental turmoil. I consider myself one of the luckier ones of my siblings to have no direct memory of that time. Yet, collectively as a family, we mourned the Somalia we lost. Although I claim London as my hometown, and I love being an East End girl, I have always seen myself as Somali. We were never far from it at home, we ate the food, we spoke the language and we were part of a wider Somali community in London. We were an immigrant family and proud. (Something only a fellow child of the diaspora would know is the strange feeling of sitting on a sofa covered with its original sticky plastic. It is so uncomfortable – especially in the summer – but as Mum used to tell us, sofas are not cheap. I used to love the moment just before guests would come around, when she would whip off the plastic so that everything looked brand-new. It was quite ingenious really.) My mum would constantly remind us of our values, the importance of education, family and hard work. She made sure that we never forgot where we came from and she would always talk about our beautiful culture back home. This is not to say our parents did not want us to be *British* – whatever that is – they wanted us to learn the language and assimilate and, for a while, we even used to play the lottery – to me, the most quintessentially British thing ever – until my mum realised it was a form of gambling and we abruptly stopped.

We were always so grateful to have made it to the UK, but back then, there was a lot of racism directed towards our family. It had become part of my lived experience.

Sometimes, I would be out shopping with my parents and passers-by would roll their eyes or whisper things under their breath. I hated the way people would look at us, and I think that is why Mum worked extra hard to instil in us a sense of pride about where we were from. It was a constant fight. The world we were living in tried to make us feel like being Somali was a bad thing. I so desperately wanted to fit in, but I am my mother's daughter, and I knew deep down I was Ramla Ali, a strong Somali woman born to a family of fighters.

Growing up, we didn't have a grasp on UK immigration law and our actual position in this country, and so when Mum would say things like, 'The British government can send you home whenever they want!' we really believed her, and I think part of her believed it too. It added to the paradox of being British and Somali, and spoke to how unsettled our life in London was. We moved a few times, and as a family, I do not think any of us ever felt we completely belonged in the UK until we eventually got our British passports, ten years after arriving here.

Still, we found our place in this country, and at least for us kids, it became home. By the time I started at secondary school, I was quite shy. I went to Plashet School for Girls, where I developed a deep love of reading. I would pore over the classics and lose myself in imaginary worlds. My favourite book was *Pride and Prejudice* by Jane Austen; the book is as English as you can get, but it reminded me so much of life in a Somali household. Mrs Bennet is always rushing around desperately trying to find her daughter a husband (something I had witnessed my own mother attempt to do for Luul and Faiza), and then the extremely independent Elizabeth Bennet is against the very traditional and patriarchal arrangement. I was like Elizabeth Bennet, not at all interested in boys or dating; I really saw myself in her – that is the power of a great book, you can really envision yourself at the centre of it. I was only convinced otherwise when I watched the film, and realised the trailblazing Elizabeth Bennet looked nothing like me.

We moved one more time to a second-floor flat on a Whitechapel estate called Ashington House, which was an attack on the senses. The school library became my sanctuary, and I often found myself craving its quiet solitude. It was a place for me to go and quietly read when I did not want to be at home. I found secondary school hard because it was clear I did not fit in. I felt so different to all the girls around me. For one, I was not interested in the same things most of my peers were – boys, make-up and nice clothes – and then there was the fact that I looked different to the other girls. My school was in a predominantly South Asian area and most of the students were either Bangladeshi, Indian or Pakistani. I was one of only three Somali girls and I found I was constantly comparing myself to my classmates. If anyone asked me where I was from, I would lie and pretend I had not come here as a refugee. I used to panic and pick a different nationality on the spot, never revealing where I was really from, and then I'd get anxiety from fear of being caught in a lie. It also did not help that ever since I hit puberty, I had been continuously putting on weight. I loved junk food and I used to spend any money I had on snacks at the corner shop: McCoy's crisps, Sour Smarties, Panda Pops. Sometimes I would stop at the chicken shop too and buy £1 chicken and chips, before going home and eating dinner. I did not know anything about nutrition, I never thought about what I was putting into my body, until I became overweight. After a while, I started to hate my appearance so much that I would get dressed in the dark. I wore my uniform baggy so that I would not draw any attention to my body.

When I think back to my school days, I think of an awkward, introverted young girl with zero confidence and cripplingly low self-esteem. I still carry a bit of that young girl with me today. There is no doubt my confidence has grown, but I still get incredibly nervous before a fight and I have always hated any sort of confrontation. I have realised that this is OK. I know that I do not have to be the loudest, bravest, strongest person in the room at all times. Sometimes the best place to be is sitting back, listening and learning. It is good to be the product of many contradicting forces, strong and sensitive, loud and quiet. Today I know when to listen, and when to speak up and fight, but back then I was so scared of the world outside of our flat. At school, I became a target for the meanest girls in the year. They were a cruel group who seemed to get a thrill out of finding innovative and heartless ways to torment me. When a new girl from Sri Lanka who barely spoke any

English joined our school, the bullies decided to pit us against each other in a popularity chart that was left on my desk after lunch one day. My name was written next to hers, and everyone in the class had passed it around after ticking the person they liked the most. When the chart was completed, there were no ticks next to my name. On the occasions where they did not feel brave enough to leave a paper trail, the bullies would just call me names, a constant stream of insults mocking my colour or my size. Looking back, they were a big part of why I felt so uncomfortable in my own skin. You realise it is impossible to feel your best when other people are constantly telling you that you are the worst. It all came to a head in year seven, when my sister Faiza got engaged and my parents threw a big traditional party to celebrate, even hiring a videographer to come and capture it all. The week after the party, everyone gathered around to watch the video together. It was a good time, with everyone laughing, smiling and talking over each other, reminiscing about how fun it had been. I could not connect with the joy in the room; I was the only one sitting in silence, stunned at the version of myself on the screen. Seeing myself from multiple angles really brought home how much weight I'd put on. Instantly a wave of unhappiness came over me, I wanted to disappear from the video, from the room. My mum could sense that something was wrong. I never had the courage to tell her I was being bullied at school – 'bullying' was not understood in my home, or in Somali culture. If I'd told her I was being bullied at school, her quick retort would have been: 'Eh? Why don't you bully them back?' I do not remember explaining to my mum how my body made me feel, but I do remember her buying me a junior membership at the local gym. My mum is strong-willed and very pragmatic; when faced with a problem, she deals with it head-on. She could tell I had put on weight and was unhappy in my body, and so she gave Faiza her bank card and asked her to take me to the gym and get me a membership. It was all done so efficiently, no hugs or pep talks accompanied my joining of the gym, but that one small act of generosity would turn out to be the beginning of a butterfly effect, gradually leading me to the sport that would change my life forever.

I had the key to losing weight, but I had never set foot in a gym before and I was far too scared to navigate that new world alone. Throughout my extremely difficult teenage years, there was one person who always had my back, my best friend Danika, pronounced Da-NEE-ka, because she was a real girl from the ends. Everyone knew who she was, the pretty Grenadian-Jamaican girl in the round-rimmed glasses who wore her hair natural and wasn't afraid to speak her mind. She was small and tough, and though she never started the fights at school – some verbal, some very physical – she often ended up mediating them. Danika was full of heart and empathy; she naturally wanted to stick up for the underdogs. The first time we met, I was attempting to stand up for myself after one of the notorious bullies had picked a fight with me over nothing. Danika saw what was happening, and walked over calmly and instantly stepped in to my defence. She stuck up for everyone. If she saw anyone being bullied, she would never hesitate to get involved. Danika had the back of whoever needed her. She had a way with words, artfully putting phrases and sentences together so that when she was cussing you out, it would really sting; nobody messed with her. I do not know exactly what she said to the other girl when I was being taunted, but she left me alone after that, and Danika and I quickly became friends. Within a few weeks, we were inseparable. We bonded over our mutual love of reading; I do not think many people at school knew but Danika was incredibly bookish. I have never met someone with such an innate curiosity, whether it is for politics, sport or technology. She reads a new book from cover to cover most weeks; she's insatiable.

Danika would often come to my house after school, where she got a front-row seat to seeing just how insecure I was. Whenever I put on a pair of jeans and would comment that my thighs were too fat, she was always there to counter my negative thoughts and shower me with love. 'You wear those jeans, girl!' she would say. 'You wear them and you wear them with pride!' If I felt down about myself, which I did a lot, she would tell me, 'Ramla, you are so beautiful, why don't you believe me? I swear it's true.' Danika knew I needed all the support possible to go to the gym so she signed up too. One day after school, we strolled up to East Ham Leisure Centre arm in arm. I had never seen anything like it, that gym was a new world; loud, smelly and full of people rushing around, who knew exactly what they should be doing. I didn't have a clue what any of the equipment did, but Danika, who loved to exercise, patiently walked me around the big silver and grey clanking machines that looked like torture devices, and pointed out what they would do for me. 'Treadmill for cardio, this one for toning your thighs, that one for the bingo wings.' Danika made it fun, and I learned that fitness, as well reading, was an escape for her. Her own life was not easy. She had been in foster care since she was two, and as a child, she moved from home to home, carer to carer, until she was eighteen and could finally live alone. I think that it is another reason why we gravitated towards each other – we knew how home could be fleeting, and something about our upbringings made us outsiders. What I love about Danika is her resilience. She has always refused to see herself as a victim. She is a fighter, and she uses the trauma of her past to be a protector for herself, her younger siblings, and for me all those years ago. She did not have any role models growing up, so she learned to be her own hero. Of course, she still has bad days, and now that we are older, it is my turn to be there for her. Outside of my family, she was the first great love in my life.

Danika and I would go to the gym all the time. Now we stuck out for another reason – always in tracksuits and leisurewear compared to the swarm of lip-glossed girls with hitched-up skirts around us. Quickly, the leisure centre became our second home. Danika would go the hardest on the treadmill and really shine. She made it look effortless, one stride after the other. She was such a good sprinter that she joined the local athletics club, Newham Beagles running club, where she ended up training alongside Olympic athlete Christine Ohuruogu. I was nowhere near as fit or as athletic as Danika, but after a few weeks of solid attendance, I could feel my body changing. My fitness levels started to improve, my muscles slowly started to push through, and most importantly, my confidence began to grow. That is an important feeling I still get when I train today. Results take a lot of hard work, but I love that achievement of getting a step closer to my goal. Even if you are only at the start of a journey, it is important to stay focused and visualise what's further down the line. I decided to try every class there was. Each one gave me more motivation and the chance to be good at something new, and I was drawn to the challenge they would provide. I had never ridden a bike before so spinning was quite difficult for me, but I gave it a shot and enjoyed it. Boxercise sounded immediately appealing. Around that time, I had had my very first glimpse of boxing when my brother T was watching a fight on television. It was between the British boxer Amir Khan and this Cuban southpaw fighter, Mario Kindelán, and it was like nothing I'd ever seen before. I remember watching the sweat fly off them and thinking how intense it looked. When I saw boxercise advertised, I instantly thought of that fight, and I reasoned that even if I did not enjoy it, at least I'd be working hard.

I did not make it to the first class I signed up to. I was

too scared, the door was closed, and instead of going in, I just peered through the glass window instead. It was completely full; men and women of all ages in the room. I was as intimidated by the really athletic-looking people as I was by the kids half my age; I was frightened of embarrassing myself if I couldn't pick it up fast enough. A week later, I forced myself to go back. Once again, I stared through the glass, but this time, I opened the door and walked sheepishly through a crowd of slender women in colourful skin-tight leggings that matched their brightly coloured sports bras. I looked at my own outfit; a big baggy T-shirt and some out-of-fashion flared tracksuit bottoms. I felt a familiar feeling and heard a voice in my head telling me I was different, that I did not belong in the class, but at the same time, some-thing about it intrigued me. I had come this far and I wanted to try it, so I found a spot near the back and waited for the class to begin. As I looked around, I noticed that everyone was expertly winding long pieces of material down their arms, snaking them in and out through their thumb and fingers and around their wrists. Boxers wear hand wraps to support the small joints and the fragile bones in their hands, and still today, I love the familiar feeling of putting on my favourite pair before a fight. They used to be the brightest of whites, but over the years, they have faded to grey after repeatedly being drenched with sweat and then washed. Putting them on is a ritual; before a fight I love watching as my coach gently wraps them around my hands and wrists. It is a chance to be calm and still; to focus mind and body

21

before you're called into the ring. Of course, back then, I did not have a clue what was going on. Quietly baffled, I stood there alone watching as everyone else set up. Thankfully, the instructor – a sweet woman in her thirties – spotted me gawping in awe at the back, found me a pair of wraps and showed me how to do it. She assured me she was there to help and that comforted me. In a flash, we started the warm-up, and it was the most exhausting five minutes I had ever experienced. I was so new to it all. After years my body is used to intense training, yet every so often with a new exercise I am back to being a novice again. I rarely master things straight away; you can practise something in training and completely forget it the first few times you try it in the ring. When that happens I'm reminded of my younger self, shy but intrigued, approaching it all with caution but a constant desire to learn and improve.

Trying something new can be hard, but the more you practise, the less difficult it becomes, and in turn, the more confident you become. Do not get me wrong, it is not always easy. Sometimes I find training brutal; the early mornings, the long nights, the frustrations when you practise a new skill in the gym but cannot seem to pull it off in a fight. Even Muhammad Ali said, 'I hated every minute of training, but I said, "Don't quit. Suffer now and live the rest of your life as a champion."' It is important to remember the process, the journey. Success does not come without a whole lot of hard work before it. That is a part of your character – your ability to try something new and commit to it. It takes bravery, because you might not be very good at it, but if you never try, you will never know. That class really pushed me to my limits, but I knew I had to be determined if I wanted to get fit. I forced the fear out of mind and focused on the instructor. She made us jump as high as we could, bringing our knees to our chest, then the instant our feet touched the ground, we had to push them behind us and slap our hands on the floor. Everything confined to one minute – and with each set of star jumps, squat jumps and burpees we had to try to improve our count. My breath was strained, and sweat dripped from every pore, but there was no time to recover. We rotated between exercises at lightning speed. The only break we had was when the instructor told everyone to partner up for some pad work; one of you wears boxing gloves, one of you wears pads for the other to hit. I panicked when she came over to me and directed me to an extremely athletic woman. I still felt at odds and wanted desperately to be paired with someone as unfit and new as I was. I knew inexperience and lack of confidence were very much my personal hills to overcome, and I did not want to hold someone back.

The woman I was paired with knew exactly what she was doing. We took it in turns doing simple exercises, she wore the pads first and I hit them, before we swapped over. I remember concentrating so hard, I am sure my partner must have thought I was scowling, but I was focusing on trying to be good. I started to really go for it – putting all the strength I had behind my punches. She was extremely encouraging, giving me advice at every instant and helping me grow in confidence. She told me to take it slowly with my motions until the combinations started to feel more natural, and it worked. We were strangers, but working together made me feel like I was part of this intimate team. I was getting what I wanted – I was dripping with sweat, but what I really loved was feeling like I was learning something. The instructor had taught us the four main types of punches. A jab is a sharp, fast shot; a cross is a more impactful punch that you throw with your dominant hand, a hook is a swinging punch delivered with a bent elbow, and finally, an uppercut: a punch delivered with an upwards motion as if you were trying to strike someone under their chin. In learning those moves, I felt part of something. I was breathless, I had lost my balance a couple of times, and my form was terrible, but I knew something else was happening which outweighed my anxieties and fears; I was having fun. It was exhilarating and exciting, I was hooked and I did not want the class to end. Years later, I would start the Sisters Club, my own boxing classes for women of all backgrounds. Whoever attends, whether they come just for one class or go on to become regulars, I always make sure they feel welcome and wanted, just like I did by the end of my very first class.

Immediately after the session finished, I signed up for another one. The class ran three times a week, but since my junior membership did not allow me to go in the evenings, I started looking for alternative gyms and times. Women's boxing was not very established back then – it was only in 1996 that women were even *allowed* to join boxing clubs – but I managed to find a cheap mixed class close to home in the back room of a red-brick community hall called the Trinity Centre. It was very rough and ready compared to the leisure centre. The paint on the wall was peeling, there was not much space and the boxing gloves we were given to wear in class were torn and smelled as if an animal had died inside them. It was mostly boys, but sporadically a few girls would attend too. None of that bothered me, I was young enough to be fearless in that respect and all I wanted to do was get better at boxing. A big burly white man with a strong East London accent led the classes. He was the stereotypical boxing coach – a brash guy who used to constantly tell stories about the highlights of his career. By his account, he had enjoyed a flourishing professional record and never lost a fight, although everyone seemed to be a little suspicious of his credentials. Junior classes cost 50p, and I attended two sessions a week if I could find the money. Actual boxing was a step-up from boxercise. It was a lot more technical, and this time there were no kind women looking out for me. If I did not grasp something straight away, which I rarely did, I had to fake it until what I was doing eventually resembled what everyone else in the room was doing. I found those first few lessons so difficult; I learned that boxing is not just about hitting – you have to connect your whole body to your punches, you have to defend yourself too. It was a lot to take in. I did not know back then that I had cognitive dyspraxia, a developmental condition that affects movement and coordination. It was only when I started university that a professor suggested I get tested. As soon as I got the diagnosis, it all made sense. I had always been so slow at picking up new movements. Sometimes a coach would say left hook and I would end up doing a right hook. It took me a long time to be able to fight properly, I had to work extra hard on my coordination skills – which are essential in boxing – but I did not give up. People say if you want something bad enough, you will stop at nothing to get there, and I didn't. I really wanted to get better, so I kept working hard. I chipped away at the parts I found hardest, until eventually something clicked.

Another big difference was that boxing classes were simply not as fun as boxercise. In the boxing gym, there was a set routine to it all. The coach would shout you through each drill, while you would rotate around the gym following the sound of his voice and occasionally you would get a go at hitting a punching bag. There was also no music or words of encouragement like I was used to in the leisure centre, but I was committed. I knew I was drawn to the sport because of how it made me feel, but here I was exposed to the competition, intensity and rituals of boxing. At the time, there was a big Traveller community who attended the classes; teenage boys with thick Irish accents and phenomenal boxing skills. Sometimes it would get heated between them and they would break into real fights with each other, but to me they were always so sweet and polite. We did not talk that much, but I loved being around them; it was the first time I had seen people my age actually box. They were not just using their arms; they were twisting their hips and spinning on their legs in the most magical way. When they made contact with a pad or a bag, the force of their whole bodies went into the shots; they even made these shouting noises, it was as if every single cell was involved in that one punch. I dreamed that I could be as good as them one day, but it was hard when the coach didn't pay much attention to me. I think he doubted my ability to stick it out because I was a girl; he certainly paid more attention to the boys. It would have been nice if there had been more of us, maybe he would have taken me more seriously, but I did not waste much time thinking about it; all I knew was that I needed to improve, with or without his help. I started watching videos online during IT classes. I would search for 'basics of boxing' and discover all these exercises to help you get your technique right. I learned that if you want to make sure your elbows are straight during a left jab, you can prac-tise against a wall. You stand at a point where your fist just brushes the wall and that gets you used to the feel-ing of having your arm fully extended. My homework started to pay off, and gradually, my technique got better and better. The act of studying is not always fun, but it is important. The more experienced you get at some-thing, the more vital it is to have a solid foundation, to make sure you have really nailed the basics. If you have not built up good balance or quick reactions, you do not stand a chance in the ring. I gained more confidence with each new drill I taught myself, and soon that started to influence my life outside of the gym. I was not afraid to show my new sense of self at school, and now if someone teased me, or talked down to me, I told them to back off. For the first time in my life, I felt strong and powerful.

Despite my growing confidence, there was one thing that instilled fear in me: telling my family. My mum gave me the gym membership to exercise, but I knew if I told her I had started boxing she would consider it haram – forbidden by Islamic law – and would not want me to continue. She would think about the sparse uniform – the short shorts and the vest that exposes your arms – and immediately dismiss me. Between us, we have always had very different interpretations of our faith, and there are many things where we do not see eye to eye. I have always prided myself on dressing modestly, even to this day, but I knew my mum's definition of modesty would be much more conservative than my own. I did not tell her or confide in anyone apart from Danika. We all have secrets we keep at the risk of hurting someone, they are not ideal but they are out of love. I knew it would hurt my mum if she discovered the truth, but it would have hurt me just as much to quit. By keeping it quiet, we were both able to maintain our happiness. I continued to train in secret for another thirteen years before my family found out; it would be even longer before they eventually accepted it and became proud of the athlete I was.

After a few years of attending Trinity, I found out they were going to shut the centre down. I was not surprised as over the years I had lived in London, I had seen the unfortunate closures of a lot of youth clubs and children's centres all around me. However, when Trinity closed, I was heartbroken at experiencing that loss of a safe space first-hand. Being young without money or a designated place to go to outside of school and home is hard. Those spaces are important, we all need an outlet from time to time; somewhere you can get away from the stresses of school and family politics. More than that, once you find the thing you love to do in life, it is important to maintain it. Instantly for me it was boxing; for my dad it is going on long walks in new cities, and for Danika it was understanding different cultures and communities through reading and learning. It does not have to be anything ground-breaking, but passions are what make a life feel full. When we first moved to London, my mum signed up for knitting classes, and it is how she made some of her first friends in this country, and where she learned to speak Basic English. Boxing was still new to me but it was special, and I knew I could not let it go. People come to things they love in all sorts of ways. I discovered my passion almost by accident. I don't recall watching women's boxing on TV, and a lot of the women boxers I've met along the way got into the sport because their dads or brothers used to do it. For me to discover boxing, I had to try it. I had to throw myself in and not be scared of failure, and that is why I vowed to carry on; when the centre finally shut its doors, I knew my journey was not finished.

I found a new gym not too far from home, and I

walked in determined to keep fighting. It stank of sweat, feet and Tiger Balm, because as well as boxing, they also taught Muay Thai and kickboxing, and the kickboxers would rub the ointment all over themselves and fight without shoes on. It was a bigger space than I was used to, packed full of people, and you could barely see the gym floor. It was loud and chaotic, but an organised kind of chaos that comes from a room of disciplined fighters who are full of energy. I attended the beginners Muay Thai classes because they were earlier than the boxing classes and I did not want my parents to be suspicious if I came home too late. Suddenly, I did not just have to hit my partner's pads, but was expected to kick them too. There were so many differences: the stances, the rhythm, the fact that your partner was trying to kick you in the face! I relished the challenge and the new chapter. Since I had been doing junior boxing classes for a few years, the coach could tell I was familiar with boxing after watching me do some partner work. After a few sessions, he asked how many fights I'd had. I looked at him confused, before realising he was asking me if I had ever competed before. He was surprised when I said none, and encouraged me to start sparring and to think about competing seriously. I did not need to think. I loved boxing, I was passionate about it, and if this was the next step I had to take to improve, I knew I had to do it. I wanted to progress, and so I was instantly excited, if a bit nervous too; sparring is the first time you are hitting and being hit by a real person, rather than a pad or a bag. That afternoon I went straight to Sports Direct and bought the cheapest gum shield I could find. It was a horrible fluorescent yellow piece of plastic that barely fit into my mouth, but I did not care. That night when everyone was in bed I tried it on in the bathroom, and I grinned a big yellow smile staring at my strange reflection in the mirror. I could not wait to get in the ring.

Sparring is the most important form of training. Think of it like a driving lesson. You are driving a real car. You are the one controlling it, and in the process, you are getting to test out what you have learned, alongside other more seasoned drivers. Sparring is not a real fight, but it is the first time you step inside the ring, and is the moment you get to test all of the practical boxing skills you have been learning against a real, live opponent. Everything you have done before in class – all that work hitting the bags, the pads, learning the combinations and the drills – it finally comes to life. The first time I sparred, I felt like I had entered a new dimension. I cannot remember the name of the girl the coach had found for me, but she was quite a few years older, a university student preparing for the British Universities Championships tournament, so she was good. In fact, she was really good. She zipped around me like a mosquito and I found it next to impossible to land any punches, especially when I also had to think about how to avoid hers, which were already raining down on me. I was spinning around trying to read her next move, but it just was not happening. I was being hit again and again and again. I knew she was not doing it as hard as she could because it was my first time, but I was bombarded by her punches and it felt like they were coming from every angle. I was desperate to get her back, just once, but I couldn't. It was a disorientating experience; I tried to listen to my coach and plan my next move as I had been taught. In my head, I was willing myself to get her, but in reality, I had forgotten everything I had learned, and I was flailing around making a total mess of it all. I started to feel embarrassed; I wondered when it would end. My thoughts were so frantic that I completely stopped listening to my coach who was barking instructions at me to 'Slip! Duck! Move your head!' Being in the ring is so different to being out on the gym floor. You have stepped inside a raised 20ft square, but it feels like you have also stepped into a new world. Time slows down and you become a different person inside the ropes. It is primal, if you do not hit then you will be hit. I realised that day that anyone can look good on the pads, but when you are sparring or competing in a fight, it is a completely different ball game. Nothing prepares you for that feeling of being punched. I was completely defeated and once I started getting inside my head, I had no chance of bringing it back.

We all get lost in our own unhelpful thoughts from time to time. Overwhelmed by a situation, it is so easy for negative thoughts and feelings of doubt to detract us from our goals. Drowning them out and staying focused is incredibly difficult. It still happens to me now; I often come out of sparring sessions feeling disappointed. My coach might ask me to work on my counter-attack and I will struggle to pull it off and feel like I am not good enough. I work with a sports psychologist who has helped me a lot. He will tell me that inside everyone is a little child, the younger version of yourself, and one who deserves to be happy; it is your job to make them proud. I try to remember that young Ramla when I struggle in training. Instead of seeing a session as a failure, I see it as an opportunity to learn, a chance to get better, and I come back for more. That is exactly what I did after that first session. I got back in the ring again, and when I did not listen to my coach, he turned his attention to the other girl and focused on her instead, saying, 'Ramla isn't listening to me, keep doing what you're doing because she will eventually learn. If she doesn't move her head, getting hit is going to make her move her head.' He was right. Often, the clearest instruction is the hardest to hear. My coach was willing me to win, giving me the tools I needed to beat this girl but the lesson was not sinking in. Sometimes we can be so focused on our own internal goal that we forget all the knowledge we have. In boxing, you do not just 'win' a fight. It takes a lot of training, you have to make sure you have both the physical and the mental strength to beat your opponent, and you absolutely have to listen to what your coach says, because they are the ones who know how you can succeed. In that moment, I learned to not let my personal doubt and my inner voice drown out my intention; I learned that when someone is telling you to move your head – you move it.

For a long time, I was really disappointed with myself. I kept thinking that I had finally found something I had fallen in love with, but I was rubbish at it – all because I had performed badly in a few sparring sessions. I have lost many fights in my career, and each of them made me feel sad, bitter, angry, but what they also did is inspire me to keep competing. The frustration is what keeps me going. It is the want to get better – the need to get better – that pushes me on. I have seen countless people spar for the first time, receive a few heavy punches, and think that's it, boxing is not for me, but I knew it *was* for me. Losing that sparring session was a defining moment for me. I didn't want to be known as a sore loser. That determination to go back for more was everything; I wanted to show my opponent that she had not beaten me. I wanted to show everyone I was not broken. The next sessions were not easy, and again I struggled, but after the third and fourth, eventually something clicked. Having sparred with that same girl so many times, I started to understand the way she fought. Finally, I managed to catch her off guard and land a few of my own punches. I started to anticipate when she was going to hit me and before her arm had even moved a centimetre towards me, I would instinctively slip, ducking forward and avoiding the impact. Then, making the most of her confusion, I would jump towards her with my own attack. Finally, I was successfully landing shots! The two of us were flying round the ring, high with adrenaline, fierce and fearless as we lurched towards each other. After all the times I had been getting it wrong, suddenly the tables were turning. No longer was I being dominated, we were fighting and we were equally matched. I felt like I was pulling off a dance routine that I had been practising for weeks. The aggression and the attack is just one element of boxing, but being able to slip or sidestep away from an incoming punch is equally important and there is something so graceful about the movement that comes with sparring. I did not want that session to ever end. Now I'd finally learned how to spar, I was so scared that if I stopped I'd never be able to do it again, that I'd lose that feeling forever, but sure enough our coaches soon signalled that it was time to cool down, and I threw myself against the ropes in elated exhaustion.

When I think about that day, I realise it was the first time that so many defining moments of my life were coming together. Years earlier I had discovered what made me happy. In wanting to change my body and feel better about myself, I had stumbled upon a passion that did so much more than help me lose weight. Boxing made me feel free. It taught me about confidence and perseverance, and it gave me a new focus, driving my attention away from the things that were upsetting me. I had found this incredible outlet that required so much of me, but also gave so much to me. I quickly learned that you could not succeed at boxing if your mind is elsewhere. You have to give it one hundred per cent of your concentration. To become a fighter, I had to leave all of my worries, my insecurities and my self-doubt outside of the ring, because if I brought them in with me, I did not stand a chance of winning.

I have noticed that time seems to move much more slowly when you are young. When I was unhappy at school, I desperately wanted to be an adult so I could leave the bullies behind and shape my own destiny. I thought that if I could just finish school, my problems would magically disappear, but rarely is life that simple. What I know now, what I did not know then, is that my issues did not start and end with those bullies. They may have exacerbated the way I was feeling, but I already had such low self-esteem, and that is not something you can fix overnight.

Gaining confidence takes time. It took my parents many years to feel at home in a new country. That sense of not fully belonging to the place you are living in also affected my siblings and me. We were a completely new generation who still needed time to connect those two ideas of home. I did not really start to feel confident in myself until my early twenties. It took a long while for me to discover my passion for boxing, and then even more time to perfect my skills and become good at it; it wasn't until three gyms and one sparring session later that my sport finally started to make sense to me, but it was worth it.

Your biggest opponent can often be yourself, your own inner voice telling you you're not good enough or you don't belong somewhere or you're about to embarrass yourself. That voice probably will not ever fully disappear – mine definitely has not – but do not be afraid to stand up to it. Do not let fear hold you back. Try things that you are interested in: dancing, painting, writing, bookbinding, performing, candle-making, climbing! Once you really love something, as I fell in love with boxing, you will learn to fight for it and do everything in your power to keep that nagging sense of self-doubt away. And once you have managed to defeat the negative thoughts a few times, you will realise that your growing confidence can easily overpower your fears, and that the love you put into it will always win.

ROUND ONE

Understand your trauma

We all go through hard times in life. Sometimes we want to block out these difficult experiences and pretend they never happened, but trauma can inform the person we become. I used to feel ashamed to admit I was a refugee, because it made me feel different to everyone else, but once I acknowledged exactly how much suffering my family went through, I realised it is what shaped us all into the fighters we have become today.

Give back

We all have goals and ambitions, but it is important to raise up the people around us too, especially if those people do not have a voice. When I was young, my family and I relied on the support and kindness of others to survive. The work I do with Unicef, Coach's 'Dream It Real' initiative, the Choose Love fund and other NGOs is to repay the generosity that so many people showed me. Try to support others in any way you can. From volunteering to fundraising, mentoring to simply checking in on your loved ones, there really are many ways to give back.

Discover your passions

I believe that everybody has at least one passion. It does not have to become your career, it could be a hobby or an interest, or maybe it is a way to make friends or relax. Whatever yours might be, make sure you look for it. Let your curiosity lead you, and do not be afraid to try new things. When you have found something you love, keep doing it! Work at it, and be open to failing; we should not fear failure, as ultimately it is what makes us stronger.

Learn how to listen

Accepting advice and criticism from others is a huge part of working hard. Surround yourself with trusted people who are going to uplift and support you. You may not agree with them every single time, but remember they have your best interests at heart, so try to take on their feedback.

Leave your comfort zone

I loved boxing from the very first time I tried on a glove, but it was not always plain sailing. There were times I felt I was not good enough to carry on, times when I thought I did not belong in the ring, but I forced myself to keep going. Do not be afraid to take risks. In my experience, the road to success is long, windy and full of traffic, but anything worth having is worth fighting for.

CONFIDENCE WILL CARRY
YOU FORWARD

*'The fight is won or lost far away from witnesses – behind
the lines, in the gym, and out there on the road, long
before I dance under those lights.'*
– Muhammad Ali

We all have to fight at some point in our lives. Sometimes when you're backed into a corner and you have
had enough, you simply *have* to. It is part of standing up
for ourselves and for others when faced with injustice;
often it is seen as negative, but fighting is a crucial skill.
Competing in the ring taught me a lot about fighting the
battles in my life that were not physical. I realised it takes
a massive amount of confidence, and sometimes that
doesn't come naturally to people. It certainly wasn't natural to me, but my confidence grew rapidly once I knew
I could defend myself, and once I felt like I had found
something to pour my energy into. One of the most
important things I learned during my first weeks at my
new gym was to believe in yourself, never show weakness and display confidence at all times. The coaches
drilled it into us as a vital formula for being a winner.
Even before you enter the ring, you are looking for signs
of confidence and weakness in your opponent. What is

the character of this fighter? Do they believe in themselves? Can you see fear in their eyes? Will they be strategic, or are they an aggressor who prioritises force over thinking about their tactics? One of the things I love about boxing is that I am constantly learning how to read people. For example, I can tell if someone is tired; it is in their face, their breathing. You have to use these moments to your advantage, to really go for it, because you know they will not be able to keep up. If someone starts dropping their hands because it's too tiring for them to hold them up and defend themselves, or if they start throwing lazy shots, that's when I know I can win. Even if you are feeling fatigued, you have to maintain your confident composure, keep going and don't let your opponent know. Fake it till you make it.

Learning about boxing became addictive. When I was not in the ring sparring, I was reading about boxing, or watching fights online. I remember watching *Shadow Boxers*, a documentary about a Dutch boxer called Lucia Rijker, and becoming completely obsessed with her; she was so strong and fierce. I read somewhere that she landed so many knockouts that the press used to call her 'The Most Dangerous Woman in the World'. In the beginning it was always a struggle to find women fighters to look up to, but as I kept digging I realised we existed. Being a woman fighter is hard. You are constantly being judged from every corner; I used to get all sorts of looks and whispers from men in the gym who did not think women belonged there. When I was starting out, there were so few of us in the sport, especially women who looked like me, that it made me wonder if they had a point. However, the fact I had found something I loved, and could not imagine being without it, told me that I did belong. The better I got at boxing, the more my confidence grew. Men could look all they wanted; I was not going anywhere.

I had grown physically and mentally stronger by then. I trained regularly and ate healthily. I was a lot fitter, and that had a huge impact on my self-esteem. The bullies at school had stopped picking on me; perhaps they could sense my new-found confidence. I was looking forward to the next chapter in my life. By the time I'd finished sixth form and started university (I went to SOAS and studied law), I was spending a lot more time at the boxing gym, training and working there as a part-time receptionist. I knew all my sparring led up to a fight, and I was eager to have my first bout. Working there was another way for me to immerse myself in boxing, and once I had made sure the place was tidy and collected everyone's money at the start of each session, I would steal a minute to sneak away from reception and watch the experienced fighters work. That was like stepping into Narnia. I loved watching the best boxers while they sparred. In those sessions, they moved like ballerinas, mirroring each other's movements and reading the other person's rhythms. I was in awe of the way they seemed to be able to simultaneously attack and defend at the same time, reacting to their partners' moves as well as planning their own.

Since the gym was often empty in between classes, one of the coaches would offer to train me while we waited for the next group to arrive. I loved these lessons. We were working one-on-one, so I was getting advice tailored to me for the first time. He would watch me while I did various drills, pointing out any bad habits and showing me the areas where I needed to improve. His tuition helped me a lot, I could feel myself getting better and it felt addictive. I started spending more and more time at the gym, showing up early for a shift or hanging around after work to see if he would have a free interval to train me.

For a while I could not believe my luck, this man was giving up his time to help me, and I was getting to train while I worked. I was so grateful to him that when I noticed he had started to behave differently around me, I forced myself to ignore it. I did not want our set-up to change, but gradually, he started to make me feel uncomfortable. It began with unwanted touching. We would be doing pull-ups – an exercise where you reach your arms up, grab the pull-up bar and use your upper body strength to lift you up above it. I had not had a proper introduction to weights and how to use them, and my arms were not strong enough, so I found pull-ups near impossible to do without support. To help me get up on the bar, he would place his hands on my bum, and hoist me up. The first time it happened, I immediately felt uncomfortable. I knew it was inappropriate but I silenced the voice in my head. I told myself what he was doing was normal and that I was being overly sensitive. It was only when I started to notice how other trainers would support you from your ankles that I realised he knew exactly what he was doing. He was not helping me, he was *groping* me, and I let him; I felt completely powerless. A separate time we had a disagreement he started to chide me as if I was a child. 'Ramla,' he said, 'you've been really naughty, you know you've been a bad girl, so now I have to punish you.' He was a strong man, and before I had time to respond, he grabbed me, sat down and put me over his legs like a child. When I shouted at him to get off, he started spanking me. It was horrible. Never before had I felt so disgusted and humiliated.

Sadly, I do not think I know a single woman who has not experienced sexual harassment or assault in one form or other, but until that day, I had never understood why victims so often place the blame on themselves. A moment like that can strip you of your voice but also your confidence, and that is exactly what happened. I convinced myself that I must have led him on, that somehow I must have flirted with him or implied I wanted him to behave the way he did, and that it was 'my fault'. I convinced myself I had been the one in the wrong, and that he was acting off the signals I gave out. I knew that particular coach had a reputation for liking younger women, but as I have grown older, I have realised that his actions should never have been written off with these kinds of euphemisms. He was the perpetrator; he had abused his power, and he had taken advantage of me. It has taken a long time for me to be able to label the situation for what it was, but I take power in being able to say it now – the man was a predator who sexually assaulted me. He used his power as a coach to take advantage of young women, and I was one of them. I hate to think how many more victims are out there. It took many years for me to realise the blame lies solely with him. I had never been intimate with a man before, and that particular day scared me and scarred me for a long time. I know far too many people who have had similar experiences, and I think after years of giving advice I slowly start to hear it – and believe it – for myself. When I think back to that day, I feel anger and sadness for that young girl, but I no longer feel the shame that engulfed my teenage years.

There was one other person I had chosen to confide in, a woman who used to attend many of the same classes as me. I did not know her that well, but since she was a few years older, I decided I could trust her. When I told her what had happened, she looked at me in disbelief. 'He did the same thing to me,' she said, shaking her head. In that moment I felt a strong sense of solidarity as she recounted all the times he had acted inappropriately with her. I knew I was not alone in this anymore, and I took some relief in that, but what happened next, I did not see coming.

At my next class with the coach, and in the middle of a drill, she started to talk to me about the incident, loud enough for the rest of the class to hear. I pleaded with her to be quiet. 'Stop talking during training!' echoed the coach; but she just flashed me a look before blurting out, 'Oh, sorry, Ramla was just telling me about how much you like younger girls.' I had no response; I was completely in shock and did not know what to say. I felt my face burning. He rolled his eyes and laughed it off as a joke, then continued to finish the class as if nothing had happened, though he was careful to avoid eye contact with either of us for the rest of the session.

I have thought a lot about why she did it. Maybe she thought she needed to address what had been going on, or maybe his attention had made her feel special in some way, and she was hurt to find out she was not the only recipient of his advances. Whatever her reasons, we did not speak after that. I was angry with her for bringing it up, and I felt humiliated and used by them both. We were both victims of the coach's advances; not only had he abused his position of authority, he had turned us against each other in the process. I know I should have acted with more compassion, given her the benefit of the doubt, and viewed her speaking up as a good thing for the both of us, but I was annoyed that she had betrayed me by saying something. She walked away after the class, I stayed at work, and I did not get to leave. I hated confrontation, and I still do. Experiencing bullying as a young child will have that effect on you.

For the rest of my shift I tried to keep my head down, working my way around the space, spraying disinfectant into gloves and putting weights back onto their stands. I was on reception cashing up when I saw the coach making a beeline for me. I prayed that he would change direction but he kept walking towards me until the reception desk was the only thing that separated us. He leaned forward and looked me straight in the eye, called me a liar and hissed at me to leave. I was silent as he accused me of lying and attention-seeking. Now, looking back, I wish I had had the strength to call him out for his behaviour, but I know he never would have admitted he'd done anything wrong. When he finished belittling me, he stormed off, slamming the door on his way out. I quietly packed up my things, knowing I would never come back. I was sad to be leaving but it was my only option. It was time to move on, and I was determined to find a safer community.

I wasted no time in resuming my training. I still had a desire to compete and I could not afford to delay it any longer. The same week I left, I turned up at another gym called Double Jab that a friend had recommended to me. Double Jab gym was a small, unassuming building in Forest Hill, with a brick interior painted over in white. The gym walls were covered in pictures of all the club's amateur boxers mid-fight, frozen in sequence. In each shot, you could see the determination on their faces. The first time I walked inside, accompanied by my friend, we walked into a human wall of people shadow-boxing around each other and on the raised platform of the ring at the back of the room, weaving through the tight space and narrowly missing each other. Getting through the crowd of fighters without being hit was no easy feat. Some boxing gyms can be intimidating places to the uninitiated, especially for women who are still a minority in many such spaces. Double Jab was very male-dominated and being a few years older and a lot more self-aware, I really noticed it this time. Being with a friend helped a lot, I felt like I stood out less because we were together, and what overwhelmed me more than the lack of women was just the sheer chaos of it all. I have been to enough boxing gyms in my career to date to understand that, often, adults are left to their own devices, but back then I was shocked by the lack of structure. I was used to being told what to do in classes or in one-to-one training with a coach. Here, there was nobody leading, everyone was just doing whatever he or she wanted. I wanted to learn, and this new environment did not instantly provide that. With no session to join and no coach to guide me, I asked my friend if I could stick with her that day. We trained together, skipping, shadow-boxing, and we did a few rounds on the bag too. I still craved the structure I'd had before, but by my next session, alone this time, I realised that training independently has its benefits too.

Boxing is actually quite a lonely sport. You work with other people but once you get inside the ring, it is just you and your opponent. If anything bad happens, you are the one who is going to have to take the fall; independence and comfort in your own company is a lesson you need to learn early on. Working alone is also how you really learn to fight. Instead of following instructions or reacting to a partner, you have to really focus on yourself and discover what makes *you* a good fighter. I spent a lot of time shadow-boxing – where you fight an invisible opponent – and it can be easy to feel self-conscious doing it when you are still new to the sport. I had to block out everyone else there and not let myself get distracted. It was worth it; in those first few weeks, I began to discover my own boxing style. I realised that I am more of a counter-boxer; rather than being the person to lead, I bide my time and wait to capitalise on someone else's mistake. Boxing is a bit like a chess match in that way; you have to analyse your opponent's move before you can make your own: being smart is just as important as being strong. Still, there was only so much I could do on my own, and eager to improve, I quickly started sparring. Since there were not many women, most of my sparring partners tended to be men. I knew there were people in the gym who didn't approve of me getting in the ring to fight with a man, but I had no other option and I told people that all the time. There was not a coordinated effort from the owners to attract women to the sport, let alone the gym. Therefore, I fought whoever was available because I had to improve. I did not mind boxing with men. I never felt scared in the ring because there was always a coach on side to stop anything, but it did prove to be difficult. Most of the men were heavier than I was; I was around 59/60kg, and there was one incident when I was sparring a man who must have been around 72kg. He hit me with a body shot with so much force that it took the air out of me, and I fell straight to the ground reeling in pain. It was an accident; my sparring partner was not used to practising with someone so much lighter. I could have stayed down on the mat and told the coaches I was out, but out of pride and a borderline obsessive determination to show them all that women did belong in their gym, I got up as quickly as I could, reassured them I was OK and told gathering onlookers, 'Let's carry on.' While I was desperate to prove myself, my coach did not see it the same way. He told me to be careful, to look after myself because it could be dangerous to fight someone that much bigger. 'You may be keen to spar,' he warned me, 'but you need to be safe too.' Blind confidence could have ended up in injury, destroying my chances of competing.

Sparring with men was a means to an end; however, if I was to ever compete officially, I needed to spar with other girls in my weight category. I used to drive to different gyms across the capital with my new coach, Richard, to find more women like me willing to spar. I remember the Lynn AC Boxing Club hosted a female-only training session for women from boxing clubs all over London, and it felt so special to be a part of that. It was exciting to finally meet the kind of women I would eventually be competing against. My joy in their presence was brief; we never talked much beyond exchanging quick and polite greetings. We were there to fight, but it gave me so much confidence to know that I was not the only girl in a very male-dominated sport; and I had just as much right to be a part of it as they did. They belonged in the ring, and so did I. Even though we were little more than strangers, seeing those women filled me with hope. Compared to all the male fighters I had watched, they seemed so much smarter and slicker. Rather than just hammering at their opponents, they prioritised speed and agility over sheer force, and it was mesmerising to witness. Still to this day, I believe that women make the most creative fighters.

My time at Double Jab amounted to just under a year before I learned that the gym would be closing. Richard found a job at a gym called Palmers in Bellingham, so I agreed to start training there too. It was far from ideal, Bellingham was over an hour and half away from my home in Whitechapel. It was sparse, small and had hardly any equipment, and somehow even in the summer, it always seemed to be freezing. It was at Palmers that I met Ricardo, Richard's twin brother. One evening when Richard had not shown up to training, Ricardo introduced himself. He had heard about me from Richard, and asked if I wanted to do some pad work with him. I enthusiastically agreed. Though they looked similar, Ricardo could not have been more different from his brother; he was much louder and more abrasive, and never afraid to speak his mind. It was refreshing to be working with someone so vocal, and from that very first pad session, I immediately knew that this man was a better fit for me than his brother. Ricardo was a lot more technical – 'You've got to turn your hips more'; 'Make sure your hands are landing at the right angle'; and, 'Ramla, it's so important you keep those hands up and protect yourself' – and it was the advice that I had been craving. He corrected my mistakes and he pushed me to do better; he was not afraid to criticise me, he was exactly what I needed in a coach. In order to get better at something, you have to learn to trust others and listen to the advice you are being given. I accepted that I still had a lot to learn, and even though sometimes his comments frustrated me, I knew they would help me in the end. It did not take much persuasion to get Ricardo to take over as my new coach, and if Richard was unhappy about it – which I later found out he was – thankfully, he did not make it too obvious. I know I should have addressed it with him properly, but I also knew Ricardo was my ticket to competing. He was an amazing trainer and he saw my potential; he helped me to see it too. When you have a goal, it is important to let other people in to support you and to hold you accountable. He believed in me, and we soon became close friends.

Ricardo was the one other person I trusted to keep my secret, along with Danika. He understood what a burden hiding boxing from my family was becoming and so he came up with an accommodating training schedule that did not keep me away from home too long in the evenings. Increasingly, my mum had started questioning why I was home late, and if I caught an injury whilst sparring, I had to hide it from my family at all costs so as not to further raise suspicion. The lying was wearing me down. I felt awful not being able to come clean to my family, and not being honest with them went against everything that I stood for. I felt like I was living two separate lives; in one, I was a good Muslim daughter. I worked hard, helped around the house and desired the same things my parents wanted for me: a good job, a suitable partner and, one day, a family of my own. Then there was my secret life: Ramla the boxer who didn't care about her career or finding a partner, Ramla who could barely tear herself away from the gym. As my confidence grew, I found myself dreaming of entering competitions and travelling around the country to fight.

I had no idea how I could ever reconcile these two different paths. Ricardo and I would discuss it for hours; him suggesting I tell my parents what was going on or move out to gain independence, and me letting him know that when it came to my family it just was not that simple. I was not ready to tell them. It was an impossible situation; I knew the second my mum found out about my boxing, she would force me to give it up. I would lie in bed keeping myself awake thinking about it, and during one of these sleepless nights I realised my mum and I shared a strange solidarity. I was not the only one living two lives: when she left her beloved Somalia, she kept a piece of it with her to survive. We had moved to London, we even became British citizens, but once you stepped inside our front door you were in Mogadishu. It was the place she had grown up and she refused to let the memories fade. Us kids still got to experience Somalia. It was in the beautiful language my family spoke, the sounds of the Somali soaps on the TV, the smell of my mum's cooking. She did not sacrifice Somalia; she brought it with her into her new life. One day, maybe, I hoped I would be able to do that with boxing. I knew I couldn't give it up.

The more advanced I got, the bigger my secret grew. Ricardo and I had only been working together a few months, but under his training, I had become a competition-ready fighter. The work was serious; we met several times a week and when we were not together, he would give me a training to-do list: running for my cardio and stamina, weights and gym routines to improve my strength. In our sessions he taught me how to nail the most difficult combinations. I was at my peak fitness and peak confidence. In sparring sessions, I was often coming out victorious. Then one day he sat me down, and said, 'Listen, Ramla, I'm going to enter you into the National Championships because I know you're good enough, what do you think?' I thought he was crazy. I may have been desperate to compete, but the Amateur Boxing Association of England (ABAE) National Championships (now known as England Boxing National Amateur Championships) are one of the biggest and most prestigious competitions in British boxing, with fighters flocking from all over the country to take part. Past winners have gone on to become boxing legends; we are talking about Nicola Adams and Tyson Fury here. I could not believe this was where I was going to make my boxing debut, with no previous competitive boxing experience under my belt. Most fighters have their first small fight between their home club and another local one. Making the jump to the national level was a jump too far. Yet, a part of me was ecstatic; I could not believe that somebody could have that much confidence in me doing well. The stakes were so high, but I could not wait to fight; and so I told Ricardo, yes, I was ready. Confidence is believing in yourself, even when the odds are stacked against you; it's choosing to acknowledge your fear but not be defined by it. In an age of social media, it can be a difficult thing to possess; we are constantly comparing ourselves to others, often we do not even realise we are doing it. It is easy to look at people excelling in our fields and think we will never be as good as them, but our confidence levels are not set in stone. If I have a fight coming up, I need to believe in myself in order to perform. Therefore, I take the steps I can to heighten my self-esteem. I limit my time on social media so I can focus. I surround myself with people who make me feel good about myself, I train hard and I put in the work. It is a combination that works every time and I might not win all of my fights, but I go in backing myself – and if I do lose, it just gives me more incentive to even the score.

The structure of the competition was simple; we were to fight 'three twos' – meaning three rounds, each lasting two minutes each. I was working at that time, and so I used to have to wake up at 5 a.m. to fit in extra sessions with Ricardo. At the weekends, I would make up for any lost training time by taking extra-long runs around London. I was pushing myself so hard to be fit, and ready. Even if my body ached and my mind was exhausted, I kept training. The chance to compete meant so much to me that I poured everything into it. Sometimes we can overcompensate, to show onlookers or even ourselves that we deserve our place in the room, and that is what I was doing. I never stopped to rest or recover, and on one of my runs, I started to feel an intense pain in my left foot. Stubbornly, I carried on, but every moment of impact between the ground and my foot sent a shudder of pain up my leg. I refused to get it checked out, blaming it on my trainers, so I bought a pair of insoles and kept running. That still did not help, so after a few weeks, I finally booked a GP appointment. The doctor examining my foot was shocked that I had waited so long and sent me to the local hospital for an urgent X-ray. It turned out I had a hairline fracture on my left metatarsal and was told I needed to rest it for at least six weeks to make a full recovery. I didn't tell the doctors I was training for the biggest fight of my life at the time, so I took their advice with a pinch of salt, and went straight back to the gym to train for the nationals. I had to wear a walker boot cast while it healed. In my mind, just because my foot was immobilised I could still train using the rest of my body, so I kept showing up and lifting weights.

It was not easy, or the smartest thing to do, and after a few weeks it had a ripple effect across the rest of my body. The pain was too much, and I found myself sitting on the gym floor in a flood of tears. I could hear Ricardo's loud voice, over my own deafening sobs. 'Ramla, I have to take you out, you're falling apart, you can't do this. I'm pulling you out of the competition.' And he did. I was heartbroken. The pain, mental and physical, was unbearable. I could not believe I would not get to fight after all the work I had put in. The injury meant that instead of going to the gym every day, I had no other option but to take a break. It was only during this enforced period of time off that I realised I had pushed myself too hard. I had been so obsessed with wanting to win that I had abandoned all sense. Instead of building up strength gradually, I had pushed my body to breaking point. In my sadness, I started to realise the importance of patience. Bodies are incredible tools that we can work with and train to do the most beautiful things; but it takes time. I ignored all the warnings from my coach and from my own body, and while my injury devastated me, it was an important reminder not to let stubbornness get the better of me. It is important to push yourself, but we all have boundaries.

Rehab is perhaps the most gruelling process for an athlete. It's long periods of resting, recovering and then gradually rebuilding strength, slowly trying to get back to peak fitness after being forced to take months off. It is also the most humbling experience. I would not say I thought I was invincible, but I did push myself to the edge of my limits. I felt as if I had so much to prove, and this was my one shot to do it. Being injured taught me the importance of healing. I had become so obsessed with training that I had lost the ability to be still. Lying down on my bed in the middle of the day felt all kinds of unnatural, but as it became a part of my routine, I realised the value of stopping. I thought back to my younger self, the one who would spend hours quietly reading. She knew how to be still in a world that moved too fast. Therefore, I channelled that young girl. Instead of feeling bitter that I would not be competing, I found other ways to distract myself. I checked in with my friends; I put my focus into my work, which I had been neglecting; I reminded myself that boxing is just as much about the mind as it is the body. I used this period to reflect on other parts of my life, for the first time I allowed myself to admit that I was not happy in my job. I began to question whether I really wanted to be a lawyer, or if I was just doing it to appease my family.

When I returned to the gym, I understood that I had to take things slowly. We decided to enter the nationals again the following year and I channelled all my energy into that, gradually rebuilding my strength and my confidence. The thought of running terrified me, I was nervous that my foot had not healed and I would never get a chance to compete. If I'd rated my level of confidence at this time, it would not have been more than a 2 out of 10 – I was so nervous that I would hurt myself again, but slowly I started to rebuild. Before long, I started to feel like a boxer again. My boot came off, and I felt able to complete my first run. It was difficult, and it was far from the fast sprints or hour-long jogs I'd been doing, but it was a start, and on the second, third and fourth times, running became a lot easier. The road to recovery was long, but slowly I started to feel like myself again. We will always have setbacks in life, and having to start again actually made me stronger than ever. As helpful as it can be to fill the future with plans and work towards goals, it is also important to learn how to adapt. We have no way of seeing what the future actually holds, sometimes obstacles get in the way and we have to find new ways to carry on. In pulling out of the competition, I became a much better athlete, one who knew how to take care of her body.

*

By the time spring 2011 rolled around, I was back on fighting form. My first amateur fight was to be in the London division ABAE National Championships, held in Feltham. My nerves were running wild; not only was this a huge, historic competition, but because there were not enough entrants (women boxers were still woefully under-represented back then), I was entering at the quarter-finals of the competition. If I won, I would progress to the semi-finals, and then hopefully the finals a few weeks later. I put a lot of pressure on that fight. Winning to me meant that all my setbacks would be worth it. The pain of fracturing my foot, the guilt of not telling my parents, and the year of early-morning runs and late-night training sessions would amount to that moment. I realised that anything worth fighting for takes a *lot* of hard work. You have to graft and graft with no guarantee that your efforts will pay off. Dreaming is the easy part; actually taking the steps to make that dream become a reality is incredibly tough – but it is also so rewarding. The morning of the fight, I felt invincible. I left the house like it was any other day – my parents assumed as always that I was going off to work – and told them I was running late when I skipped breakfast. The night before, I had packed my kit and some snacks in my bag, and I left the house to meet Ricardo round the corner.

The first years of my career, seeing other women box was always a revelation for me. I was always used to either being the only one or one of a small handful in boxing gyms. Representation is important, especially in sport, and to see other women like me gave me immense hope and confidence to keep going. Surrounded by so many women boxers under one roof that day, I knew that even if I lost, I was proud to be there and to have a small part of it. We arrived in the morning, but I was not competing until 4 p.m., so after my weigh-in, I walked round the large hall taking everything in – there were competitors shadow-boxing to warm up, or huddling with their coaches and teammates. My opponent was a girl called Debbie Tyrell. She was a stunning fitness model, incredibly athletic, and much taller than I expected, which dashed my hopes of being the bigger fighter. I remember Ricardo saying to me, 'You can't lose to a model!' which is ironic to think back on as now I am also a model, and why shouldn't the same woman who fights in the ring also appear on the front pages of magazines? I knew that I had a very real chance of losing; she was incredibly fit and I knew that she would have amazing stamina. After a few hours had slowly passed we warmed up, and then I waited for them to call my name. I was so nervous that my stomach started to feel as though the peanut butter sandwiches I had eaten had been made with lead, but as Ricardo talked me through what to do in the ring, I willed myself to focus on his words only, zoning out all of my fears.

A crowd of roughly two hundred people were in the stands, but as far as I was concerned, Debbie Tyrell was the only person in the room. Gloves on, we walked to the middle of the ring from opposite sides while the referee read out the rules. I have heard them a hundred times now, but that day I could barely hear the referee say, 'No holding, no pushing, protect yourself at all times, make it a clean fight,' over my heart pounding in my chest. This was it; I was about to be in my first ever fight. When I first saw Debbie, I smiled and she flashed a quick grin back at me, but in those final seconds before we broke away to our separate corners, we just stared into each other's eyes. This stand-off is a pre-fight ritual that has existed as long as boxing itself. You have to be so full of self-belief that you radiate confidence. It is your chance to show your opponent you are here to win, while looking for signs of weakness in them. I have always remembered Mike Tyson speaking about this in his documentary, when he talks about the art of looking at your opponent just before you fight. According to him, if they are not able to hold eye contact, or if they blink or look away, you know you have already won. When I looked at Debbie I saw nerves. Minutes earlier, my own anxiety had been through the roof, but in that second face to face with her, my nerves fell away as the adrenaline of the moment kicked in. There was no inner voice of doubt, there was no racing heart, I felt unexpectedly calm and ready, and I knew I was going to win.

When the boxing bell rings, you get to work. Your instinct is to get in there with a jab, but it is often best to hold back and wait for your opponent to move; you want to get a sense of how she is going to fight. Debbie was taller than I was which made her a harder target to hit. I had to get really close to her to land a good combination of blows; one to the upper body followed by a left hook to her side. Every time I did manage to hit her, she would almost certainly hit me back, it was a well-matched fight and the constant back and forth was tiring us both out quickly. By the second round, Debbie and I were still fighting blow for blow. We were locked in a battle of endurance, making it hard for one of us to outfight the other. In the ring, everything happens at lightning speed; you are constantly reading your opponent and anticipating their next move. I tried to draw on my instinct to read her, but she was so fast it was impossible. If ever there was a time to dig deep it was now, but before I was about to strike my next blow the bell rang and I went back to my corner. You have sixty seconds to speak to your trainer, and most of that time goes by in a blur. In that moment your coach and trainer gives you sips of water, checks your face for cuts, and most importantly, gives you a tactical talk. Those talks are vital. Your coach has watched the previous round looking for any signs of weakness and opportunity. You are exhausted, urgently trying to catch your breath, but you have to take in their every word. They will tell you where to aim for, whether you need to back off or be more aggressive; it is hard to take everything in but if you listen carefully enough, they are the ones with the key to winning. Ricardo made it clear to me how close the fight was, and that whoever wanted to win was going to have to show it in this round as it would ultimately decide the fight. With his words still ringing in my ears, I knew I had to make the final two minutes count. Physically I was exhausted, but I refused to show it; I knew if I did, Debbie would be all over me. I replayed the past rounds in my mind; every time one of us would hit, the other would follow up with a counterpunch. I knew in that final round I needed to be much more assertive, I needed to get a combination of clean punches in and take the lead. I charged at her, hitting her three times, twice to the body, and once in the head. I put myself in the lead with that, but part of my tactic was not to give Debbie the opportunity to even the score and hit back. I decided not to go in for the attack again, being greedy would make me vulnerable, so instead I kept moving around the ring. I became a moving target, so that Debbie found it near impossible to hit me. It also meant she was using up energy and growing tired trying to chase me. Spinning, dancing and floating around the ring, I too had to fight off the fatigue I was feeling. I could not see the clock, but I kept moving, my feet switching to get me out of range while Debbie desperately tried to get closer. This game of cat and mouse continued until I heard the final ding of the bell. Back in my corner, relieved at the chance to rest, I collapsed onto the ropes. In that moment all of your adrenaline finally starts to drain away as you try to process the fight. I always ask my coach if I have won, you can usually tell from their reaction if you have done enough; only someone on the outside looking in can call the result.

Debbie and I touched gloves back in the middle of the ring, while we waited for the results. I shot her a quick glance; both of us were still desperately trying to catch our breath, and were both glistening with sweat. Before the referee made his announcement, I shut my eyes and raised my arm to the sky, a sign Ricardo had taught me: it signifies that you think you are the rightful winner. In that moment, time slowed down. I felt a strange sense of calm wash over me as I waited and waited for the results. The roar of the crowd felt so distant, I completely blocked it out so that every cell in my body could focus on one sound only, that of the referee. Finally, the confirmation came. 'The winner is . . . Ramla Ali!' The crowd erupted and my eyes filled with tears. I had done it; I had won my first ever fight.

ROUND TWO

Confidence comes, confidence goes

We can never feel a hundred per cent confident a hundred per cent of the time, and it is important to accept that. The way we feel is fluid, not fixed, and confidence, like other emotions, will come and go. Be gentle on yourself if you do have low self-esteem, and when you are feeling good, take note of what makes you most confident. I feel at my best when I'm surrounded by the people I trust, when I'm not spending too much time on social media, and when I'm reflecting on the things I'm grateful for.

Trust your gut

When my coach took advantage of me, I knew instantly that he had done something wrong. I felt it in my heart and in the pit of my stomach. I should have held on to that feeling, but instead, I blamed myself. Intuition is a beautiful thing; if your body is telling you something feels wrong, listen to it. If you feel uncomfortable, remember you have the right to speak out. Find some-one you trust and tell them how you are feeling.

Don't be afraid to be the first

Representation is so important. For the first few years of my boxing career, I rarely saw other women training or sparring in the gym, but I knew that they were out there. Sometimes because of being the only one existing in a space, you become a beacon for people, and it signals to a new generation that it is OK and you do belong there. Your presence could create a completely new community, so do not be afraid to be the first.

Learn how to be alone

Growing up in a big family it was so rare for me to spend time on my own. It was only when I started training independently that I quickly learned how to work hard without an audience. It can be hard sometimes to be by yourself, with only your own thoughts swimming around your head, but there is value in listening to them and really getting to know yourself better. I appreciate those moments when I am alone; they make me think about what I want to get out of life.

Be adaptable

Patience is a virtue that does not come easily to me. I like to work hard and constantly feel like I am progressing, but sometimes unforeseen obstacles get in the way. Learn to accept the setbacks. When I hurt my foot and had to pull out of my first fight, I was devastated, but it taught me the value of taking stock and sitting still. If you are able to adapt to change, chances are you will come back a lot stronger.

BE YOURSELF

'If I, being a mother of two, can win a medal, so can you all. Take me as an example and don't give up.'
— Mary Kom

What followed after that fight was a blur. I was so proud of myself, and after experiencing my first win, I wanted to stay and soak up the atmosphere; being in a boxing tournament felt like home; I belonged in that arena surrounded by all of those athletes. We should have gone straight back – I knew Mum would be wondering where I was – but I was so high from the win I couldn't leave straight away. We stayed to watch the fight after mine, the 57kg quarter-finals. The moment one of the competitors entered, I was immediately transfixed. 'Who is that?' I asked Ricardo as she waited in the centre of the ring with the referee. She was so muscular; her body was this incredible embodiment of how hard she must have trained. 'That's Valerian Spicer,' he said. 'She's one of the best boxers in the country.'

You can't get good at anything living inside a vacuum. Whether you love sprinting or painting, writing or dancing, coding or cooking, watching others excelling in the same field is a great way to improve and to understand your own place in that world. It can be easy to see other people purely as competition; but when I see a phenomenal boxer, I choose to be inspired instead of jealous. I was never going to be Valerian Spicer, I had to become my own fighter; but we existed in the same arena, and I couldn't wait to watch her. When her fight started that day, she obliterated her opponent with each and every shot. There was so much force behind her punches I could almost feel her power, even from just sitting in the stands. The thought of fighting her filled me with equal amounts of dread and desire. It was addictive to watch her; it made me excited about the boxer I could become. A few years later, I would become friends with Valerian Spicer myself, and we would spar together. She is as incredible a person as she is a fighter; kind, supportive and always honest about her performance. Working with her has taught me that we are all human. The idea of meeting your heroes can be terrifying – especially the thought of training alongside them, but those scary experiences are opportunities to learn. We never got to meet that day, though. When you're already living something of a double life, hanging around competitions after your fight is a massive risk, so while Valerian stood victorious in the ring, I headed back to Whitechapel. By the time Ricardo dropped me home, all I could think about was the next fight.

After my victory at Feltham, I went on to snatch another win in the semi-finals, before heading to the final round of the National Championships, which were being held in Manchester. I travelled up by coach the night before with Ricardo, Richard and Emily, another girl from Double Jab who I had sparred with a couple of times. I didn't know her particularly well, but she was keen to watch me compete and I appreciated the extra support. By the National Championship finals, your body is pretty much running on empty. You've already battled your way through the quarter-finals and the semi-finals, which are exhausting, so having other people around to support you really fuels your fight. I'm so grateful for anyone who has ever come to watch me in the ring. I know buying a ticket and travelling around the country to see a fight that lasts less than ten minutes can be quite an undertaking. That's why I never take anyone in the crowd for granted.

Ricardo told me I'd be competing with a girl named Amy O'Kane from a club in Bristol. He hadn't been able to find out anything about her, so I was going in completely blind. Luckily, she wasn't too difficult to fight. Even though I'd only competed twice before, something told me I was the more experienced boxer. I knew she couldn't read me, so I threw fake shots to confuse her, before sneaking up to land a slick combination of blows. By that point, I'd had it really drilled into me that you have to use your head in boxing just as much as you're using your body. In stressful situations, it's vital that you consider the other people in the room, not just yourself. What are they thinking? What will they do next? After round one, the scores were 9–2 to me.

Back in my corner with Ricardo, I felt in control, but I was careful not to get complacent. 'You've got this,' he assured me. 'Keep doing what you were doing; she's not putting up much of a fight, but just watch out in the next round.'

The bell rang and we went again. In the second round, Amy tried to even the score. She was bold and unafraid, and though her shots were a little messy, she kept coming for me with a wild determination. Somehow, she was full of energy for the third round as if she'd been holding back, but I stuck with her like a magnet, striking out, then repelling myself away and leaving her no opportunity to hit me back. Amy seemed to have burned out by the last round. She made elementary mistakes, letting her guard down, which allowed me to score some more clean shots. The bell rang and we waited for the scores. I tried to catch my breath as I took in the hundreds of faces watching us. I was feeling quietly confident when I heard something that made no sense. 'The winner by unanimous decision . . . in the blue corner, it's Amy O'Kane.'

On hearing her name, my world collapsed around me. Out of nowhere she had won, a result I simply couldn't compute. I looked at the referee and at Amy; neither would meet my eye. I felt a furious combination of injustice and heartbreak spread through my body; I hadn't slept properly for days, I'd near starved myself to make weight, and I knew I'd put in the winning performance, yet still somehow none of it counted.

Nobody prepares you for a loss, or for the unfairness of a badly scored fight. Nobody tells you how to feel or what is going to happen afterwards. You have every right to be hurt, especially if you don't feel the score reflects the fight, but it's important to maintain perspective. One defeat – fair or not – is not the end. You have to find a way to accept the situation, and to move on. We drove home in stony silence and I remained irritable for days afterwards, sulking around the house like a moody teenager, but I knew I needed to let it go. Boxing is not a perfect sport. The judges are often volunteers who aren't paid to be there, they might miss a shot or unfortunately show bias towards a competitor. I had to accept that this was the nature of the sport, and all I could do was keep showing up and keep doing my best. In the days that followed, I slowly picked myself back up. One wrong score wasn't going to stop me. Instead, I made the rash decision to quit my job; the next time I won, I wanted it to be very clear to every judge and every spectator in the room that I was the unanimous winner, so I needed to find a job that would allow me to focus more time on training. I hadn't ever really wanted to study law at university, I'd done it to make my parents happy, but now that I was working full-time in a law firm, I felt even less motivated. I hated the work and I dreaded what was supposed to be my end goal: becoming a solicitor. My parents wanted me to have a good salary, but six months into paralegal work, I realised that no amount of money could buy the happiness I felt from handing in my notice.

When it came to my career, I really wanted to make my parents proud. While it's understandable that we want to do the best by the people around us, we shouldn't let others dictate our lives, especially not at the cost of our own happiness. Since my mum had been robbed of her own career as a businesswoman, I could see why she desperately wanted me to find a skilled job and a safe profession that paid well. I think for her, it was about me having the freedom to live a life that wasn't solely dedicated to caregiving, like hers had become. At the end of the day, while we can (and should) listen to the advice of others, when it comes to making decisions, there is only one person in the driving seat. I had a lot of pressure on me to get a good education and a good job. There may be certain expectations placed on you – from the way you look to the company you keep, to the lifestyle and the career you choose – but remember these things are simply choices. My mum would be disappointed, but I knew I was doing the right thing by being honest and telling her how I felt.

Surprisingly, she was more understanding than I'd predicted. When I told her I wanted to leave the law firm, she accepted it on the condition I found something else; I agreed and we found a way to compromise. After quitting, I tried every different job under the sun. I applied for roles I'd never even heard of, but with each new job came the same sense of boredom. I tried to keep an open mind; we are the sum of all the different experiences we try, and I knew there must be a career out there for me somewhere. I treated my job search with the same open-mindedness that I treated my early days at East Ham Leisure Centre: try everything until you find that thing you love.

I worked in HGV (heavy goods vehicle) licence sales – which is even less exciting than it sounds. I did a stint as an administrative assistant at the Royal Mail canteen, and for a while I was as a telemarketer for Save the Children. My longest job was as a coordinator for another charity. Although I was only doing administrative work, it did at least feel meaningful and I got on well enough with my colleagues, but like everything else that came before, each job just seemed to affirm the fact that I didn't want to spend the rest of my life staring at screens in badly lit offices. My career, or lack of, started to fill me with anxiety. My life wasn't taking a direction, and I hated the thought of disappointing my parents even more. If you wake up in the morning filled with dread and have to drag yourself to work every day, you reach a point where you start to ask yourself, is this worth it? That's exactly how I felt and it was a constant battle just to get myself to the office. I compared this to my energy for boxing, where even if I was tired and my body hurt from the session before, I could ignore all of that. I was so passionate that I'd bounce out of bed to get down to the gym. I realised I couldn't keep enduring jobs that made me unhappy. Boxing taught me I needed to be doing the kind of work I was invested in rather than just interested in. While wanting to please my parents meant so much to me, I realised I had to put my own mental health first. As hard as I tried, sitting behind a computer all day made me feel bored and unsatisfied. I was starting to become increasingly miserable and I knew I had to find something else. So much of our adult lives are spent working; if your career makes you unhappy, it's important to think about a new alternative.

This time period of trying to find the right job taught me a lot about myself – what I valued, and what I desired, and ultimately what I wanted from work and life. When I started listening to my feelings the path became clearer, and I started to let go of the feeling of failure that was surrounding me. Sometimes it can be hard to prioritise your own desires, when so many other factors come into play. I worried about earning enough money, about making my parents proud, about trying too many jobs and never succeeding at any of them. Although my concerns were valid, I had to block them out. I had to be confident and really think about what I wanted. I loved sports, and the more I trained the more I found myself learning about my own body. Boxers take a lot of injuries; aside from the obvious cuts and bruises to the face, it's easy to sprain a wrist, pull a muscle, or fracture your foot like I did. Inspiration is everywhere, and I realised that my own rehabilitation had fascinated me as much as it frustrated me. Learning about the series of stretches I had to do in order to rebuild the muscles in my foot had slowly triggered an interest in the world of sports physio, so I started to research how I might train to become a physiotherapist. It meant I would still be close to athletes and the world that I loved. I'd be helping people to be their best, and I could work flexibly enough to still compete. When I was fully qualified, maybe I could even become a specialist for boxers and work with the GB team.

When we make goals, it's important to see the path that will lead us to them. Even today, I try to break my ambitions down into manageable steps. At the time, to become a physio, I discovered that I would have to go back to college part-time to get science A levels, and then do a degree in physiotherapy. I'd been saving up since graduating and my only real outgoings were a small amount of rent to my parents, and boxing costs, so I would be able to afford the course if I did it part-time. I had a long road ahead of me; even if all went to plan, I wouldn't be a trained physiotherapist for at least four years, but I was ready to put in the work. For the first time since graduating, I felt excited about my job prospects. I made sure to follow through on my plans, and when I got accepted onto a physiotherapy course at King's College in London (on the condition I did well in the A levels), not only was I thrilled, but my parents were happy for me too. I enrolled at Birkbeck to study maths, chemistry and biology, and got a job as a receptionist at Virgin Active in Cannon Street to fund my studies.

In between work, school and boxing, I had zero free time, but I was in a rush to get the A levels I needed and start my degree course. Some people complete the course over two years, but I was determined to do it in one. My job at Virgin Active gave me a free gym membership, and so I trained before or after each shift if I couldn't make it to Palmers. Sometimes I used to daydream that boxing could be my career, but back then, it was completely unthinkable; women's boxing was still so small because nobody had really given it much of a chance. As is the case with a lot of sports, if a woman did turn professional and was lucky enough to be paid a proper salary, there was still a massive gender pay gap, as there is today. It's a complicated situation, with so much of it coming down to demand. If Anthony Joshua is fighting, he will easily sell out a whole arena, but there's not that same level of enthusiasm and demand for the women's fights. For there to be a change in pay, for the sport to become more inclusive and on the verge of selling out arenas, it's not just on us as fighters to create change; we need more fans to start supporting women athletes. I hope that I can encourage more people to back us, to come to a fight and be enthralled by the action, because there really is nothing like watching women's boxing live. I remember the first time I saw a big live fight. It was during the 2012 Olympics in London and a few of us from Palmers had managed to get tickets to the women's lightweight quarter-final where Ireland's Katie Taylor was fighting Natasha Jonas from Team GB. The ticket prices were absolutely extortionate, especially for me on little more than minimum wage, but I saved for weeks and it was the best fifty quid I'd ever spent. Watching those two women fight gave me goosebumps, the way they flew around the ring was so graceful, but the minute one would take a shot at the other, you'd feel the air being knocked out of her lungs like a slashed tire. The atmosphere was beyond electric, I'd never heard a crowd make that kind of noise before and by the end my throat was hoarse from screaming. That fight holds the official record of being the highest decibel level recorded at the London 2012 Olympics – 113.7 decibels. Katie was deservedly declared the winner, and as I watched her waving and smiling to the crowd,

I remember thinking, Wow, that could be me in the future.

Our lives are littered with these kinds of incredible moments – moments that make you feel alive. You don't have to be in an arena with thousands of people to feel something; some of my most special memories are of me and Danika hanging out and making each other laugh in my childhood bedroom. These are the memories I treasure the most because those good days and good times inform who we are, and help us get through the harder times when they come. The feeling I got from being in that stadium never went away, even when I got to experience the difficult sides of boxing.

The summer after the nationals, Ricardo went to Jamaica for a month, leaving me to train on my own. Occasionally the other coaches would take pity on me and offer me some pad work, but mostly I worked solo. I was so exhausted from work and college that I found training alone difficult. Missing my regular coaching was one thing, but not being able to spar made me feel like I would stop progressing. Ricardo would always get me in the ring at least once a week, and that was when I'd get to put all the skills I was working on to the test. With Ricardo being away, it was the longest I'd ever gone without sparring and I worried I was forgetting how to fight, so one morning when the gym was quiet, I pulled my old trainer Richard aside and explained my situation. He didn't take much persuading; he told me to come back later that day and he'd put me in the ring with one of his clients.

I had to laugh when I saw the guy I would be fighting. He was huge and must have weighed at least 20kg more than me. His body was completely ripped, and he was tall too. Still, it was hard to find a woman to spar with, and I relished the challenge. As we slipped under the ropes, the guy barely acknowledged me. I introduced myself and he replied with a grunt and a nod of the head without making eye contact; I still don't know his name. We must have looked strange; he was large and moved gradually towards me, I was faster and seemed to have the upper hand when it came to speed and agility. I was glad; I did everything I could to get him to chase me around the ropes and to avoid being hit by his giant arm. I landed several strikes on him, but he was so hench he didn't even flinch. It was exhausting, and when he did get me in the ribs with a sneaky left hook, I suddenly felt myself being propelled to the other side of the ring. There was no time to catch my breath; he was hitting me again with what I was sure was his full strength, because every shot felt like being struck with a slab of marble. I slipped to his right, thinking I was safe; I wasn't.

I'm not really sure what happened next, but whatever he did knocked me straight to the ground. Richard says he hit me square in the nose with full force. I tried to get up, but the force of the blow made me dizzy and confused. A crowd of onlookers flooded the ring. 'Are you OK? Ramla, can you hear us?!' Through blurred vision I saw Richard's concerned face. It took me a moment to remember where I was, and then the shock of being grounded subsided, and the pain suddenly hit me. My nose, which felt like it had just been struck with an axe, was throbbing and gushing blood. Slowly, I stood up and went to look in the mirror. Richard tried to stop me. 'Wait a minute,' he said, grabbing my arm. 'I don't want you to panic, but . . .' Alarmed, I twisted out of his grip and walked straight to the mirror. I didn't even recognise the reflection. Where my nose used to be was a wonky twisted bloody and bruised lump; I fought back tears as Richard desperately tried to console me. 'It won't stay like that!' he said, though I was sure he had no idea either way. He passed me an ice pack apologetically. 'Here, this will help with the swelling.' Armed with painkillers, I took the bus home, and only when I was back in the safety of my bed did I realise the man who had probably broken my nose hadn't even apologised.

In boxing, the first big injury you receive presents you with a dilemma – it's make or break. A lot of people choose not to get back inside the ring after realising how dangerous it can be, they realise it's not for them and that's OK. Sometimes in life when you experience knock-backs, you have to make the right decision for yourself and live with that. I was so passionate about boxing, it had taught me not to let fear rule my life; I had to be brave and keep fighting.

I spent the next twenty-four hours trying to hide a mild concussion and a broken nose from my parents, but of course my mum saw it. I lied to her, saying I'd tripped and fallen over as I ran for the bus, and since she was so worried about my injury, she didn't bother to interrogate my story. When I went back to Palmers the next day, Ricardo was back from Jamaica, and both him and Terry, the owner of the gym, were fuming over the events from the previous day. Terry focused his fury on the fact I'd had an unequal opponent, and that a much larger man had used so much force against me. Meanwhile, Ricardo was just as angry that I'd sparred without his permission. He took one look at my wonky nose, and asked me a question I already knew the answer to.

'Are you going to quit because of this?'

I was offended he even had to ask. 'Of course not,' I replied.

'Good. Do you want me to fix it?'

I nodded. I knew that whatever was about to happen was going to hurt, but I was stubborn and always felt as if I had to prove that I was serious about boxing. To me, whatever was about to happen next was just another test. I closed my eyes, swallowed the fear, and patiently waited for the onslaught of pain that I knew was coming. Ricardo cradled the broken bridge of my nose between both his hands. Even the slightest touch made me wince.

'3 . . .' he said. I took a deep breath.

'2 . . .' My body started tensing up in anticipation of the pain.

'1.'

In a flash his hands flicked from left to right. There was a loud cracking noise, quickly followed by the most intense pain I have ever experienced rushing through me. It was far worse than the blow that caused the damage, and when Ricardo removed his hands this time I couldn't hold back the tears. The pain was completely overwhelming, it hurt to cry and to breathe, but to be fair to Ricardo, he had done it; my nose was straight again. I could fight on.

I had to take six weeks off from training while my broken nose healed, but as I'd come to learn from my previous injuries, it was an opportunity to rest and reset. I had dealt with injuries before, and I knew that this was nothing more than a setback that I needed to overcome. When training started building up again, my mum grew suspicious about my schedule and the return of the late nights coming home. Part of me wanted to tell her about boxing, but it wasn't just about her disapproval; my mum would have been heartbroken if she'd found out I was boxing, she would have felt completely betrayed, and I wasn't ready to inflict that suffering on her. Ricardo knew I was worried about her finding out, so he ran an idea past me to switch gyms so I could be closer to home. There were a lot more women than I expected at Fitzroy Lodge in Elephant and Castle. And by a lot more, I mean there were at least ten women boxers who attended regularly, compared to the fifty or sixty men. It was a start, and a sign that times were changing. There is no accurate measure of how long true change takes – sometimes it happens excruciatingly slowly, sometimes it's instant – in both instances you just have to be patient, and never lose sight of what you're hoping for.

I was so excited to get to know the other girls. There was Rachel, the painfully organised police officer who never talked in sessions – and she made sure we didn't either. Isra was the feistiest and loudest of the girls who wouldn't let anyone tell her what to do. Leanne and Bianca were frank in that way too, they always said exactly what was on their minds, and often they would cause me to laugh until my stomach hurt. Iris, who joined after me, came to London from Spain, and for a long time she was very shy, but she soon became a core part of the group. Us girls would stick together, and soon she was very much a part of our crew.

I adored these women. We were completely different, but the fact that we were there in that club all together at a time when there were so few women in boxing really brought us closer; we became a family. For the first time, I'd get to go to women-only sessions where all of us got to train together. It was a lot of hard work but it was also so fun; we got to have a laugh but we also pushed each other to achieve our goals. We were all training for different competitions but we shared the same day-to-day experiences, everyone trying to make weight, everyone battling nerves and trying to be their best. If someone was training on their period (which is the worst), we knew what they were going through and we knew to give them an extra push. The funny thing is we spent so much time together that eventually all our periods synced up anyway. Those women are still some of my closest friends today.

Having such a strong and supportive unit taught me two things – the importance of community and the importance of accountability. Accountability goes hand in hand with community. In that group we were all committed to each other, and we've maintained that bond. I respect that everyone is busy, but I've learned that real friends always find a way to make time for you when you need them. Such people are hard to come by, and when you find them, it's important to keep them close. We supported each other inside and outside of the gym. We raised each other up and pushed each other forward, and I felt proud being part of a group of strong, dedicated fighters.

That same sense of community underpins the work I do at the Sisters Club — a not-for-profit initiative I founded in 2018. It started as a London-based regular weekly women's boxing class. Any woman was welcome, but I targeted it at Muslims in particular, because I wanted to create a safe space where they could train with or without their hijabs, free from discrimination. Within a few weeks, Sister's Club drew in women from all backgrounds. Some had come from abusive relationships or didn't feel safe walking alone and wanted to learn self-defence, others loved the idea of training and competing, and some just wanted to get fit. Whatever their reasons for attending, we became a proud community of fighters.

Ricardo and I soon got into a rhythm of regular competitions. I fought at several club shows; both at Fitzroy Lodge and other neighbouring clubs such as the Haringey Box Cup, an annual tournament that attracts some of the country's best boxing talent. Competing is hard work. The training that goes into it is exhausting, but it's also a huge mental strain too. You're constantly thinking about the next competition, worrying that you haven't done enough and imagining all the things that could go wrong. I was grateful to have the support of my friends and my coach, and as my boxing career developed, so did my character. I found myself becoming so much more resilient as a person. Even in the toughest moments I pushed myself and didn't give up. I felt proud of how hard I worked and in time I grew to really back myself; I was growing into a strong woman and an accomplished fighter, I was exactly where I wanted to be.

But despite all of this, something was missing – I was constantly craving the support of my family, and I decided to confide in my youngest brother, Yahya. I knew I could trust him and I needed a confidant to help me keep boxing a secret from my family. Yahya was amazing; when he wasn't guarding the bathroom door while I snuck out through the window, he'd be covering for me when Mum wondered why I wasn't answering my phone, and he'd always give me a heads-up if she was wondering where I was. It was Yahya who helped me compete in my very first international tournament, an annual competition called the Golden Girl Championship. When I told him I wanted to enter, he found a football competition that was taking place over the same dates in Stockholm, and we told my mum that Yahya had been invited to play. Since he was a few years younger than me, we said I would be going to chaperone him. We managed to pull the whole thing off without raising any suspicions, and for the first time, I got to experience having a family member cheering me on from the side-lines. The older I've got, the more I've realised how important it is to have people you can confide in, whether that's friends or family members. I'm a naturally private person, I always will be – and for a long time I used to keep my worries bottled up, I didn't want to burden other people with my feelings – but when I started to tell people how much I was struggling keeping boxing a secret, I felt so relieved once I'd shared my worries. Even if these people didn't have all the answers, just the act of talking to someone can make you feel heard, and it reminds you that you're not alone.

Shortly after Yahya and I got back from Sweden, I was asked to compete in an all-female amateur boxing gala. I was so excited for that fight; it felt like there was a real spotlight on us women fighters after years of being ignored. The TV channel London Live had recently launched, and when Ricardo and I arrived, a woman from the station with a headset and clipboard introduced herself and asked to do a quick pre-show interview with me. My heart sank. I was always so careful to keep my fights a secret. I used to trawl through social media for hours making sure nobody had uploaded any pictures of me, and if I ever saw anything, I'd immediately untag myself and ask whoever posted it to take it down. I was used to dealing with the odd photographer at a fight, but it was rare for women's boxing to be televised, and I had no idea London Live would be recording that day. To my relief, the producer was understanding. She told me it was fine for me not to do the interview, and assured me that my bout wouldn't go on air. I thanked her and headed to the ring.

I lost that fight. I remember my opponent had her whole family in the crowd to support her, and her victory was met by the most rapturous applause. They clearly adored her, and the pride on their faces made me wish so badly that I could tell my own family – I could only imagine what it might feel like to see my mum and dad cheering me on from the front row. When Ricardo and I left, I was relieved to sink into the passenger seat of his car. Leaning against the window, my eyes grew heavy and I was almost asleep when the sound of an incoming text cut through the low hum of the car radio. I glanced down at my phone and saw my sister Faiza's name flash up on the screen; she was asking what time I would be home that night. I sighed; instead of inviting them to fights like other contestants, I was constantly living in fear that my family would find out what I did. I replied to Faiza saying work had finished late and that I'd be home in ten minutes, and then closed my eyes to the world.

Ricardo dropped me off round the corner from the house like every other time. I entered my house and opened the living room door to find my whole family gathered there. I instantly knew something was wrong. 'What's going on?' I asked, while scanning the room for answers. My mum was stood up, hands on her hips, looking agitated. My dad was on the sofa staring into space and desperately trying to ignore the gathering happening around him. Yahya avoided my eye contact too;

and it was my eldest brother T who broke the frosty silence. 'I saw your boxing match,' he said, before Mum cut in, yelling at me about how I had been dishonest and had brought shame to the family. It appeared London Live had televised the fight after all; T had seen it, and had gone straight to my parents with the video. Apart from the odd word or phrase, Mum doesn't really speak English. I don't speak Somali all that well, so when we communicate, it's a jumbled mix of the two plus a whole lot of gesticulation, but that day it didn't take much for me to understand what she was saying about the sport I loved. Boxing was haram, it was not for women, it was wrong, how could I have done something like this? She was so angry, the list of my transgressions went on and on; how could I have gone behind her back, why would I wear such immodest clothes, who had put me up to this? Then came the emotional blackmail: 'Your father is so old, what are you trying to do? Do you want to put him in an early grave by competing in such a dangerous activity?' At this, my dad shook his head. 'Just leave her alone!' he pleaded to Mum. 'Let Ramla make her own decisions, you can't keep telling her what to do; at the end of the day she's a grown woman, she needs to make her own mistakes.'

I appreciated Dad trying to help, but of course it didn't work. I couldn't get a word in to defend myself, so I found myself staring at the painting that hung proudly above the mantelpiece. It's a beautiful scene; a huge bright blue wave is crashing against the shore, spluttering rocks onto a deserted sandy beach. Faiza painted it the year we moved from Mogadishu to London. She couldn't speak a word of English, but at school she had to sit her GCSEs regardless. She failed almost everything, but art was the one subject she got an A in. That A meant the world to my mum, she couldn't have been prouder, and so, twenty-five years later, encased in a wooden frame, Faiza's painting of the beach we used to go to in Mogadishu still takes pride of place.

'Ramla!' barked Mum's shrill voice as she stepped in front of the painting, obscuring my view of Somalia. 'Are you listening to me?!' I felt sick. It was a heartbreaking decision, but I knew I had no choice. All I could do was give up boxing or give up my family, so I agreed to quit. If I didn't, I would have been disowned by the people I loved the most. That evening, the emptiness I felt turned to anger, which turned into guilt; I had lied to my family, I had let them down. Everyone makes mistakes; from time to time, we all mess up. When we get caught out, it feels horrible. Seeing my mum so upset made me feel deeply ashamed for hurting her, but at the same time, I couldn't bring myself to fully regret my actions because boxing had brought me so much joy. In the aftermath of my family confronting me, I learned that life isn't always fair. I had no doubt about how much my family loved me – my parents risked their lives to save ours – and yet in that instance, my happiness came secondary to their belief system.

While part of me was so full of frustration and sadness; I didn't argue with my parents. They taught me from a young age that I must respect my elders, and in our family, we never talk back to my mum and dad.

Disagreeing with the people you love the most is so crushing, but learning to accept other people's differences and finding a way to co-exist with them is part of succeeding as an adult. We don't always get our own way, and though I didn't agree with my parents' decision that I had to stop boxing – out of respect, I promised that I would. I loved them, and after all the sacrifices that they had made for me, I was ready to make one for them. It took an enormous amount of courage, but I chose to put my family first. That evening at home was horrendous, but things only got worse for me. I had lost the thing that made me happy. I had lost the love of my life. It may seem dramatic but that's the only way I can describe it. Imagine, the early stages of dating someone. They enter your life and change it irrevocably. You think about that person 24/7, daydreaming about travelling the world and growing old with them, you'd spend every minute you have in their company if you could. Then imagine, just as things are getting started, they disappear overnight; just like that, they're gone from your life. That is how I felt. Boxing was gone in a flash. After spending so many hours a week at the boxing gym, trying to establish a new routine was difficult. I'd wake up, go to work, come home, eat, sleep, and start all over again, but my existence felt empty. I was spending more time at home, but home didn't feel like home. I was on house arrest, I felt suspended, out of place and hopeless.

I tried to fill my spare time by going on runs or doing fitness classes at the local gym; the closest I could get to actually boxing. I made more of an effort to see friends.

Danika tried to cheer me up by taking me out for dinner or going on walks, but I knew I was horrendous company so I stopped replying to her invites. I read books and watched TV, but none of it even began to fill the void that boxing had left. Every now and then Ricardo would text me: 'Ramla, why don't you come back? You can't let your family decide your future, why don't you move into your own place? I'll help you.' But he didn't understand, I had to put family first. Slowly I slipped into a depression. I thought about boxing every day. I missed the camaraderie with the other girls at the gym, the satisfaction of landing a clean combination, even the overpowering smell of stale sweat when you walked into Fitzroy Lodge. When I went online, I could see my friends were progressing, they were travelling around the country and winning competitions. I was proud of them, but it was also too painful to see. I stopped checking social media and I didn't reply to their messages. I stopped responding to Ricardo too, and eventually he stopped trying to persuade me to come back. I became a ghost.

Six months had now passed since I'd quit boxing. I was sinking lower and lower with each new day, as my memories of being in the ring began to feel further away. I felt able to speak to my best friend again, but Danika was going through it too. After years of battling several mental health struggles, she had been sectioned under the Mental Health Act. I felt so guilty for the times I hadn't responded to her messages. I desperately wanted to visit her, to share books and go for a run like in our school days, but visitors weren't allowed in the hospital. I prayed for her to get better, and when she was occasionally allowed to call me, I did the best I could to let her know that I was there for her, that she was loved. Friendship is so magical, and when you know somebody so well, inside and out, like Danika and I do, it's easy to think you know what's going on in their head. But I didn't; I could never fully understand what Danika was going through, nor could she with me.

After quitting boxing, I'd been strict with myself, and I had kept the promise I'd made to my family – but once the six-month mark had passed and I still felt depressed, I started to let myself entertain the idea of returning to the boxing gym. Even just thinking about it gave me a flicker of hope and helped me get out of bed in the mornings. I'd imagine myself putting on a glove or stepping into a ring, and for the first time I didn't force myself to push the thought out of my head. Gradually the idea felt realer and realer and I wanted it more and more. I questioned everything – could I start boxing again? What if Mum found out? Would she kick me out? Could I survive without my family? Where would I live? What swung my decision to go back into the ring was the realisation that I had been living Mum's life, not mine. She was the one who thought boxing was haram, she was the one who thought it wasn't for good Muslim women, but I had never shared those views. For as long as I can remember, we've always interpreted our faith differently. Like my younger siblings, I have a less strict understanding of Islam, a more liberal interpretation. I don't always wear a hijab, I go to the mosque less often than my parents, but it doesn't make me any less of a Muslim than them. I pray, I give to charity, I respect my community, I fast during Ramadan. To me, boxing has never been in conflict with my religion, only my family. I wasn't rebelling against my family to go out drinking – like my older sister Luul used to – I was rebelling because boxing brought me a community, it helped me feel confident and become a better version of myself. Boxing made me dream about my future – I started to think about the bigger picture; maybe one day I could compete for my country, I could become a positive role model for other young British Muslims, who like me had felt different and lonely and lost. I had a good case for wanting to disobey her. After a week of mulling it over, I had my answer. I couldn't keep living my mother's truths when I had my own to face. I had my own life to live. I had listened to my family, and now I had to listen to myself; I had to be the real, authentic me, not the one my parents wanted. I had to start boxing again.

In the spring of 2015, I walked back into Fitzroy Lodge like a student on the first day of term. I kept it secret from my family, but luckily I'd met my second family at that gym. I still worried what they would think about me abandoning them for so long, I didn't know how I would be welcomed. But the girls made me feel like nothing had changed. They knew why I'd left, and not a single one of them asked me questions or made me talk about my time off. It was exactly what I needed, and I was so grateful for the way they handled my return. My routine of training and sparring quickly got back to normal. I threw myself into it, eager to make up for lost time, and perhaps to drown out that nervous voice in my head that was telling me I had abandoned the others. The only thing that felt off was my relationship with Ricardo. We had communicated before I came back and he'd assured me I was welcome, and that he wanted me back, but when we saw each other in person for the first time his tone was short. He didn't ask how I'd been, and he spoke in short, direct sentences that made me feel as if he was harbouring a grudge against me, and that he resented how long I had been away despite knowing my family predicament. At times when we're faced with very difficult decisions, we can't rush them. I had made the hardest choice in my life back then to quit boxing; and I'd needed those six months to realise who I was. I found out that during my time away from Fitzroy Lodge, Ricardo had fallen out with one of the coaches and had been offered a position at London Community Boxing (LCB), a gym located under a railway arch in Peckham. Though things between us felt off, I agreed to go with him. Despite my friends being so welcoming about my return, I too felt like I needed a fresh start.

LCB had been set up by Lee Bruce, a city type, an ex-investment banker, who loved boxing and had wanted to do something for his local community, hence the name. When he found out I was studying and saving for university, he offered me a part-time job on reception, and it was from working there that I got a real sense of the place. LCB was a melting pot of people, in a way I'd never seen at other boxing gyms. Amateur boxers about to turn professional would train among those completely uninitiated to the sport. I met fighters from working-class immigrant backgrounds like my own, and others who'd arrived there with the gentrification of Peckham – being situated near Goldsmiths, part of the University of London, the place attracted a bunch of art and fashion students and photographers. There was even a neuroscientist who trained at the gym, who talked to me about brain scans and boxing injuries. Just like I'd found with each new club, more and more women were joining too.

I've always loved getting to know people who grew up with completely different experiences to my own; it's easy to stay in your bubble and only ever mix with people who look and think the same as you, but once you throw yourself into unfamiliar territory, you learn so much about the world and the people in it. It was refreshing to be part of such an inclusive and welcoming community, and I'm so glad that I live in such a multicultural city that celebrates difference instead of using it to divide people. One of the first friends I made at LCB was a woman from Bangladesh called Zee. She used to come to some of the evening classes, and she enrolled her two young kids into junior lessons. We bonded over our strict parents; her mum and dad had kicked her out when she started dating a Black man, which went against their plan of finding her a fellow Bengali husband. I confided in her about my own conflict with my family, and she completely understood where I was coming from – we shared the same burden of our rebellions and it made us both feel less alone. Talking to people who share similar experiences can be such a powerful interaction. I used to feel as though no one understood my struggle, but there is always somebody out there who can relate to you; sometimes it's just a case of finding them.

With an amateur boxing career that had been defined by constant stops and starts, I was desperate to compete again. I'd got a taste of competitive boxing, and I realised it had become a part of who I was; all the qualities I needed to excel in the ring were becoming qualities of my personality: dedication, strength, fearlessness, and most of all, a ruthless refusal to quit. I was a fighter, and being in the ring was where I belonged, though my experiences also taught me how to be outside of the ring too. The first blow came when Ricardo refused to enter me into the 2015 National Championships. During my time out, he had started working with a new girl and he wanted to enter her instead. That stung, but we entered the National Novice Championships instead, a tournament for boxers who have competed in fewer than fifteen fights. In the end, I would go on to win the novices, but the competition and title didn't satisfy me, partly because I was adamant I should have competed in the nationals, and it didn't feel like a real achievement because a lot of the competitors had pulled out in the weeks leading up to the fights, meaning I only had to beat one girl to win the competition. Ricardo promised to enter me into the nationals the following year, which would make it four years since I'd last competed for the title. This time, with renewed energy and focus I was determined there was no way I'd be leaving empty-handed.

When Ricardo handed me a crisp manilla envelope one evening after training, I panicked that he might be kicking me out of LCB. It looked so official and I dreaded opening it. When I asked him what it was, he kept his hand outstretched until I took it. I pulled out the piece of paper and I saw it instantly – the logo for Great Britain Boxing – the letter was an invitation for me to attend a training camp at GB Boxing's training facility in Sheffield. My eyes skimmed the rest of the letter, but I'd taken in all I needed to see; the GB boxing team trains throughout the year, and during their training camps, they invite non-members to participate alongside them. This was an invite to do just that, to train with the coaches and meet the team. It was a huge, pivotal moment in my boxing career. To get that letter, I must have been on the radar of some important people: someone had seen me fight and seen potential in me. My mind started racing; maybe one day I could be on that team, the pool from which the Olympic fighters are drawn. For the first time, I felt like I'd been noticed. I had always boxed for myself, and I did it because I loved it, not because I thought I ever stood a real chance of fighting for Great Britain. Now, suddenly my world had grown bigger and I would have to rise to the challenge. The prospect of training with Team GB was beyond what I could have even dreamed; it made me think about all the times I'd had to get up at 5 a.m. to go for a run before college or work, the exhaustion and pain, the day-in-day-out training; it all felt worth it, my hard work had been rewarded. It made me see that success cements the journey, because it reminds us that we're on the right path. 'This is real, right?' I asked Ricardo.

'Yes, Ramla. Team GB wants you to go train with them.'

I arrived in Sheffield on a dreary afternoon and saw little more of the city than the train station and surrounding area, because for the next three days, every minute of my time was spent in the English Institute of Sport (EIS). It was a huge complex with Olympic-sized swimming pools, multiple basketball courts, and a strength and conditioning facility about triple the size of any gym I'd ever seen. We'd leave the training centre as the sun was setting, only to walk back to the athletes' housing across the road from the EIS, which consisted of dorm-like rooms where we'd cook dinner and get to know each other the best we could before desperately needing to sleep. I thought I had trained hard before, but Sheffield was gruelling. We had to be on the track at 7 a.m. for running or sprinting, then back for breakfast and a quick break before going to the gym at 10 a.m. for strength and conditioning workshops. The afternoons were my favourite; that's when we'd spar, and it meant I was finally getting the chance to fight a whole host of incredible women, including my personal hero, former Commonwealth Games champion Lisa Whiteside. The first time I got in the ring with Lisa, I was all kinds of overwhelmed. I had followed her career and had looked up to her ever since the first time I'd seen her fight back in 2011. Watching her was one thing, but actually getting to spar with her was completely intimidating, even though I loved every second of it; she was so fast. I had to react to her every move with razor-sharp precision, or I'd find myself getting completely dominated. The first session was genuinely frightening, but by day three, we were a lot more evenly matched. Lisa came up to me after that last session, and grabbed me by the arm and told me, 'You're fucking annoying!' I was completely speechless. 'You're just so good with your feet,' she continued. 'It was so hard catching you.' Relieved, I couldn't help but smile.

'Thank you so much. You know, you're really annoying too.'

'What do you mean?' she asked.

'Every time you caught me, it really hurt! You're three kilos lighter than me but your punches are so strong.'

And just like that, I'd made my first friend on Team GB. That camp pushed me to the edge of my limit, and out of my comfort zone but it's in those moments that true heroes are born. You realise what you're made of when you force yourself to do the things you didn't know you were capable of. I was in no way the fittest person or the best boxer there, but I was there for a reason, and I was proud of my performance over the weekend. I was given a chance to step up, and I had given it everything I'd got.

*

April 2016 and I was back at the nationals. There were no other London competitors, so I skipped the regional divisions and joined in at the quarter-finals. The pressure was really on, as not only did I have something to prove inside the ring, but out of it too. In the height of training I'd had to sit my A level exams to make it to King's to study physiotherapy, and while I'd passed chemistry with flying colours, I was two marks off the grade I needed in biology. That meant that I'd lost my place at King's; it was a huge setback in my career plan and I felt like I'd let myself and my parents down. I realised too late that I'd taken on too much. I had put too much time into training and not enough into studying. I was crushed, thinking I'd thrown away my time and money. I had made plenty of sacrifices to get to this point, so I took all of my energy and frustration and poured it into my next competition. I needed that focus in that moment – allowing me to power forward, and fuelling my reason to fight – and reassessing my career could come later, once the competition was out of the way.

That year the nationals were taking place at the Echo Arena in Liverpool, and this time the quarter-finals, semi-finals and finals were happening over three consecutive days. I told my parents I was staying with my friends for a long weekend, and I didn't let the guilt of lying consume me on this occasion. I had made my choice, and I was standing by it. Sometimes the decisions we make for ourselves impact the people around us. I had to accept there was a chance my family could find out that I'd started boxing again; that was the risk I took, and I was more prepared to accept responsibility for my own actions. In the same way my training had affected my education, me competing could also hurt my family; I needed to acknowledge that, even though the thought scared me. I was choosing to compete, even though I didn't have the backing of my family, so I had to back myself. I was fully in that fight, regardless of what might happen; I needed to say it with my chest.

I'd competed for the National title before, I'd even competed for it in the same space, but everything felt bigger that year. Women's boxing had come a long way. The stakes were higher, the audiences were larger, and as I watched competitors warm up in the wings of the stadium, I felt proud to be a small part of it. I won my first two fights, against a woman called Jade from Middlesbrough, and then I faced Kim Shannon, a very distinguished fighter. I could see in the faces of the other competitors around me that they'd already written me off, but I backed myself even if nobody else did. It was a close match, but when I won that second fight against Kim Shannon, I showed the boxing world I was there to be taken seriously. I wanted that win so badly I worried that I'd only dreamed it, but my phone was exploding with texts that grounded me in an exciting reality. My friends from the gym, Bianca and Leanne, had been streaming the fight and my phone was full of missed calls from them. 'That was incredible! We're coming to watch you in the finals!' read a text from Bianca. They arrived a few hours later, and since they didn't have anywhere to stay, the three of us shared my hotel bed that night. I didn't mind being squashed, I felt so grateful that they had come to support me, and the fight against Kim had completely exhausted me, so there was no danger I wouldn't fall fast asleep.

I woke up early the next morning and walked over to the stadium alone. The hustle of merchandise vendors setting up their stalls and fighters queuing to be weighed had begun to feel familiar, and I paced around the stadium a few times before I had to weigh in so I could clear my head. It was my third fight there in three days, but still the sheer size of the arena amazed me with each visit. I was waiting to be called up to the scales when one of the referees walked past. 'Ladies!' he said with a smile to me and the other girls signing in. 'Look what you could be winning today.' I followed the direction of his outstretched arm, and there, perched on a podium was the winner's belt: a big black leather piece with a bright red rim. In its centre was a massive silver medal bearing three lions: the England Boxing logo. It looked so stiff and shiny; obviously being brand new it had never been worn. In reality it was quite an ugly thing – it was audacious and impractical, and I had no idea where I would even be able to put it if I took it home, but I would have done anything to win it. When the stewards finished weighing me, I left the arena and came back to the hotel for a pre-fight breakfast of scrambled eggs on toast.

While the other competitors chatted away, I was quiet. I was nervous. Before every fight it's the same – my ritual of solitude. I've come to learn there is no clear way of me ever overcoming my nerves before a fight. As I've progressed in my career I've found yoga and meditation forces me to slow down my thoughts and to focus on the positives and lean in to the possibility of winning rather than letting myself be consumed by nerves. I have to sit with them and accept that raw nervous energy is part of the process. I acknowledge the adrenaline sweeping through my body and welcome it. Your nerves stem from the same energy source that drives you to win, and you have to learn to embrace that. We only get nervous when we really care about something, and that means we're in exactly the right place in our discomfort. I don't try to distract myself from the intense feeling; instead, I make sure I get a few minutes of privacy before the fight. I need to be alone, nobody talks to me, I am quiet and I am still; I preserve my energy.

However, there was something about my opponent that day that made it even harder to stay calm. Rachael Mackenzie was a few years older than me, and something of a dark horse in boxing. I hadn't heard of her before that week; Ricardo hadn't been able to find out any information and it seemed as if she had just come out of nowhere and suddenly started beating everyone. It turned out that she'd only recently switched to boxing. But she was no novice; before boxing, she'd had a lucrative career in Muay Thai fighting. She was the first European woman to compete in a traditional bare-knuckle fight in Thailand before a knee injury brought her to boxing, and then to the nationals. I managed to watch her in her own semi-final fight. She'd beaten a really strong competitor, and there was something completely unorthodox about the way she fought. She seemed to have this way of constantly making her opponents fall short; the other girl couldn't seem to get into a rhythm with her, which made Rachael almost impossible to hit.

The first time we met was when we were in the ring together. I tried to stare into her eyes, hoping she'd look nervous or try to avoid eye contact, but she looked right back at me, grinning a wide, toothy smile. Nobody had ever smiled at me like that before, it was unnerving. I didn't know if she was trying to be threatening, but it certainly made me feel uncomfortable. When the fight began, I charged towards her. I was the first one to land a hit, and there it was again, that smile. It threw me ever so slightly – how could you smile after being punched in the face? Was she trying to throw me off? But then I realised, it doesn't matter what your opponent does when they're hit, it doesn't matter how many people show up for you in the audience, or who has worked harder to be here. All that mattered was what I did in those eight minutes, I had to do the work. If I lost my focus, I would lose the fight.

As I'd seen in her previous matches, there was something strange and difficult about fighting Rachael. The way she moved was completely unexpected, and we'd often end up in a hold where one of us would lock our arms around the other in a desperate embrace. It went like this for two rounds, me stealing shots wherever I could and her charging around me with bullish determination. By the third round, I had stepped up. I was faster on my feet and I played it to my advantage, not letting her get away, hitting her hard and fast before getting out. In tense moments when the audience were quiet, I was sure I could hear Leanne and Bianca in the distance screaming my name. Most competitors bring their whole family to the national finals; to this day I've never been able to do that, and so in those moments, hearing their voices meant the world to me. By the time we were into the fourth round, I had finally found my rhythm. I was flying around the ring landing every punch. As soon as the bell rang, Rachael and I embraced in a hug, and for the first time, I saw that smile for exactly what it was: genuine warmth. Here was a girl so passionate about our sport that the fear of losing or getting a black eye or worse . . . none of it mattered, she was so happy simply being in the ring. 'Congratulations!' Rachael whispered in my ear. I looked at her, confused because we still hadn't heard the scores. 'Look, I know you won that,' she explained. 'You fought better than me.' I know it must have taken a lot to say that, I felt so humbled by how gracious she was; it was a smiling reminder that even in the heat of competition life goes on beyond the ring.

Rachael was right; I had won, and this time the judges confirmed it. I finally held the National title. All my setbacks instantly became insignificant in that moment – having to pull out in 2011, being refused the title in 2012, having to give up boxing for my family in 2014, Ricardo refusing to enter me in 2015; none of it mattered, the setbacks were all worth it. I held the National title, and the feeling was indescribable. I risked everything to be there, but rather than let the pressure and the nerves get to me, I had to summon the strength and courage I needed from within myself, and to remember why I was doing this. My friends piled onto me as soon as I was out of the ring and I knew I couldn't have done it without them.

As much as I slated it, I loved the feeling of putting on that belt. You're presented with this brand-new thing, but once you wear it, it immediately gets covered in your sweat, sometimes your blood, and it becomes something completely different, an extension of you as a fighter, and a talisman for the next battle. You feel so strong, as if the world is yours for the taking. Maybe it all seems a bit showy, the booming announcer, the gaudy trophies and the slightly ridiculous belts; but for a misfit who never thought she'd find happiness, that ceremony was one of the first times I felt seen for who I really was. That fight taught me that in the moment, you have to be yourself and believe in your own power.

ROUND THREE

It's your life: live it

There are so many different forces at play when it comes to dictating what we should want and who we should become. Sometimes it comes from people we care about; growing up, I had my parents constantly instilling in me the importance of having a good, steady job. Other times, it comes from strangers; as women we're constantly being told by the media how we should look, how we should dress, what lifestyle we should subscribe to. People can have their opinions and try to encourage you to be one thing or the other, but at the end of the day, only you can live your life, so be active not passive in the choices you make. If you love something, sometimes you have to just go for it.

Forgive

People will wrong us, even the ones we love. Staying angry with a person uses up a lot of energy that could be directed into something more positive. A man broke my nose in a way that could have been entirely avoidable if he hadn't used his full strength. That annoyed me, but I chose to forgive and focus on the future rather than be bitter and wait for an apology that would never come. My family and I have had to forgive each other many times, even if we haven't always acknowledged it. I harbour no resentment that they made me quit boxing, and

I know they forgive me for living a secret life for all those years.

Keep an open mind

Closed doors can be dangerous. Whenever I have hit difficulties – in my education, my career, my relationships – I have realised the best way to overcome obstacles is to remain open-minded to solutions. For a long time, I struggled to get on the right career path; sometimes I would force myself to stay in jobs I hated, or give up at the first setback. What actually helped me the most was taking time to really evaluate my skills and passions. I had to ask myself what I was good at, where could I really see myself? It made my journey to career satisfaction longer, but it was one hundred per cent worth it.

Honour your friendships

I really believe that friends are the family we choose ourselves. I only had a few close friends at school, I hardly made any at university either, but take it from me – in a planet with over seven billion humans, your people are out there. I met a lot of my best friends through boxing, and in the hardest times, I have really appreciated how invaluable their support is.

EMBRACE YOUR VULNERABILITY

*'Rhythm is everything in boxing. Every move you
make starts with your heart, and that's in rhythm or
you're in trouble.'*
— Sugar Ray Robinson

I've always been independent. In my younger years, a combination of the tough love of my parents and the feeling that I was different from other people at school taught me that I shouldn't depend on other people for emotional support, that I had to look after myself. Growing up in my family, showing one another love meant making sure everybody was provided for: meals on the table, a roof over our heads, good education. My parents showered me with love in a way that centred around making sure my physical needs were met, but when it came to emotional needs, none of us found it particularly easy to express ourselves. My parents rarely talk about the trauma they went through during our final weeks in Somalia; it's too painful so they shut it out, and instead focus on the future. My siblings and I have naturally adopted that same way of thinking and feeling. We were taught to overcome our problems by getting on with it and moving forward. In some ways, I'm still like that today, I find it difficult to talk about the things that bother me. I used to put up walls and not let people know what was going on inside my head as a way of protecting myself. I thought if I kept people at arm's length, they couldn't hurt me, but I eventually realised I couldn't face everything alone. Understanding how to navigate your own mental health is so important, particularly for diasporic communities where at times trauma is never addressed. I've learned that there is a silent power that comes from sharing your struggles with others, from allowing yourself to be vulnerable, and from letting in the people that you trust. On the occasions that I did open myself up and let love in, whether to my friends or my partner, I've been lucky enough to experience deep human connection in the most powerful ways.

When the man I would go on to marry first walked into my life in the spring of 2016, my first two words for him were: 'Go away.' It happened shortly after the nationals tournament. I'd been doing more training camps in Sheffield, and with the dream of fighting for Great Britain constantly in the back of my mind, I was more committed to boxing than ever before. Because I had won the nationals, I had been selected to represent England in the English Title Series, in October 2016, my next big fight. That competition would mark a lot of firsts for me; the first test of my ability as a leading champion, and the first time I would be fighting with an England vest on my back. So when I encountered Richard Moore (also for the first time), I had a lot on my mind. The one thing I wasn't thinking about at all was my love life. I was the modern-day Elizabeth Bennet; I didn't need to find a partner. Through boxing, I had learned to be happy by myself, and I saw dating as something other people did to fill their time. I was determined, and I knew what my goals were, and what I had to do to achieve them, to the extent that I thought having anyone else involved in my life would become a distraction. I was doing pad work with Ricardo, when Richard came over to ask if he could watch us train. My initial reaction was one of mild irritation. This kind of thing had happened a few times: I had been made captain of the gym and I'd just won a big fight, so sometimes people would ask to watch my technique. It was flattering, but I felt uncomfortable with the attention, and on that day, Ricardo had been constantly correcting me and I didn't appreciate having an audience while we bickered. Reluctantly, I agreed to it. Richard stayed far too long for my liking, and I remember thinking, Who *is* this guy? Why is he watching us? 'Go away,' I muttered under my breath, still hammering away at the pads.

The following Saturday, I had to be at the gym at 7 a.m. to start work. The trains didn't run as frequently on the weekends, and to avoid being late, I always arrived half an hour early and waited until one of the managers came to unlock the gym. I quite liked starting the day thirty minutes before my shift began; it was a chance to be alone and to clear my head before the chaos of the gym started. But that Saturday, I wasn't alone. There he was, lying outside the door of the gym, the man who had watched me on the pads with Ricardo. I sensed he was going to try and talk to me so I quickly rooted around my bag in search of my headphones. I put them on and carefully avoided any eye contact.

'Hi!' I heard his sheepish voice from a few metres away. I sighed.

'Hi,' I said, reluctantly removing the headphones; he'd already stood up and was walking towards me.

'I thought the gym opened at 6 a.m.,' he said with an embarrassed grin. 'I've been here for ages, I didn't think it was worth going home just to come back so I thought I'd try and sleep; it didn't really work.'

'Oh,' I said, flatly. 'That's annoying for you.'

'I'm Richard,' he continued. 'I saw you doing pads the other day, you're really good. Why did Ricardo keep stopping and starting like that though? I feel like he didn't properly let you get into a flow?'

For the first time I got to take a proper look at Richard. He had a sly smile, dazzling blue eyes and brownish-blonde hair that probably would have been curly if he'd let it grow longer. He was clearly confident; he spoke with a boyish charm that made him hard to ignore, as much as I was trying to in that moment. I didn't want to engage in conversation, but it was hard not to when he kept firing question after question at me. Richard and I laugh about that day now, that everything about my body language was telling him to back off, but ever since he'd first seen me in the gym, he'd been waiting for a chance to talk to me. This was his opportunity; and there was no way he was going to waste it.

Reluctantly I found myself warming to this persistent stranger. He was friendly, kind and clearly passionate about boxing; but I had no idea that he might have liked me. I thought he was just chatty – a bit too chatty – and on that day, I had too much on my mind to let myself engage. Meanwhile, his tactic was to try and *keep* me talking, until I eventually thawed; but unluckily for him, it also happened to be Ramadan so I was fasting. I was hungry, tired and definitely not in the mood. I was relieved when Chris, one of the managers, showed up just before 7 a.m. to open the gym.

Richard and I parted ways; I went straight to reception as he headed off to the men's changing room, but later that day I found myself thinking about him whenever I had a spare minute. If I was clearing up after a class, I'd linger a little longer to watch him train, being careful that he never saw me. One of my jobs at LCB was to offer teas and coffees to the parents who were waiting for their children to finish junior classes. Only Zee was in that morning. Since it was a quiet day and Richard had finished his session with Chris, I offered him a drink too; he had been outside since 6 a.m., after all.

Looking at him again, I noticed he had this reddish-brown glow to his skin. I pointed out that he looked very tanned, and he told me he'd just come back from Los Angeles, where he'd been living for the past few years. He worked as a producer on commercials and documentaries, and since I was once again feeling anxious about my own career, I was interested to hear how he came to his profession. As we spoke, I realised

Richard knew a lot about boxing. He'd been doing it since he was at school in Brighton, where he grew up before moving to London with his mum. His dad was an amateur fighter, and his great-grandad was Archie Sexton, a former British champion who still to this day holds the record for most knockouts in the country.

As we talked it was clear that Richard was what my mum would call 'a bit of a bad boy' – it's how she referred to my dad when he was younger. At school, Richard had got into his fair share of trouble, and was eventually expelled. He'd got into the film and TV production world at sixteen, and since setting up his own company, he hadn't looked back. While Richard told me everything about his life, I wasn't so quick to open up – my nerves put my defence barriers up immediately. We can all put up a wall for many different reasons; it's scary to let somebody new in, in case we get hurt or are abandoned down the line. So instead we build psychological barriers to protect ourselves; it's a defence mechanism. I didn't want him to know about my family and what we'd been through because to share this with someone always made me feel exposed. At school I was worried that people would judge us for being refugees, and though I was proud of everything we'd overcome, I'd been hurt by my experiences of being bullied as a child. I still had some of the same lingering fears when it came to revealing intimate details about myself. I knew I would have to confront this fear of my past – to keep it locked up was to dishonour the journey my family had taken, and I knew that if I continued to keep everything bottled up I would explode. Believe it or not, boxing is never an outlet for my rage, quite the opposite. It's about poise and control; you need to be able to take whatever is going on in your personal life and not let it impact your performance in the ring.

When Richard left to go and train, I felt Zee's eyes on me as she tapped me on the back. 'He likes you,' she said, conspiratorially sipping her coffee. 'No way,' I scoffed back at her, and I really meant it. Tall, handsome, blue-eyed Richard looked like he belonged in some kind of teen movie, and I'd watched enough teen movies in my life to know that the Richards of the worlds didn't seem to end up with the Ramlas. Boxing may have given me more confidence, but I'd endured years of bullies telling me I wasn't good enough, and deep down that's still how I felt. Now when I look back at it, I see how deluded I was for thinking in that way. I believed Richard was out of my league, but of course we have always been equals; I just wasn't confident enough to see it yet. It's easy to put people on pedestals before we know them, but it's important to have perspective too. Instead of instantly assuming someone is more successful or more talented or smarter than us, we should celebrate our own qualities, the ones we actually know we possess.

What Richard saw that day was a strong, talented woman; of course he wanted to get to know me, so much so that he came back to the gym that same afternoon. Zee rushed over to me with the news. 'I told you he liked you,' she said. 'It's not like he's an actual boxer, why else would he come in twice in one day? I'm telling you, he's definitely into you.'

I wondered if there might be some truth in what she was saying. It *was* only the competing boxers who trained twice a day, and I knew Richard didn't compete. I tried not to think about it; I didn't want to let myself entertain any ideas in case I ended up disappointed. And yet, I couldn't help myself. Crushes are often dismissed as silly fantasies, and it's true that they are an exercise of the imagination, but they're also a way of showing you what you want. Why do you find yourself thinking about this person constantly? You don't know them, so what are the important qualities you're hoping and imagining they have? Kindness? Empathy? I can see now that what you project onto a person is a reminder of what you might want from them. I think a part of me was looking for someone who I could be myself around; it just took me a while to admit it.

I hoped the regular training camps would be a welcome distraction from thinking about Richard, but the more time I spent in Sheffield, the more I'd find myself wondering about him. He seemed so interested and supportive of my boxing career in a way that no one else had been before, and in turn that helped me feel extra confident. Spending time around people who uplift us is so empowering; sharing our goals with others can help us to analyse them and stay focused on turning our ambitions into a reality. I used to never think beyond my next competition, but Richard would often ask me about my plans for the future. From early on he seemed excited about my potential, which made me start to consider new possibilities I'd never dared to dream about before. Could I really join the GB team? Could I become a professional boxer instead of an amateur one day?

On the days that I was back at LCB, I'd hope that I might run into Richard, even though I was starting to dread spending time with Ricardo; as time went on our relationship was becoming increasingly fraught and more hostile. I made sure not to let him know about my developing relationship with Richard, as I sensed he would disapprove. I really felt like I was becoming stronger as a boxer, but that only seemed to make Ricardo harsher as a coach. He'd been happy for me when we'd first got the GB letter, but I'd had to confront some difficult truths. I realised that our dynamic had always worked because he held the power. We weren't equals in the relationship; in our coaching sessions, he would tell me what I had to do, and I'd do it. If he criticised me, I would always accept what he said because he was my coach and I knew it was in my best interest to listen to him, but that was becoming almost impossible to do. We'd begun to argue a lot; I did not feel that his criticism of my performance was justified.

That summer, Ricardo and I both knew that his influence was declining. He was my coach during the week, but with a lot of my weekends being spent in Sheffield on training camps, I was working more closely with Amanda, one of the England Boxing coaches – meaning Ricardo had become my secondary trainer. I could tell it bothered him. Amanda would often send him notes about the areas she'd like him to work on with me, but he bridled at being told what to do. Unlike Ricardo, Amanda's sessions never involved shouting or pointing out my flaws. Instead, she'd calmly show me ways to alter my technique, and once I was working more efficiently, she'd praise me. Her approach wasn't at all radical, but I'd never worked with a coach that caring before. Boxing is so often about toughness and breaking the fighter down so that they submissively take in their teacher's every word. A coach has a lot of responsibility. If they're consistently disparaging, it can hurt. If I'm working with an aggressive coach I tend to shut down; I get so in my own head that I can't take their feedback on board in the same way. I know that I need the calming and positive energy that a coach like Amanda brought to every session. With Amanda, it felt like we were collaborating; she was a kind, passionate woman who always wanted to get the best out of people. She helped me to be confident and to see my own potential. Working with her made me realise that empathy guides what I do, and I'm drawn to working with people who are caring and understanding. It's a value I wish more people operated with. I'd never felt Amanda and Ricardo's differences more sharply than when I had a sparring session with a girl from another gym. She'd been boxing for less than a year so I knew I needed to take it easy on her. I didn't hit her with maximum impact, and when it felt like she was still recovering from my blows, I deliberately missed opportunities where I could have come at her again. This was the same level of respect I'd been lucky enough to be shown when I'd first started sparring. It's such a new and frightening experience to go through, and you don't want to overpower a person so badly that they never want to get in the ring again. I also knew I had nothing to prove, while she needed to build up her confidence and skills over a different period of time. I felt a responsibility to look after her; to be her 'big sister' in this experience as opposed to her opponent. We should all be so lucky to have someone looking out for us in this way – whether in the workplace or the gym – solidarity as well as physical and psychological safety is so important in these dynamics. Seeing more women in boxing – regardless of level of ability – genuinely excites me. We have to stick up for each other and I'm committed to making a welcoming environment for the new generation coming through.

Sadly, Ricardo didn't recognise the bigger issue of mutual respect at play. As we sparred, he constantly jeered at me from the sidelines, saying that I wasn't putting in any effort and that I needed to hit her harder. I tried to ignore him, but as time went on, I could feel him growing more and more agitated until he was yelling at me in front of everyone. Eventually he snapped, abruptly stopping the session and demanding that I left the ring. Before me or my sparring partner had a chance to climb under the ropes, he grabbed me by my headguard, pulling it off and throwing it across the floor. My hair had been caught in it and I felt the back of my head stinging. It was so humiliating. I could feel the eyes of the girl and everyone from her gym on me, waiting for me to react, but I didn't. I knew trying to reason with him would never work. If I stood my ground I was worried he might ignore me for days, refusing to train with me. I couldn't afford to lose my coach with the English Title Series on the horizon, so I said nothing. I felt powerless. The relationship had turned toxic. Looking back on it, I should have stopped working with him then, but I didn't. I've grown to learn that everyone has the right to feel safe and supported in any kind of relationship, be it a professional one or a friendship – trust and respect are the fundamental basics, and the moment you start to feel those basics are not there, you have to get out. Ricardo had stopped showing me both those values, and the way he coached me had started to make me feel incompetent and undermined.

Where Ricardo made me feel small, luckily Richard continued to make me feel supported. His kindness was energising to be around, especially when I was dealing with so much animosity from my coach. We'd been getting to know each other for a few weeks, when he invited me to a barbecue at his house. I went back and forth on whether I should go; I was shy and wouldn't know anyone else there, but as the day grew closer, I found myself excited about the prospect of spending time with him outside of the gym. On the afternoon of the barbecue I was relieved when Richard appeared from outside his terraced house to greet me. At the time he lived with Charlie, his housemate and best friend, and as he led me to the garden, he told me about how Charlie's mum had moved to London from Nigeria in the seventies, eventually buying this house from the council. When she'd moved out of London a few years previously, she'd left it to her son, who, from what I could tell, hadn't redecorated since; the place was full of spare furniture and half-packed boxes he hadn't got around to moving. When I met Charlie it made sense; he had this busy, scatty energy, but he knew exactly how to make me feel welcome. You can tell a lot by a person's friends, and Richard's were a real motley crew of misfits. None of them had what my mum would call a 'proper job': they were surfers, skaters, personal trainers, artists and freelance photographers. I liked his friends; none of them seemed to work in offices and they were full of stories about travelling all over the world. Like theirs, Richard's life seemed so limitless. He didn't have to answer to his parents and it seemed like there were no financial implications of throwing caution to the wind and booking the next flight out of the country. I wouldn't have changed my upbringing for the world – it taught me the value of working hard – but it was interesting meeting all these people who I sensed had had a very different background to me. There was something inspiring about the way so many of them had managed to turn their passion into their careers: the sky really was the limit.

I learned that Richard was similarly always on the move. He told me about living in California and travelling around North Africa where he discovered a deep love for Islam. Richard and Charlie had visited a mosque in Morocco, where some Muslim men had invited them to pray and had introduced them to Islamic teachings. Their words had stuck with Richard, and after that trip he'd been thinking about converting to Islam, so he had a lot of questions about my faith. At the time my parents were in Mogadishu which meant for once, I didn't have to rush home, so I stayed until most of the others had filtered out and the sky had turned black and enveloped the garden, and even then, I wasn't ready to leave, but I knew if I didn't go soon I'd miss the last Overground. Charlie welcomed me to stay the night in the spare room instead of travelling alone after dark, but there was no way I was staying; my parents might have been on the other side of the world but they had a way of finding things out and I didn't want to rebel against them any more than I was already doing. Instead, Richard offered to walk me to the station, and so, shoulder to shoulder, the two of us wandered to Peckham Rye in a comfortable quietness. As we neared the station, I don't think either of us was ready to say goodbye, and I spent the train journey home gazing out of the window and replaying the evening as south London sped by. When he messaged to check I'd got home safe, I felt silly about how excited it made me, and when I saw him a few days later at LCB, he flashed me a smile from across the room. Later that day, he asked if I wanted to come over for dinner that night, and once again, we ended up staying up late and setting the world to rights with Charlie.

With my parents away, Richard and I continued to spend more time together. He would ask me about my family and why I couldn't talk to them about boxing, and slowly I learned to trust him enough to open up. The first time I did, admitting my fears and insecurities, I felt completely naked. I had no walls to hide behind and it was something I'd never done. It was scary, I worried he would judge me or think of me differently. It was like jumping out of a plane and hoping the parachute would open. But in the aftermath, it felt good too, he didn't run away or see me differently and I felt relieved. The more we shared about ourselves, the more I fell for Richard; he was caring and supportive, and spending time with him made me feel so good about myself. He really backed me as a fighter, reminding me to see the bigger picture and encouraging me to aim higher with boxing. When we weren't at Charlie's or LCB, we'd spend hours just wandering around Peckham, where I also felt myself falling in love with south London. We'd watch beautiful Black queens walking out of the hair salons with fresh weaves and wigs and listen to the hundreds of languages and different dialects that made up the sound of the high street. It was during one of our longer walks that Richard suddenly sat me down on a bench and told me exactly what I needed to hear – that he liked me.

That weekend, we went on our first real date, one that we both laugh about now. We went for dinner at Negril, a Jamaican restaurant in Brixton, where we both thought we were being so fancy, sat across the table from each other eating jerk chicken with a knife and fork instead of our fingers. We were trying to impress each other, but we needn't have bothered because we both already cared about one another, and neither of us wanted the other to change. When I'd read *Pride and Prejudice* at school it had made me believe that having a partner meant you sacrificed a part of yourself, but I now realise that shouldn't be the case. I don't believe in meeting your 'other half' or finding 'the one', but if you have a healthy relationship with yourself, and if someone does come along – someone who shows you respect and support, friendship and love, someone who can help you be the best version of yourself – then opening yourself up to the prospect of letting them into your life can be a great thing.

Of course, the most important relationship is the one that will always be there; the one that you have with yourself. It took a lot of work for me to feel confident and proud of who I am. I had to force myself to celebrate the positives; the friendships I'd made, the competitions I'd worked hard to be part of; even the times when I'd got up early and run that extra lap. Learning to celebrate the small wins is a useful skill, because the small wins lead to bigger wins, and the big wins take a lot of self-love to achieve. As my romantic relationship developed, I found myself confiding in Richard in a way that I'd never done with anyone before. It wasn't because he had become my boyfriend, but because he had a way of sensing when something was on my mind, and encouraging me to open up. At first, I'd been reluctant to let my guard down but he was persistent in wanting to get to know me, and when I was stressed or upset, he seemed to know exactly what to say to calm me down. I realised that if I let him in, I didn't have to face all of my problems alone. Sharing your feelings with someone you trust isn't always easy, but I have discovered how powerful it can be if I'm struggling, to know there are people I can share my inner thoughts with. When I tell Richard, or Danika, or Dave – my sports psychologist – about what's upsetting me, they have a way of reminding me I'm not alone. They might not be able to solve my problems, but they certainly make them seem more manageable. They take the load that I think I carry alone, and break it down, making it seem more bearable, and supporting me through it.

My relationship with Richard moved quickly, but it felt right. It had only been a few weeks when we admitted we loved each other, and we soon found ourselves planning a whole new future that neither one of us could have ever imagined. I found myself experiencing love at a time when the world seemed to be full of hate, as that same summer, the UK had voted to leave the European Union, and just a few months later Donald Trump would win the US presidential election. We talked about Brexit a lot; as it felt like anti-immigrant sentiment was suddenly everywhere. Racist politicians would go on talk shows to spout hate, while immigrant-owned businesses were being vandalised. All my life I had known that racism existed; I had experienced it first-hand many times, and while the reports of rising hate crime didn't shock me, they did sadden me.

That same year, the Great Britain boxing team were regularly inviting me to training camps. Until then I'd wanted nothing more than to represent my country, but now I was asking myself if that same country wanted me here. 'Yes,' Richard would tell me, over and over and over again. We would talk about the horrible forces in the world, and realise that it was both of our responsibilities to fight against them. I felt like a misfit, but a proud one. I grew glad that I stood out. In the face of hatred, I was committed to standing up, being proud of where I was from and spreading positivity and love. It's simple – representation matters, and seeing somebody who looks like you succeed is an invitation for you to step up and achieve greatness yourself. My passion for boxing also became my responsibility, something I had to be accountable for; if I won the English Title Series, I would become the first female Muslim boxer to do so, and I knew that would send a strong message out into the world. I wanted to show every young person of colour that came after me, every Muslim or minority, that we are here, we are champions, and we are a force to be reckoned with.

A few weeks before the English Title Series, Richard told me he had converted to Islam. He deliberately waited until after he'd said his shahada (a declaration of his faith) to call me so I couldn't talk him out of it or tell him to wait. He knew I would think he was doing it solely for me, but he promised he'd made the decision on his own, and said that he'd been thinking about it for a long time. Islam, he told me, was the religion that had brought him the strongest sense of peace during the most chaotic moments of his life. He told me that he wanted to be part of something bigger than just himself, and I understood. Having faith is an intensely personal commitment; he'd been on his own journey in the same way I'd been on mine. Though my faith looks different to my parents', I have always been a proud Muslim. Through Islam I have learned about the importance of charity and giving back, it's taught me infinite things about patience and commitment and love, so I was happy for Richard – he had become a part of something incredibly special. Of course, it did help us be together too, and in late July, our relationship reached new heights when in the middle of the day, in the middle of the street, he got down on one knee and asked me to marry him. He was so calm, as if he was asking what I wanted for dinner, not what I thought about spending the rest of our lives together. I stared at him in shock. It was nothing like a romcom, the proposal was so unantici-pated to me that my fight or flight response kicked in and I could have easily run away – but the shock gave way to sheer joy. I was laughing and crying uncontrolla-bly before I eventually managed to force the words out: 'Yes,' I told him. 'I cannot wait to marry you.'

Of course, there was no way I could do that without the permission of my family, and at that point, they didn't even know he existed. Richard wanted to elope, and I loved his spontaneity, his innate sense of adven-ture, but I was firm; there was no way I would marry him if my family didn't agree. I love my family and I couldn't imagine a life without them. When I'm ill, all I want is a cuddle from my mum. I was young and head over heels in love, but still, my family came first.

The day I told my mum I'd met someone, she was at

home, midway through making a vegetable curry. The fear I felt was ten times worse than any pre-match anxieties. Half of me wanted to run up to my bedroom, but I held my nerve. I told her I needed to talk with her, and we sat down at the kitchen table, my hand holding hers. Learning to face your fears is one of the hardest lessons there is, but being in the ring has done a lot to prepare me for the most difficult moments. Deep down we have to believe that the best things in life are worth fighting for, and being brave is a commitment you make to yourself first and foremost, and a true testament to what something means to you. So I pushed through my insecurity and fears, and was honest with my mum. I blurted out that I'd met someone, I told her everything I could, only omitting the fact we'd met at a boxing gym. I explained that Richard was gentle and kind, that he was hard-working and made me feel happy and loved. To this day, my admission is one of the rare times I've left my mum speechless. I tried to make the most of the silence, the final moments where it was all up in the air and everything might just work out in my favour. When she finally spoke, she asked me if he was a Muslim, and I told her he was. I watched as her face erupted into a smile before we both started laughing. What followed was a flurry of questions: where did I meet him? How long had I known him? What did he do? Where was he from? Were his parents still alive? What did his parents do? When could my parents meet his parents? The interrogation was full on, but she was so excited; I loved seeing her like that.

As promised, we arranged a meeting. First for Richard and my family; later, for his dad and my parents. It was an overwhelming series of introductions which was going well until my parents told us they didn't approve of us getting married. It was too soon. It wasn't my mum saying no, rather to slow down, take time and embrace learning about each other for a little longer. My mum reminded me of my brother, the son who was taken away from her too soon. She told me that she couldn't let the same thing happen to me; that she knew nothing about the man I wanted to marry and that she needed to know him before I had her full blessing. My parents were right, and I now see that this was an important lesson in patience and empathy for both Richard and me.

Richard dropped the fantasies of eloping, and he instead promised to put in the hours getting to know my parents and siblings, and learning about our values as a close-knit family. For the next few weeks, Richard and I continued to put in as much effort with them as we could. Things were going well, both my parents seemed to like him, and after they met his dad, slowly, talk of marriage started to come up again. It had been a whirlwind few weeks for my personal life, but I also had to wrap my mind around the fact that in just over a week, I had the English Title Series to compete for. I felt an intense amount of pressure to win because of what was going on around us, and the risk involved in being there; I needed to prove to myself that it was worth it, that I could leave victorious.

As the fight date grew closer, my nerves really took

hold of me, and for the first time I really felt alone. I couldn't talk to my family and Richard had to take a two-week production job in America. The morning of the fight, I felt like I didn't have the strength to get in the ring and perform to the best of my abilities. I was panicking so much as I packed my bag with water, snacks and the England vest I'd be wearing to defend the title. I laid the top on my lap – it was just a simple black vest – but I analysed it for way more detail. In wearing this vest, I would be representing the country I had grown up in for the first time. It wasn't lost on me how monumental this was – and as much as I was proud, it didn't stop the negative thoughts starting to creep in. I was overwhelmed with the fear of failing, and whether I really deserved to be there. Imposter syndrome can rear its ugly head at any moment – no matter how capable you know you are. My way through in these moments is to force myself to focus on how I can win – visualising each step of the way and reminding myself that I have everything I need within me. Changing negative thought processes doesn't happen overnight – it takes time. As well as envisioning your end goal, you have to begin by breaking down your self-doubt, and replacing it with self-love. When I have a quiet moment, I like to write down what I like about myself, the achievements that I'm most proud of, the way my body carries me through competitions. I'm not always the most positive person I can be, but reading back over those affirmations reminds me of how much I have achieved.

*

The fight would take place at York Hall in Bethnal Green – the mecca of English boxing. York Hall is such an intoxicating experience for any boxer. It's a proper East End institution. If those walls could talk they would reveal a legacy steeped in history – prizefighters since the 1700s have fought there, and everyone from Anthony Joshua to Nicola Adams has stepped between its ropes. As soon as I walked in that morning, I could feel the powerful spectral presence of hundreds of boxers who had been there before me; maybe, just maybe, I wasn't alone after all.

The other thing I love about York Hall is that it is only a five-minute walk from my parents' house, which made me feel like I was destined to be there in that moment. On my way to register and get weighed, I walked past the same pubs, fruit and veg stalls and my favourite Indian restaurants, which I must have passed by a thousand times. Those streets are my home; filled with black and brown and white faces, a whole melting pot of cultures who don't just tolerate each other but who co-exist proudly together in one area. That to me is London at its finest. I was home from the weigh-in before any suspicions could be aroused. I ate a big breakfast and tried to sleep to conserve my energy but I couldn't; I was full of apprehension and every minute passed impossibly slowly.

Danika called in the afternoon to wish me luck, and I felt full of love. She never watches my fights because she hates the idea of seeing me get hurt. She once told me that it makes her want to climb in the ring and help me defend myself, and Danika is so loyal it's the kind of thing I could imagine her actually doing. Hearing her positive mantras soothed my nerves. She reminded me that whatever happened in the ring, I would always have a best friend waiting for me at home. Having someone in my corner that day extended to Amanda too. Because I was representing England, I'd asked her to be my coach for the fight. Ricardo was there too, but purely for support – and whether he wanted to be there or not, I did appreciate the fact he had shown up. Leanne had also come down to watch me. That day, I remember feeling so loved and emboldened by the people who showed up for me. It really helped; my confidence levels started to rise and I remembered the things that would fuel my fight. I *had* beaten my opponent Rachael Mackenzie before, I told myself, though I knew that for her to come back from a defeat and want to fight me again meant she really wanted to even the score. Rachael was an unpredictable fighter and difficult to beat; I had my confidence back, but I wasn't going to let myself become complacent.

With less than ten minutes to go before we went face to face, Amanda and I found a space to be quiet. We sat in silence as I began to narrow my focus and continued to drown out the flurry inside. There was so much resting on that fight; I wanted to show Ricardo I didn't need him anymore and I wanted to show Amanda that I really was England material. I also wanted to prove to myself that this was worth the emotional pain I was putting myself and my family through. I wanted to make them proud too, one day, and I wanted to show my country that I belonged here. With the sound of the audience buzzing in the background, I prayed for a safe fight, and when my name was finally called, I let everything in my head go. With a deep breath, I calmly stepped up to the ring. This time, I couldn't help but smile back at Rachael as we locked eyes and the referee read us the rules – but as we took our corners, I had my game face on.

The bell rang. My guard was up, my head down. I let her come to me with that bullish charge, drawing her close and then trying to hit her with an unsuspected right hook. Rachael was much faster this time, she'd become even more agile and athletic; she was clearly there to win. I felt myself falling into the same trap as at the nationals; disorientated and unable to predict her jarring movements. I forced myself to stay calm, because if you panic in the ring, you waste mental energy, which is just as valuable as the physical. I needed to be fully present in the moment; completely focused on my body and hers. Gradually, I started to find my rhythm and gain confidence and control. When she'd come for me, I'd swiftly leap back out of her reach. On my own attack I was elastic; light on my feet, but fast and ferocious, moving around the ring like a flame.

When the bell rang signalling the end of the first round, I collapsed into my corner as Amanda appeared by my side. She admitted that I'd had a bit of a shaky start, but praised me for my performance in the second half when I had become noticeably more confident. Amanda warned me to stay alert, advising me to give two shots and then step out of Rachael's reach straight away. If I got into too much of an exchange with her it wouldn't pay off; I had to be both predator and prey, darting in and out of the action and striking her without being caught myself.

The bell rang for the second round, and I kept repeating Amanda's advice clear in my mind; give two shots, step straight back out. I lurched towards Rachael, landing a blow to the head followed by a blow to the body and then propelled myself away from her long arm as it swung back towards me in retaliation. The next time we were back in range, I twisted towards her on the ball of my right foot, hitting her with a heavy backhand. Rachael flew to the ground and I gasped. I was so relieved when she immediately got back up – it meant she was OK – and kept my distance as she staggered towards me. Instantly, I knew something was wrong. Before we could connect again, her coach threw in the towel signalling the end of the match.

The threat of physical danger is not why I got into boxing. I don't fight to cause pain. You can prepare to get injured during a fight, but to hurt someone else badly is an impossible feeling to plan for. After seeing Rachael fall like that, I needed to know she was alright. I found her after the fight and was relieved to see her walking with her coach; luckily she wasn't injured. She gave me a massive hug. We congratulated each other, and on sensing my hesitation, Rachael promised me that she was fine. She congratulated me on my performance; since I had knocked her down and ended the fight prematurely, I was the winner. Hearing the all-clear, I breathed a sigh of relief, but it wasn't until I was back in the safety of my bedroom that it really hit me: I had defended the English Title, and I had won.

When I think about the English Title fight, I think about the two moods that bookended that day. In the morning, I'd woken up feeling scared, nervous, alone. The same night, I was absolutely buzzing with joy, I was so proud of my successes and grateful for every person who had helped me along the way. I realise now that I couldn't have experienced such a high without having also gone through the lows. It was sitting in my fear in the morning that made me feel that much prouder in the evening, because I knew I had done something brave. I used to perceive fear and vulnerability as weaknesses, but a vulnerable person is someone who is strong enough to allow themselves to be open, so that they can live a full life. Of course, there is always a risk of getting hurt, that's especially true when it comes to relationships, but taking risks can be extremely character-building. It's easy to take the comfortable route, but no one achieves their goals if they don't seize the scariest of opportunities. Even if it does backfire, you'll feel hurt, but living life is about experiencing a full spectrum of emotions – loss, wins, good and bad. I don't believe everyone is happy one hundred per cent of the time; happiness and comfort tend to be punctuated with moments of frustrations, sadness or hurt, maybe even hatred or grief. Experiencing these emotions, hard though it may be, teaches us emotional intelligence. We become more empathetic people and better friends, partners or teammates to those around us. When I came home that night, I had the strongest urge to burst into the living room and tell my family: 'Mum, Dad, I just fought for England, and I won.' Imagining their pride felt so good but I knew it was completely out of the question. Instead, while the night grew dark and I waited for sleep to come, I closed my eyes and whispered the same words to myself. One day I would be able to share my wins with them, one day they would be proud.

ROUND FOUR

Love yourself

Loving yourself is more than acts of self-care, it's about backing your actions and decisions and being confident in your choices, even when others doubt you. It's about being proud of yourself when you're doing well, and gentle on yourself when things aren't going great. It's something we all need to work on, because your relationship with yourself is the most important one you'll ever have.

Be vulnerable

It took me a long time to learn that you can't face every problem by yourself. When things get hard, seek help, talk to people, ask for advice. Like me, you might not feel comfortable sharing your feelings with your family, but that doesn't mean you're alone. There are people out there who are the most incredible listeners – friends, counsellors, therapists, teachers – your job is just to find them.

Find your people

To be the best version of yourself, to really become your own champion, the key is to surround yourself with brilliant people. People who raise you up, people who are there for you when you really need them, and people who will hold you accountable to your goals. It took me a long time to really understand who my best friends and most trusted confidants are, and I had to be open and selfless to foster these relationships. Be there for the next generation too. Respect the younger people in your field; offer them the same level of advice and support that you have been given.

Compromise

There are a lot of things my parents and I don't see eye to eye on, some that we never will, and yet we consistently find a way to make our relationship work. Conflicts can be hard, even more so when they involve the people you love, but it's these difficult disagreements that teach us how to compromise. We don't all see the world in the same way. Try to see the other person's perspective; it's often a great opportunity to learn.

DEAL WITH DEFEAT

'Winners never quit and quitters never win.'
– Vince Lombardi

One of the qualities that I am most proud of is my drive to keep going, and my stubbornness to never give up on the things I want the most. October 14th, 2016. Seven days after I took home the English title, I got married, moved away from my childhood home and began my new life. When I looked back on all that I had achieved in the years that led up to that moment – winning the English Title Series, being scouted by England, meeting Richard – those highlights were broken up with at least as many setbacks and struggles – having to hide boxing from my family, the competitions I didn't win, failing my exams. It was tough, there was hurt and heartbreak, and it took everything to keep going. That rugged perseverance, the ability to continue to bet on yourself – when it pays off, it's as if a huge weight slips from your shoulders, allowing you to embrace the lessons and challenges up to this point; it makes it much more worth it too. Marrying and moving in with Richard allowed me a new sense of freedom. Living with my parents and their disapproval had hindered my boxing career: the constant stops and starts, the several international fights I turned down, as well as the tournaments outside of London that involved overnight stays. Even when it came to training in Sheffield; on the occasions that Mum was suspicious about me going away, I would turn down the training camps, a move that could make it look like I wasn't serious about competing. The fact was, by now I should have had way more fights under my belt, and I didn't – which made me feel like an underdog. The situation was especially frustrating, because I started to wonder if my parents suspected I was still boxing anyway. I frequently came home with visible injuries, and once my mum had even seen me slip into the house carrying boxing gloves. She hadn't said anything – I think neither of us could face the heartbreak of another confrontation – but I'm sure it was in the back of her head. I knew so much of her issue with my boxing revolved around what the community would think, and on moving out, I would be free from any judgement, and freer to train and compete. On the flipside, this was my family I was leaving. My parents had endured so much pain and suffering, they had watched the destruction of their beloved home before embarking on a terrifying journey that took over a year. Once they finally made it to the UK, they had to start their lives all over again. They experienced so much trauma and sacrifice, and yet they never gave up. They had survived so we could excel. They took menial jobs so we could find better ones, and though I may not have always seen eye to eye with them, I knew that every decision they made was always in the best interests of their children. Their strength has stuck with me. It's in my nature too, because of them. When I refuse to quit, I am summoning the courage I learned from my parents. I had lived with my parents forever, and so my excitement at the start of a new life was also tinged with sadness at the thought of not waking up every day to the smell of Mum's cooking. When it came down to it, I would miss it all; even the constant questioning I got from my mum, and the fact that the flat was never, ever quiet. There would be no more Somali TV streamed on YouTube. I'd grown up watching the strange soap operas that my mother loved – they were like a kind of African *EastEnders*, trashy as anything, but my parents loved them because it was something that they could understand.

Being part of Somali culture has taught me the value of respecting your family and your elders. I think a lot of children of the diaspora will feel the same sense of duty to obey their parents, never talking back or arguing with them. Although it was probably drilled into me through fear of punishment, I'm glad my parents taught me to behave with respect. It's easy for the younger generation to think we know it all, especially when we can harness the power of the internet to do and discover anything we want. We may have some advantages over our parents when it comes to using technology to learn about the things we're interested in and to connect with like-minded people all over the world. However, what the older generations have over us is a lot more lived experience, and it's important to respect that – even if we see the world differently to them.

When I woke up the morning of the wedding, I felt invincible. Just a few months earlier, I had met the man who would change my life forever, but for a while, it had felt like nobody was on our side. Even his best friends had agreed with my family; Charlie had tried to talk Richard out of proposing because he also thought it was too soon. We were moving too fast, he'd told Richard; we didn't know each other well enough. Nobody seemed to understand that we would have spent our every minute together if we could. We'd had to hide our relationship from Ricardo, from my family, but after today, we could finally be free. A Muslim wedding ceremony is known as a nikah, and as is custom, the ceremony took place at home. It felt fitting; as we officially welcomed Richard into our family, it was also a chance for me to say goodbye to the place I'd grown up in and the people I'd spent my whole life with. Nikahs tend to be very simple ceremonies – forget the cakes and the speeches – it's purely about vows being exchanged and the marriage contract being signed; the partying comes later. The bride doesn't even have to be present as long as she sends two witnesses, so I didn't come home till after my training session. I was still wearing my tracksuit bottoms and a T-shirt, then I slipped on my hijab, and I couldn't have felt more like myself. All of the Somali weddings I've been to have always been very spiritual affairs. They're rarely showy, but stripped back, and with the focus being on the joining of two people and two families. The men and women have to be separate, so once I had told the imam I accepted and signed the contract, we split the house into two. Richard, a few of his friends, my brothers and cousins were downstairs while the imam read from the Quran, and all of us women went upstairs into my mum's room, where in hushed excitement we waited for the marriage contract to be signed. It was at that point that one of the men came up to tell Luul, my older sister, who passed it on to all the women by basically running up the stairs screaming, 'Ramla is married!' Then, in my favourite Somali tradition, everyone joined her in making this sharp, high-pitched noise: 'Lilililili!' I can't explain it but to me it's the sound of pure joy. Being reunited with Richard felt amazing. I came downstairs to find him, along with my family, where we both belonged. We had done it the right way; we had waited for my family's approval but not given up on our own dreams.

Shortly after the wedding I was met with exciting news: Amanda had selected me to compete in the European Championships with the GB team, my first big international competition. Back then, because there were only three women's Olympic weight categories – 51kg, 60kg and 75kg – those were the only groups funded to be in the GB squad. It meant for the tournaments outside of the Olympics where there were a lot more weight categories, they had to draft in other boxers to compete alongside them. So, along with two other girls, I'd been invited to join the Team GB girls for the competition in Bulgaria. I couldn't believe I was getting to fight as a boxer for England. I was over the moon, but completely terrified too. I had less than a month to train, so the pride that came from being picked was laced with the biggest bouts of nerves I'd ever faced.

I felt like my boxing career was balancing on a knife edge. If I could progress and keep fighting with England, then I would be fulfilling my dreams and freeing myself from Ricardo, but if I messed up now, everyone would lose interest in me, and I'd be back to square one all over again, trying to earn my place. I felt as if one bad fight would automatically lose me the opportunities I'd worked so hard for, and I'd be finished. It wasn't a positive way of thinking at all, and another example of how we put way too much unnecessary pressure on ourselves. Now, when I find myself placing emphasis on one event to define my entire future, I remind myself to take a second to pause, zoom out and look at the bigger picture. In the thick of it, it may seem impossible; however, I tell myself that *I can* afford to lose a few fights, *I can* mess up in training, *I can* get injuries, and *I can* take time off to recover. For a boxer, and indeed anyone, there are things that are inevitable – that's why I try to replace the unnecessary doubt with a stronger voice that reiterates: some things will just happen, they are allowed to. In the grand scheme of things they don't pose that much of a problem and I can get through them and keep going.

In November 2016, Richard and I finally moved into our own place, a two-bedroom apartment on the second floor of a Greenwich new-build. The deposit was most of my savings, but we adored that flat. It had a little balcony overlooking a quiet, leafy courtyard, and was just metres away from the River Thames. When we got the keys, neither of us could believe our luck. I had grown up living in crowded council houses, sleeping in a bedroom I shared with my sister and never knowing when we'd next be asked to leave. Now we had our own peaceful little corner of the world, just for us. Moving into that flat was a huge reminder of how dramatically your life can change. It taught me the power of dreaming beyond your circumstances; I may have grown up in temporary accommodation and council housing, but there I was, having changed my circumstances and getting to travel to Europe to do the thing I loved. I had put in the hard work, years of it, and now I was finally getting to experience some of the rewards. We furnished the flat with a mattress my parents gave me, which went straight on the floor because we couldn't afford a bed yet, and we used upturned cardboard boxes as temporary bedside tables. Because I'd been living at home my whole life, and Richard had moved from LA to Charlie's, neither of us owned any furniture, and for a long time we lived out of bags and boxes. It would take us a few years to turn that flat into a real home, but we slowly did it, one cushion and one plant at a time.

We'd longed for our own space for so long, and in those simple moments where we cooked dinner in the kitchen or woke up together, life felt so magical. We were barely able to spend much time there which made it feel all the more special. I was taking on extra work at Virgin Active, and using the time before and after my shifts to improve on my strength and conditioning away from Ricardo's judging eyes and disparaging comments. I could get a free membership for Richard too, so sometimes he'd join me at the gym. He was shy at first, not wanting to step on my toes while I trained, but when he started supporting me by offering all these words of encouragement while I raced against the treadmill or lifted weights, it had a real impact on me. He was so invested in my boxing career, and his passion fuelled me to train harder, to keep pushing myself that extra bit. Whenever I wasn't at Virgin Active, I was at LCB, where I still had my reception job on the weekends. I rarely had a day off, and Richard had taken a full-time job at a creative agency as the head of production so that we'd be able to cover the costs of our flat. His work was intense; the hours were long and he often had to travel for shoots. After a few months living in Greenwich, the novelty began to wear off a little. I was often home alone in the evenings, and I started to feel lost without the constant noise and bustle I was accustomed to. At my parents' house, though I used to crave a moment to myself, I was rarely alone. Mum would always be in, shouting to be heard over the noise of the blaring TV and there was always somebody going in and out. In Greenwich, there were times I'd find myself feeling completely alone, lying on the mattress, gazing up at the ceiling contemplating how much my life had suddenly changed. Loneliness can affect even the most popular of people.

You can feel it when you're surrounded by others, and even though I was seeing Richard every day and my family were only a phone call away, there were times when I did feel completely alone. To combat the loneliness, I forced myself to get up early and get out of the house before I noticed the quiet. Being around people, even strangers, helped me to feel connected, and I always had training to look forward to, where I could be surrounded by friends. It wasn't the easiest of times, but I tried to focus on the positives.

The last training camp before the European Championships was in Tamworth, a town in Staffordshire. There were two other girls who had been selected to represent England outside of the team: Raven Chapman and Demie-Jade Resztan. Demie was younger than me and Raven. Having just turned nineteen, she was full of puppyish enthusiasm. What she lacked in age, she made up for by being completely fearless. I learned a lot from her; when Raven and I would have to battle nerves before each fight, Demie would approach hers with sheer excitement. She'd been boxing since she was just seven years old, and now that she was finally able to compete, she couldn't wait to get in the ring. While I always dreaded the thought of losing, Demie never even let herself entertain it. I envied her youthful energy and fearlessness not in a way that made me jealous, but in a way that made me want to embrace the same attitude. We can learn lessons from anyone around us, as long as we are open to them. Demie's attitude towards competing was so inspiring, and I really took something from that. She was able to override the fear by focusing on how lucky she was to be there.

By that point, I knew Raven pretty well. She usually fought at a heavier weight than me, but we'd been in a lot of the same training weekends at Sheffield, as well as the same tournaments. We'd started texting when we weren't together, talking about training and our upcoming fights. I liked Raven. She was a straight-talking mousy-haired girl from Brighton, and we'd started to bond a lot over our shared sense of terror when it came to competing. We both loved it, but we found that our nerves could be so debilitating we worried that fear would destroy our performances. Being around each other calmed us down. She was such a great boxer that I knew if she suffered from pre-fight anxiety and still won, I could too. Through Demie and Raven I was reminded how comforting it is to open up to other people. Often the women close to me in the sport share the same anxieties as I do. I've discovered the power that comes from talking about my worries with them, as I've found it's a good way to break these worries down; we share things and help each other come up with ways to cope. At the very least, I take heart in knowing other people can relate.

A minibus took the three of us and our coaches on the two-hour drive from Tamworth to Stansted airport, where we joined the other fighters. I was thrilled to see Lisa, who would be competing at flyweight (51kg). Sandy Ryan was the lightweight fighter (60kg), Chantelle Cameron classed as light-welterweight at 64kg, and Natasha Gale fought as a middleweight at 75kg; they were all there waiting for us in matching black tracksuits. It was a surreal moment, being alongside the GB team. These women represented the country at the World Championships and the Olympics, the biggest amateur boxing competitions on the planet. This was the Great British team, the best of the best. At that time, the competition in Bulgaria was the most important fight in my life. I kept thinking that if I performed well, one day I might be able to join the GB team myself. I'd never fully let myself dare to even dream about it before, but there I was, eating lukewarm soup in Pret a Manger in Stansted airport alongside the country's finest boxing talent.

While we may have been at the top of our game, the trip to Bulgaria was a testament to how unglamorous the world of women's boxing could be. We boarded a Ryanair flight with a randomly allocated ticket, finding our spaces next to the appropriate strangers. Four hours later, we landed in Sofia airport, where we were greeted with a sign that read 'Team GB'. I was an official part of the squad. Seeing those words in bold sent a pulse of electricity through my veins; this was our moment.

Our hotel was a huge grey building which always had a massive cloud of cigarette smoke outside the front doors, where a huddle of guests would congregate to smoke. Amanda didn't want Demie to be on her own, since she was the youngest, so she and I agreed to share a room. I'm not fussy about where I sleep, but I hated that hotel. The smell of smoke seemed to drift in and cling to the walls, and the bedsheets may well have been older than me, but the journey had exhausted me enough to tolerate the surroundings. Each morning, we had to be up and dressed by 7 a.m. for Team GB to weigh us. I'd barely eaten, but at that first weigh-in, I was marked as over. The competition started the next day, so I had twenty-four hours to lose half a pound. It's an impossibly frustrating situation when that happens; in its very nature, boxing requires you to eat a considerable number of calories to have the energy to maximise training sessions and win fights. And yet, the weight categories are so specific that if you're even slightly over the stipulated weight, you won't be allowed to compete. I only let myself be weight-conscious and stricter with my diet when I'm training for a fight, because getting into the habit of checking my weight every day isn't healthy. There needs to be balance, so when I'm not in training camp I let my body relax and indulge a little. In the early years, my weight was everything to me. I held on to my experience of being bullied for being overweight. I embraced boxing for what it did to me mentally as well as physically, however I still held on to apprehension around my weight and the anxiety of being too heavy for a competition, to the extent that I developed an unhealthy relationship with my body.

Every night before the European Championships, I took a long, hot bath which would make me sweat profusely. I limited my calorie intake, and I pushed myself to the max in each training session. My unofficial mantra was 'Restrict, restrict, restrict,' and I admit it wasn't a sensible way to lose weight; it also negatively affected my performance. Before the Bulgaria fight, I was exhausted, but I was training every minute I could in the hotel corridors because we didn't have access to a gym in Sofia. We were forced to be scrappy and make do with what we did have. We made it work; holding planks outside our rooms or sprinting around the corridors. After a few days of that, we couldn't wait for the competition to get started, and I was relieved to learn I'd be fighting on day one.

Amanda came to my room to give me a briefing. She told me that my first bout of the tournament was against a girl called Marielle Hansen from Norway. It had taken me years in the UK circuit to get even the vaguest sense of who the toughest opponents were or how somebody's style might differ to mine. Boxing at international level was a whole new world; 129 boxers from 28 nations were competing in the European Championships. I only recognised a handful of names, and I realised that this is where having a good coach is vital. Amanda explained that she was going to be learning everything about the girl: who she had fought before, who her trainer was, and most importantly, her fighting style. Amanda assured me she and the other coaches would leave no stone unturned as they carefully watched old video footage of her previous fights. She asked if I wanted to join them in the video analysis, but I told her I wouldn't watch. I trusted Amanda's judgement and promised I'd do exactly what she told me to; that way, I'd have something to focus on. I didn't want to scare myself by watching loads of footage of Marielle.

We reconvened the next morning once Amanda had watched the videos with the other coaches, and I had finally made weight successfully. Amanda warned me that Marielle was an extremely strong boxer. She had been competing for a long time, and had a lot more experience than me. The pit of my stomach felt heavy, but Amanda promised me she saw a way for me to win the fight. As we discussed tactics, I locked into Amanda's every word, making sure I didn't miss a single beat. 'This is how we're going to get this girl. I need you to wait. I need you to be really patient, and then when she comes . . .' Amanda slowly moved her hand through the air. 'That's your moment, then you go, go, go!' she said, pointing her outstretched fingers towards me. 'Wait for her to come in, and then you counter.' While Marielle may have been more experienced, Amanda also noted that she was shorter than me. That meant that if I kept my distance, I should be able to make contact with her first, landing quick jabs and crosses while I was still out of Marielle's range. I listened intently to everything Amanda said, repeating and memorising each point until it felt like second nature. In the ring, I would do exactly what she asked of me. The wisdom of a coach can appear in many forms. In that moment I was grateful for having someone on my side, and I trusted her to show me the way forward.

This was my first international fight wearing an England vest, and I was determined not to disappoint. Walking to the stadium that morning, I went over Amanda's advice again and again, making sure I knew every note about my opponent's movement and style by heart, and by the time I was in the ring, I felt confident and ready. From the second the bell rang, I set to executing Amanda's every instruction. I admit it didn't feel natural instantly, but I waited for the right opportunities to present themselves. I stayed calm, I lured Marielle into the middle of the ring and I'd hit only when I knew she was within range. I fought defensively, but it made it difficult to take any kind of control. Marielle was fast; she would lean one way to get me to react and then attack me out of nowhere on the other side. So much of boxing is about reading your partner, anticipating what they're going to do next. I only had four two-minute rounds to outshine her, but I couldn't predict her moves. My instincts told me I should be more aggressive, I wasn't landing enough shots by staying back, but I also knew I had to follow Amanda's instructions. Being torn between these two approaches, I was lost in my own head, rather than fighting and reacting; my performance was patchy at best. I have realised that in my most crucial moments, focus is everything. If I take my mind off my opponent, even for a second, I can slip up. I can't afford to waste a second doubting myself, and that's where my training comes in. You have to do the work before those key moments. You have to be prepared and ready, so that you have the confidence to go out there with no negative thoughts, because there's no time to second-guess yourself, there is only time to do your thing – and win.

I lost that fight, and the result hit me like a ton of bricks. Through experience and agility, Marielle got the better of me. I forced myself to accept the loss graciously, congratulating my opponent and contorting my face into a smile, but inside I was defeated and deflated. Most of the GB team had come to watch me, and my overwhelming sense of shame made it almost impossible to look them in the eye, least of all Amanda. I covered my face with my hands, wanting to disappear, wanting so badly to be home, but knowing that home was a thousand miles away. That night I felt numb. I still had over a week left in Bulgaria while the others fought. They were all still in the competition, performing and progressing in a way that I hadn't. With each passing day, I dragged myself out of bed, I watched the girls fight and tried to train, but it was hard to be motivated after leaving the championships so early like that. I watched as they all won their first fights and tried to celebrate their achievements, but I was constantly reliving my own loss in my head. The situation reminded me of failing my exam, and the subsequent reset of my plans. I felt like both my boxing prospects and my career prospects were disappearing before my eyes.

I spoke to Richard every day, and he tried his best to make me accept what had happened and move on. 'It doesn't matter,' he'd try and reason with me. 'You'll be home soon, you're bigger than this, we're going to get through it together.' He was really trying. I could hear his words but I just couldn't take them in. I felt guilty and heartbroken. I'd lost fights before, but something about this one hit me harder. Let's face it – any loss is hard, and losing opens the door to all your negative thoughts rushing back in. You have this voice in your head telling you you're inferior and that you should never have been in the competition in the first place. The loss hurt so bad that a part of me wanted to give up. The thing that got me is that every single person on the team apart from me had won their first fight. They might not have gone on to win a medal, but they could at least leave with one win under their belts. Everyone but me. I couldn't seem to move on from this. In the end, Richard flew out to console me. I was supposed to stay with the team at all times, but I snuck out to meet him and stayed at his hotel for one night. Having him motivate me in person, the sting of losing felt less raw and the pain began to melt away. I knew I could come back from this. What I needed to do, hard as it was to admit, was to swallow my pride before letting go. Losing was a natural outcome of my fight – it stung because I knew I could perform better, and it lingered because I felt as if I had let myself and my team down. My biggest obstacle to seeing reason in the moment – and allowing what someone else was doing not to impact me – was myself. The minute I got past that brick wall of pride, I felt lighter.

Natasha would go on to win a gold medal, while Lisa and Sandy both picked up bronze. In the end, I loved seeing them achieve their wins. Losing and letting go of pride also gave me an opportunity for more perspective. I was far from the first boxer to lose a fight: it was part of our sport. I realised that they both had years of experience on me, and I still had time to learn and to fight and to grow into being a champion. I wasn't going to let myself fall at the first hurdle of defeat. I had chosen to follow my dreams and that also meant I had chosen not to give up. To not let one setback determine my future, and to not give it the power to. One bad grade, one mistake, one lost fight won't change the course of your life unless you let it. Always try to zoom out, and see the bigger picture. To remember the reason you turned up in the first place. To see that a bad day is just a bad day.

Amanda used my spare time in Bulgaria wisely as an opportunity to train me for my next fight. She set me up with sparring sessions with some of the best women fighting in Europe at the time; women who, like me, had been knocked out of the competition. Here was another example of a positive outcome from what appeared to be a setback. If I hadn't been knocked out so early in the competition, I would never have got all the invaluable sparring practice in. The chance to still compete at a high level and improve without the pressure of winning. In many ways, it was almost the better outcome, although it took me a while to be able to see it like that.

When the tournament was finished and we all flew home, my heart no longer felt heavy, even though I was dreading going back to LCB. I hadn't spoken to Ricardo but he would know I had lost my fight. Still, I returned to the gym a little rejected but ready to work. In the end, he didn't say anything about Bulgaria, but he told me he'd made a plan to accommodate all my trips to Sheffield. I was to train with him Mondays, Wednesdays and Thursdays when he was in, but on Tuesdays, Fridays and the weekend, he told me not to come to the gym. Since it clearly wasn't up for negotiation, I agreed to his terms and for a few weeks, tried my best to make the new arrangement work – but when one of my days off at Virgin coincided with a day Ricardo wasn't at the gym, I decided to come into LCB to use the bags. I planned on training alone, but since it was a quiet time, I asked my friend Luis, one of the junior coaches, if he would do some pad work with me. Luis was younger than me, a laid-back south London teenager who I got on well with, and I knew I could trust him not to tell Ricardo. He was working with a client when I approached him. There's a strange sort of hierarchy that comes with boxing gyms. At LCB, competing boxers would pay a low weekly fee of around £5 to use the facilities and work with the trainers. By competing, they're promoting the gym and pushing its reputation, so in return, they don't have to pay much. Then there's the members; the gym's non-competing men and women who generally attend for fitness over fights. They're the ones who bring the money into the club, so coaches need to prioritise them when it comes to dividing their time.

Luis told me I needed to check with the member first – an older man who I didn't recognise – which is exactly what I did. He was kind about it and said he didn't mind at all. I thanked him and promised it would only be for ten minutes. Sometimes we get so caught up in our goals that we put our needs first when we should consider other people, and that's what happened. I never should have interrupted a member during their training. I may have had a competition on the horizon, but that didn't make me any more worthy of Luis's time than someone who might just have been starting their boxing journey.

When Ricardo called me later that evening, I instantly knew he'd found out I'd been at the gym. Reluctantly, I answered the phone. Immediately, he started shouting at me for being in the gym, and for training with Luis. He called me manipulative, which stung, however Ricardo was right on one thing. I shouldn't have interrupted someone else's session for my own gain, I knew it then and I know it now, but something about my next competition had completely blindsided me. I knew I had to own up to my mistake, and apologise in the situation, and I did. When I told him I was sorry, I meant it. However, when the call finally ended, my attention turned to whoever had told Ricardo behind my back. I felt betrayed by their lack of trust, and their ability not to see that I didn't mean to overstep my place or disrupt things. I just wanted to box. Luis was my friend, he would never have told Ricardo, and nobody else in the actual gym would have had Ricardo's number to let him know, apart from the new receptionist. I didn't know her particularly well. She'd only recently joined the gym, and between getting married, moving to Greenwich and travelling to Bulgaria, we had barely crossed paths. Yet I knew she and Ricardo, it seemed, had become quite close. I was sure it was her, everybody else would have had my back, and I realised he must have told her to alert him if I showed up on the wrong days. I grew angry at the prospect of being spied on.

I was still annoyed about it when I next came to the

gym for one of my allocated sessions with Ricardo. The receptionist greeted me when I signed in, but I couldn't bring myself to be polite, and I didn't respond. My relationship with my coach of six years was already on a knife edge, and I hated the fact that she'd interfered. I couldn't tell her that in case she told him, so I said nothing. I looked straight through her as if she were a ghost. I knew it wasn't the right way to behave, but I've always hated conflict and I didn't want to confront her about what had happened. That day, I let my anger get the better of me, I took out my frustrations with Ricardo on a girl I barely knew. Deep down I know that I shouldn't have reacted towards her like that. Despite your anger or frustrations, it's important to treat others with dignity and respect. In dismissing her, I gained nothing, and of course, word of my attitude got back to Ricardo. I was at the start of my training hitting the bags when he bowled over; it was clear he was even more angry than he'd been on the phone. In front of everyone in the gym, he accused me of being rude and ungrateful. I tried to apologise, but I could barely get a word in to respond, and in an outcome I could never have expected, he told me I had to leave the gym indefinitely. I was completely lost for words, but I knew it was not worth arguing about with him. Our situation had been boiling up to this moment. Of all the instructions and advice he had given me recently, this was one I adhered to immediately. I walked away, packed my bags and sprinted out of the gym, desperate to put as much distance between him and myself as possible. My air of calm slipped when

LCB was completely out of sight. I stopped, and began to feel my breath speed up, and panic took over. I remembered that I had the GB Championships in less than two weeks and I had just lost my coach and my boxing club.

I called Richard to tell him what had happened; he was training at a Virgin Active gym and told me to come straight away. Inside, instead of talking about it – we trained. The sheer power of endorphins never ceases to amaze me. Exercising in the gym, unlike in a fight, gives you a real channel for your emotions – here I can draw upon my anger of any moment, whereas in a fight it's important to be calm and focused. After an hour at the gym, I started to feel more in control. I realised that losing my place and Ricardo as my coach was no bad thing. It might not have happened in the best way, but finally I was free.

I went back to LCB one last time to collect my things, where I was met by the smiling face of the new receptionist. I was done with being silent and I decided to calmly confront her. When I asked her why she'd told Ricardo I'd been at the gym, she immediately became defensive. I realised I was the one who needed to let it go. True, I was a fighter, but I had to pick my battles when I could, rather than be in conflict with everyone. There were a million things I wanted to say to her, but instead I looked her straight in the eye and told her it was all in the past, that I was looking forward to a fresh start. I wasn't going to leave any part of me behind. I took every medal I'd ever won for the club, as well as a framed picture of me that hung on the wall from when I won the National Novice Championships, packed them all carefully into my bag and said goodbye. It was finally time to move on.

I faced a very difficult situation. I'd been kicked out of my club and I'd lost my coach just before one of my biggest fights. Even though I had no idea what to do next, I knew I couldn't give up. I could feel the panic deep in my stomach, but I remained determined. Determination is so important. As long as we can see the end goal, it's OK if the road to it changes, or in my case becomes completely blocked. It's important to keep the faith; we have no idea what the future will bring, but with the right attitude I truly believe we can accomplish so much more than we even dare to dream of achieving. That's why I didn't let the end of my time at LCB become the end of my journey. I didn't know how or where I would train, but I took a leap of faith and trusted that things would work out. Never give up, there is always a way.

ROUND FIVE

Channel your anger for good

We all get angry from time to time. It's often considered a negative emotion, but sometimes anger can help fuel us to fight and to keep going. My experiences of anger are usually born out of injustice. It's OK to be angry, but be careful what you do with that anger. The next time you feel angry, I challenge you to try and harness your emotion and turn it into a positive experience.

Your goals will guide you

I can't stress enough how important it is to have goals. Even if they're small or vague, even if you find that they are constantly changing, having something to work towards is such a powerful motivator. When I was kicked out of LCB, I didn't know what my end goal was, but I did know that I had to keep boxing and keep competing. I wanted to excel, I wanted to get better, and that was enough; my ambition to carry on drove me forward, even when everything else seemed to be holding me back.

Respect your elders (and youngers)

Lived experience and emotional intelligence come with age, and people who possess those qualities can make great mentors. My family taught me the value of respecting those who come before you, and in boxing I wouldn't be where I am today without the pioneering women who fought to make boxing more accessible for future generations of women. I've been inspired by younger fighters too, who have shown me what true fearlessness looks like. Take note of the people around you – just because someone leads a different life from you doesn't mean you can't learn something from their experiences.

Learn how to say sorry

I can be really stubborn; I get it from my mum. When it comes to arguments, in the heat of the moment, it can be really hard to see the other person's point of view, but disagreements and most conflicts are an opportunity for us to learn. Nobody is perfect, and it's important to recognise the times that we slip up. Being able to say sorry and being able to forgive are vital qualities to learn for anyone who wants to succeed; you have to be able to move on.

Take time out

It took me way too long to understand the importance of slowing down. On the most basic survival level, humans need enough rest to function properly, especially if you're working your body to its limits. I started to learn this as I watched the ways in which my body recovered from injury, but what took me much longer to comprehend is the fact our brains need rest too. I used to spend so much time training and obsessing about my

next competition that the anxiety would end up negatively impacting my performance. In reality, my best
fights are the ones where I am fully prepared. Of course,
that involves a lot of training, but it also means that I
enter the ring rested, recharged and ready to go.

LEARN TO FAIL

'The phoenix must burn to emerge.'
– Janet Fitch

We hear so much about the success of others, we're living in a time when all you need to do is scroll through Instagram to be greeted by a sea of new pioneers – young high-flyers, overachievers, dancers and poets, athletes and entrepreneurs. In many ways, it's amazing to see talented young people being celebrated, but often we're not getting the full story. I'm no exception to this new rule. Often people hear about me one of two ways: I'm 'Ramla the boxer' or 'Ramla the model' – both accolades present an easy story to tell, and a shiny palpable version of my life, but neither reflects the whole truth. I'm often presented as a beacon of success; another simplified version of my story is that I went from a refugee fleeing Somalia, to a champion boxer, to a model. I've never forgotten my past and how it has created a path for my future, however taking my isolated successes on their own isn't even half of my story. With every single achievement came many more failures, and it's important for people to know that. I own each of my failures – from failing at competitions, not getting the grades for the course I really dreamed of enrolling in, being kicked out of my boxing club, not being picked by the GB boxing team, select fashion shoots or editorial features, the list goes on. I don't tell you these things to get sympathy. I'm telling you this version of my life because every winner has experienced a loss, and there is something to learn in all the lows. All successful people fail. Take Oprah Winfrey – she was fired from one of her early jobs as a TV news anchor in Baltimore; actress Carey Mulligan was rejected from every single drama school she applied to; and after waiting years for a record deal, Lady Gaga got dropped by her first record label in just three months. I have no doubt that every person reading this has experienced some kind of failure too. These moments can be crushing, but they can also be incredibly useful; failure reminds us what we really want and sets us on the right path. It can be such a horrible, desperate feeling that it motivates us to get better, to learn and improve, to get stronger, smarter, fitter – whatever we need to do to achieve our goals.

In the weeks that followed my final conversation with Ricardo, there was no time to process what had happened. I knew I wasn't in the best position; I'd lost my last fight, I had no coach, no boxing gym, and the GB Championships were coming up in a matter of weeks. I felt so uncomfortable; I wasn't in the place in my boxing career that I wanted to be, I felt like I'd just taken ten steps back. There was no other way of looking at it; on paper I had failed, but that discomfort of feeling like a failure really spurred me on. I knew the odds were stacked against me, so all I could do was train the best I could. Sparring would be impossible – I didn't have a boxing gym to do it at – I also didn't have any pads or equipment in our flat, but I did have Richard, and he knew his stuff. Together, we worked out a programme to keep my fitness and stamina up. The only thing missing was the actual boxing, but training in that way taught me to be resilient and resourceful. Sometimes in life we have to be scrappy, the situation might not be ideal, or how we expected it to be, but we have to work with what we've got.

Every day we ran outside, or we'd go to the gym and do circuits. Admittedly, I would have loved to have been training in a boxing gym with bags and pads and other amateur fighters, but sinking into the reality that that wasn't going to happen just wasn't going to help my situation. Instead, I trained with Richard and worked twice as hard. Richard wasn't a certified coach, but he'd been boxing his whole life, and he knew me better than anyone I'd ever worked with – that had to count for something. We started going for long runs along the river to build up my endurance, and I practised my boxing combinations the best I could outside the flat, jumping around the courtyard, chasing my invisible opponent into the shadows. I put my trust in Richard, and he became my stand-in coach. We found a way to make it work, taking my bad situation and turning it into a positive one. He was constantly coming up with vigorous new routines in the gym to help me with speed and strength, and whenever I told him I was doubting my abilities – which was quite frequently – we'd talk and talk about my fears until they didn't seem to scare me any longer. To this day, he's still the most important coach I've ever had.

In the swiftness of everything – my new routine and my underlying anxiety about throwing myself into it – I didn't reach out to my England coach, Amanda. In hindsight I know I should have told her what was going on and asked for her help. I didn't put my finger on the word for our relationship at the time, but she was a mentor to me and she offered me guidance and support. We'd worked together enough in the past for her to know what I needed. She would have given me advice and training ideas, maybe even put me in touch with a coach, but I admit I didn't want to trouble her – and I think part of me worried about how she would react. Instead of catastrophising about what might happen, I should have taken a beat, thought about the people who always had my back, who had helped me grow, who wanted me to be better, and asked for help. My impulse has always been to fend for myself rather than let people in, I've done this ever since I was a kid, even when the situation is snowballing out of my control. But sometimes, a burden is too heavy to bear on your own, and that's the point when you need to let others in. Remember, you're rarely as alone as you think. Life can be full of unexpected twists, and we all need some help along the way.

The GB Championships took place where so many of my training camps had been, at the English Institute of Sport in Sheffield. In the lead-up I found myself fixated on the fact that everyone else would have been sparring for weeks while I had only been training in the gym. Social media has definitely made the comparison culture worse. In 2020, I took three months away from my phone, and it was one of the best things I've ever done for my mental health. It removed the impulse to constantly see what others were up to, the second it happened. I wasn't completely devoid of friends, of course, and it gave those around me a chance to have deeper conversations, as opposed to fleeting ones. Away from my phone, I found I had more time than I thought. I used it to read books – something I never usually made time for – mostly on breathing and meditation. I learned some amazing techniques over those three months that have really helped me get into a good headspace before a fight.

As was often the case, I still had a few grams to lose to qualify for my weight category, so when I arrived at the hotel the day before the fight, the first thing I did was run a hot bath. It was a cold afternoon, and as I slowly immersed myself into the small white bathtub, the shock of the heat hit me like a bunch of pinpricks all over my body. I leaned back, gripping the sides of the tub as a shiny layer of sweat spread over my face. Slowly, I grew accustomed to the temperature, and as I closed my eyes, I embraced the sense of exhaustion that came with the steaming water. I saw Amanda later that evening. She greeted me with a warm smile and asked me how training had been going. As we sat down in the hotel lobby, I think she could tell something had happened before I began to explain. I told her about Ricardo;

how he'd kicked me out of the gym, how Richard had stepped up the best he could. When I finished, I was surprised at how relieved I felt, even more so when I clocked that the look on Amanda's own face was one of complete empathy. She was glad I'd opened up to her, she sympathised with what I'd been through, and assured me she would ask around and help me to find a new coach and somewhere to train. Amanda encouraged me not to worry about the past, and instead focus on the future; there was the video analysis of my opponent to go through, pad work in the morning, and the fight ahead to approach. I promised to leave it all behind me. I was here now, and had to focus.

Back at the hotel, my mind raced back to my fight in Bulgaria and how I'd been the only one to falter in the first round, how I'd not been able to get out of my own head, how I'd failed. That was the last time I'd seen the squad, and I admit I was terrified that it would happen again in front of the entire GB team. Some of my friends from LCB had come to watch too; and in my head I conjured a voice delivering my bad performance back to Ricardo: 'Ramla froze in the ring; she cracked under the pressure and hasn't been able to recover from losing you as a coach.' When I spoke to Richard that night, I relayed every potential nightmarish situation one after another – a long list of what ifs, buts and maybes. Worrying about the worst-case scenario never achieves anything, a much better focus is that positive outcome, reminding yourself that it's in reach; but that time, I couldn't picture it. Sometimes the pressure gets too much. It's overwhelmingly stressful, and one part of coping with stress is accepting the things we cannot change. I will always get nervous before a fight, that's a given, but what I can do is identify the causes, feelings of inferiority, fear of failure and try to change my negative thought patterns. In the end Richard told me I was putting way too much pressure on myself. I knew this, I always know this before a big fight; however, there's also a part to feeling nervous that lets me know I'm human, it reminds me to stay humble, to know that I'm not complete, that I'm not guaranteed to win. I go through these feelings before every fight – even now – and it's a constant process of learning how to overcome myself when faced with anxiety. I take time to sit in those feelings; I acknowledge that fear is an inevitable by-product that comes with taking risks and having dreams, and then I try to realign my focus. A lot of the techniques that help me the most are to do with visualising a win. It's a way of distracting me from any unhelpful thoughts and reminding me that I am prepared, that I have what it takes to win.

I slept really badly that night, and I was almost late to meet everyone in the hotel lobby for the first day of the competition. We were kicking things off with a team walk; all the coaches and the competitors, along with the other staff, the nutritionists, sports psychologists and junior trainers. It's nothing too strenuous; just ten minutes around the block with the idea of clearing our heads and warming up our legs while bonding as a team – that's important. Boxing by nature is a solitary sport, so it's a reminder that you really are part of a community. As we meandered through the industrial backstreets of north-east Sheffield, Amanda slipped back from the front to discuss my tactics. I was going to be fighting the Scottish champion, a girl called Stephanie Kernachan who had won the Elite National Championships the year before I had. 'Listen,' Amanda said. 'Remember what I said. I don't want you to let the past few weeks get to you.' I nodded in agreement, although it felt like an impossible task. 'It's all in the past,' she reiterated. After, she talked me through Stephanie's boxing style and we discussed the best way to approach the fight. Amanda was on my team, she had my back; and her confidence in me reminded me that one failure wouldn't define my boxing career. And it didn't; nobody ever writes about the time I lost my first fight at the European Championships; people move on, sometimes you have to as well.

We arrived at the stadium as a team, and one that I felt proud to be fighting with. I knew the venue well, but to be competing there felt different. I was seeing it with new eyes and I took in the sheer scale of the place in awe. Where there was a basketball court, two boxing rings had been erected, each with its own set of separate stages for commentators and judges. Stretching upwards from the two rings were rows and rows of audience seating, right back to the ceiling. A surge of gratitude overcame me; I couldn't believe I was fighting at this level. I was in a position where my passion allowed me to travel the country – and occasionally beyond – competing in huge venues while being watched by thousands of people. I thought back to the timid schoolgirl I once was; a teenager so desperate to be part of the crowd, that she never even dreamed about being the one on the stage.

'This is where you're going to do the entrance,' Amanda said, pointing out a long gangway that led from an exit to where we were standing. She beckoned again towards the ring. 'Go ahead,' she said, 'if you want to test it, you can go in and test it.' I didn't need telling twice. I scrambled between the ropes and felt the soft elasticity of the floor beneath my feet as I took in the world around me. I felt so small at the centre of that cavernous stadium; I was on a raft in the middle of an ocean and there was a horizon of seats everywhere I looked. I began to shadow-box, lightly moving around the ring and feeling the grip of the ground beneath my feet. I ran through some combinations, jabbing at the air and imagining how it might retaliate. Alone in the ring, I took my time. I hadn't been myself for a while, and it felt good to be back between the ropes.

The GB Championships are a proper, televised event, and by the time we were back at the arena that afternoon, the place looked completely different. People rushed in and out of the commentators' boxes, and everywhere I looked were bright lights and entire crews carrying cameras and other equipment. It made me think nervously of Mum, flicking through the channels and suddenly being met with her daughter's face on-screen, but since I'd moved in with Richard, a man she had learned to love and trust, my whereabouts seemed less of a priority for her. I still wished there was some way she would come around to me boxing. Her support would have meant so much, but what can I say, us Ali women don't back down easily, and I knew she would be hurt by the thought that I was still boxing. Luckily, I had the rest of the team watching me compete. For the GB Championships, I got to select a song to walk on to, an exciting part of the fight that made me feel like a *real* boxer. Because the fight was taking place in Sheffield, I had chosen an Arctic Monkeys song, because I thought a hometown band would be my way of showing appreciation to the supporters in the stadium who had bought tickets for the fight. I knew a lot of them would have no idea who I was. The people filling those seats were there because they loved boxing; and many of them would have been local. They didn't have any loyalty to me and I needed to gain their support and earn their respect, but I also needed to thank them for showing up. As I waited to walk up to the ring, I heard the opening bars of my song, 'Brianstorm'. It starts with these thundering drums and a rousing bassline and it completely set the crowd off. That was an incredible feeling, suddenly seeing everyone standing up, some people climbing up onto their chairs to get a better view of the ring. In that moment it felt as if everyone in the room was on my side, roaring down to me from their distant seats. The more I have progressed in boxing, the bigger my audiences have grown, both in the stadiums, and online. Though I haven't met the majority of the people in these spaces, I really value the opportunity to connect with them when I can – be it in person, through a comment – some way to let them know I see them, and that I'm thankful for their support. Their interaction is a strong reminder that we are never alone. Support is a two-way street – they see something of themselves in me, and in accepting their support, I do my best to stand up and fight for them.

I didn't meet Stephanie until we were both face to face in the ring and our eyes locked for the first time. As we headed back to our corners – her in the red corner, and me in the blue – I noticed she had this shy smile, but I knew it didn't reflect her abilities. As my gloves were put on, I thought of everything that Amanda had taught me. I closed my eyes and prayed, as I always do before I step into the ring; not for a win, but for self-belief and a safe fight.

Then it began, the moment I'd been waiting for, the moment I couldn't wait for, the moment I got to prove my worth to myself and the thousands of people filling the stadium. Stephanie was ruthless. She came at me quickly and furiously, but I found myself slipping away from the worst of it, ducking under her outstretched fist and propelling myself away from her incoming shots. Dipping and weaving, I twisted away from her like a snake, and drew her closer for my own incoming punches. I was winning – I was sure of it – but then a wave of panic hit. It was like I was back in Bulgaria. I felt myself judging my moves split seconds after they were happening. I just couldn't stop thinking and then *BAM* – she hit me square in the face. Why had I not seen that coming? It was a messy and difficult fight, but through the power of evasion, somehow, I managed to snatch a win. It didn't feel like a win though; and I couldn't have felt like less of a champion. I knew I hadn't fought well. I had been so lost in my own thoughts that I had failed to properly act and react in the moment. I had been judging myself throughout the fight, waiting till I slipped up and then punishing myself for it. Mid-performance is never the time for doubting and dismissing yourself; you have to allow yourself the freedom to do your best. The spark that I always brought to the ring seemed to be dwindling with every fight. The others congratulated me; so did Richard who had been watching from home, but it felt hollow. I think they must have thought I was mad for not being satisfied after a win; only Lisa seemed to understand me. She admitted that it definitely hadn't been my best performance, reminding me that everybody has their bad days. I really appreciated her honesty, she's never been one to sugar-coat the truth, whether she's talking about her own bout or somebody else's. She knew that fight wasn't my best work, but to me it felt like more than just a down day. My performance in my last two fights had been underwhelming, and it made me worry about the future.

In the weeks that followed the GB Championships, I fell into a hopeless slump as I came to a bleak realisation. Usually, if a boxer wins the National Championships or the GB Championships, they are called up to have a trial to join the GB squad. That's how it works; it even says so on their website. I had won the nationals, and though my performance hadn't been great, I'd won the GB Championships too. I'd been regularly invited to Sheffield to train with the squad, but despite ticking all the boxes, no call had come: I really had failed. I found myself constantly staring at my phone or checking the GB Boxing website in case I'd made a mistake, but it just confirmed what I already knew; I should have received the call, I should have been asked to attend a trial. Every day that I didn't hear anything, I lost a little more hope. There was no other explanation, and as the days turned to weeks, it became evident that GB just didn't want me, which meant in my eyes I couldn't progress. That was it, I told myself; my journey stopped there. My confidence had taken a huge blow from the last two fights, and mentally, I was out. When I arrived back in London I fell into a depressed daze, I couldn't face competing at a lower level and just like I had before, I decided to quit boxing again. I'd go to work at Virgin Active in the morning and come home like clockwork in the evening. I did nothing to fill the spare time; I became more and more withdrawn, and Richard became more and more concerned. I hated my job, but I didn't have enough savings to resit my biology exam and start the physio course.

Everything felt hopeless, and I took to eating, all of the time. I'd have huge lunches that would leave me feeling full and lazy, and I snacked on crisps and chocolates and fizzy drinks until I felt their sugary coating across my teeth. I had trained and worked and starved and fought with my body for years, and now I identified it as the thing that had failed me, so I pushed it to a new extreme by completely overloading it, which stripped me of my energy and made me feel sluggish and low. When your goals slip from your grasp it's devastating, especially when you've tied them to a sense of your self worth. In my mind I wasn't a good boxer because I didn't get a call from Team GB. Bringing back your focus and reminding yourself of who you are is essential; however, you also have to give yourself permission to fail. I didn't do that in Bulgaria, and I wasn't doing that now. I believed that the only right outcome was winning. I didn't make space for the natural possibility that I could train hard, fight my best and still lose. Allowing yourself to fail is different from having a defeatist mentality. It's leaning into the fact that you are a brilliant multi-faceted individual who has the capacity for life's highs and lows.

I stayed in that slump for a long time, feeling like I'd failed and let myself and the people around me down. When my mum called me one afternoon, I felt like I didn't even have the mental energy to pick up, but she worries so much if she can't get hold of us, so I didn't let it ring too long before I answered. The voice on the other end immediately started chatting away. Something had been on her mind, she told me, which we needed to discuss. It was my wedding party. Since the nikah had been a few months earlier, she thought it would look suspicious that we were yet to throw a party. I sighed. While Richard and I were already officially married, the next part would be a big celebration with all our friends and family. My mum was worried people would talk about the fact we hadn't had one yet; she didn't want there to be rumours that I was pregnant. When we hung up, I stretched out onto the sofa and shut my eyes; the last thing I felt like doing was celebrating, but a few days later, my friend Saffiyah turned up on my doorstep to take me dress shopping – she had been sent by my mother. I couldn't help but laugh at my mum's dedication. Saffiyah had been my brother T's girlfriend before they'd broken up a few years back, but she still remained a part of our family, and when it came to my wedding, Mum and Saffiyah both knew exactly what they were doing. We went to a shop called D'Amore in Harringay. It wasn't much from the outside, an inconspicuous high-street store sand-wiched between a dessert parlour and a wedding-cake shop, but inside was like stepping into Narnia. Every wall was full of floor-length gowns in the brightest col-ours; vibrant reds and deep-sea blues. Obediently I strolled down each aisle, passing hundreds of gowns with intricate lace details or panels of crystal embellish-ment, glitzy tiaras and dangerously high stiletto heels. I've never been one for dressing up, and in my baggy jeans and an old faded hoodie, I couldn't have felt more out of place.

Saffiyah was determined. 'What about this one?' she said, passing me a long white silk dress with a chiffon overlay. I shook my head, hunting out the simplest dress I could find. Eventually, I located a fairly plain option; it was made of green silk with long, oversized sleeves. I picked it off the rack and waved it at Saffiyah. Her nose wrinkled and she tilted her head to one side. She gently prised the hanger from my hand, put the dress back and led me across the shop. As I absent-mindedly skulked my way around the shop, Saffiyah zipped up and down the aisles until I heard an audible gasp. 'Look at this,' she squealed, pulling out a dress. She rushed over and held it up against me. I took a step back so I could see. It was a terracotta nude colour with cream lace details, slightly fish-tailed in its cut, and *very* fitted. I thought it was too much – too fancy, too dressy, not me – but Saffiyah convinced me to at least try it on. Once I put it on, I felt differently. I couldn't remember the last time I'd worn a dress, and while it couldn't have felt more different from my usual attire, it felt good. I realised it was nice to step out of my comfort zone from time to time, to dress up and see myself differently. I used to think fashion wasn't for me. I'd see beautiful clothes in magazines or on billboards and it felt like a whole different world, one that I couldn't afford and wasn't welcome in. Sometimes I used to treat myself to new clothes, but since I lived in my gym kit, I'd never seem to find an occasion to wear them. Eventually any nice pieces I owned would be taken by one of my sisters who would say if I wasn't wearing it, it was theirs. They had a point, I didn't socialise that much, but every now and then, when I did have to dress up – usually for a family event like a wedding – I really loved the feeling of putting time and effort into my appearance. My sisters would do my hair and make-up and I'd get to wear something that made me feel good. Clothes are a form of self-expression, and allowing yourself to try new things can be fun. Six days out of seven I'm in gym clothes all day, but when I do wear a dress or heels, it reminds me that I have another side to me, that I'm not only defined by boxing. We don't have to be one thing, all the time. Sometimes branching out and trying new things can make us feel confident.

When I tried the dress on, it fit perfectly, but when I look at pictures of myself from the wedding party, I was feeling so insecure about my stomach that I've got one hand on my tummy in almost every shot. In the weeks after we went shopping, I continued to binge on food until I felt ill. I have mixed feelings about the celebration. I loved being surrounded by friends and my family more than anything, but I was on a downward spiral. I felt like boxing had been taken away from me, like I'd reached the end of the road and I had no idea what I was supposed to do next.

It was a relief to get some distance from home for a few weeks, when Richard and I went to LA to decompress. The emotional toil of not getting picked for the GB team was still continuing to hit me hard and for the next two weeks, I didn't want to think about any of it. I had run away to LA, not to follow my dreams but to put them behind me. I just wanted to let go, and for a while I could. To me, LA was this strange parallel world full of excess; one full of expensive boutiques and glamorous restaurants on every corner. It was nothing like my London life, and so it was the perfect place to forget about my worries. That's how I felt as we touched down in Los Angeles International airport – and for the first week, I loved our American adventure. We stayed in a plush hotel with a rooftop pool and incredible views of the city. We'd go for walks to the Hollywood sign or along Venice Beach, where muscular men would hurl themselves up onto outdoor gym equipment. We ate picnics by the sea or had meals out with Richard's friends, where I'd order burgers and fries and the kind of thick malt milkshakes you just can't get in the UK. It was after a few of these dinners that I realised how much Richard's life had changed; the man his friends described was one who was out all the time, constantly chasing parties, the first one at the club and the last one to bed. 'You wouldn't have recognised me back then,' Richard said to me one night, when I brought it up back at the hotel. 'I wasn't looking after myself, I'm so much happier now.' He made sure to point out he'd been able to recognise his self-destructive behaviours and change them. I knew what he was insinuating – using himself as an example to show his lifestyle switch from self-destruction to self-care. Where I was ravaging my body with food, he'd done the same thing just a few years earlier with alcohol. It hadn't made him feel better. Instead he had realised the hard way that partying had not brought him happiness. He gave up drinking, he changed his diet and he found religion. A small part of me recognised his point that I should go back to my old routine, which had made me feel good about myself, but it was a routine I'd adopted for boxing – and that wasn't a part of my life at the time, and I still didn't think I was good enough to carry on. In my eyes, I had failed.

One evening over dinner, Richard tried again, this time in a much less subtle way. 'Hey, do you know Wild Card?' he asked me.

'Yeah, of course I know it,' I said, with a slight snap to my voice. Wild Card is a famous boxing gym, run by a legendary retired boxer named Freddie Roach. It's full of world-renowned fighters and, as Richard pointed out, only costs $5 a day for non-members to attend. If you're lucky, you might end up training with some of the best coaches in the US.

'I'm on holiday,' I warned him, and he knew not to push me.

It wasn't until we were back in London, safely in the privacy of our flat, that Richard finally said everything he'd been holding back for the last two weeks. 'Why are you punishing yourself?' he asked me, with a sudden urgency. 'If you're really serious about quitting boxing, fine, quit boxing. But you need to stop because it's *your* decision, and not because someone else has made the decision for you. If Team GB doesn't want you, fuck them!' he pleaded. 'This doesn't have to be the end, Ramla. Turn professional! You don't need to continue with amateur boxing, and you certainly don't need to punish yourself in the process.' He looked so upset. I realised that my own sadness had completely penetrated him too. That night was the most worked up I'd seen him since my parents had told him it was too soon to get married. We were a team; not only did I feel like I was falling apart, but I'd also been hurting the person I loved the most in the process. I couldn't face him, so I went for a walk to clear my head.

I knew Richard was right; I had been punishing myself, because I thought I'd failed, but he didn't. For the first time in two months I felt a glimmer of hope. If Richard could believe in me, I could believe in myself. I realised I had been so harsh on myself because of my last two fights, when I should have been extra kind to myself. That's the way I look at my life today: if something's going wrong, I acknowledge it and since it's already upsetting me, I don't punish myself even more by entertaining negative thoughts. Instead I try to be practical and think about how I can make things better. That day, I decided I *needed* to keep going, though I still didn't know what carrying on looked like. To 'turn pro' is a huge responsibility. I knew I wanted it, but I wasn't ready. While it sounded great to become a paid fighter, unknown boxers only make a very small amount per fight, and they're also tasked with selling a proportion of their own tickets; if they don't sell enough, they won't even break even. Pro fighters box to different rules – the fights are longer and they're not allowed to wear protective headgear – it's a big leap. Back then, the broken nose and concussion I'd suffered from sparring were still fresh enough in my mind to keep me cautious.

Then the answer came to me. I would start my career again as an amateur boxer and I knew exactly how I was going to do it. I burst back into the flat eager to tell Richard. He looked at me with a confused expression while I started rooting around through my rucksack and coat pockets in search of a small scrap of paper. I found it, carefully unfolded it and read the biro-scribbled words aloud. 'Samm Mullins – Nemesis Gym!' I blurted out, waving the paper at his face. It was the contact that Mick, one of my coaches who worked with Amanda, had given me while I was in Sheffield. I was going to call him and start training again, I was going to give it another shot. I knew going back to boxing wasn't going to be easy. My existing problems still stood stark; I wasn't going to be welcomed into the GB team, I didn't feel ready to turn professional, and yet, I had had enough distance from boxing to know that I needed to get back, at least to the gym. If something makes you happy, sometimes you don't need all the answers at once, you just have to trust the process. I decided to start again, that would be the first step, and then I could reassess my goals down the line.

Nemesis was set up by Samm Mullins. Samm was a passionate boxer and head coach at Lynn AC Boxing Club in Camberwell, and had decided to set up his own gym in Vauxhall, which was the London-based offshoot of the bigger Nemesis Gym in Crayford, Kent. To get things started he brought a small squad of amateur and professional fighters, and he was looking to add to his list. I hadn't even heard of Crayford until I typed it into Google, but Samm told me if I joined, we'd need to visit the Kent location once a week, as the Vauxhall space didn't have a ring to spar in. I agreed, and we set a date in a few weeks' time to work together, but as the date grew closer, I slipped back into the habits that stalled my progress and exacerbated self-doubt. I wasn't exercising, and though I had started eating healthily again, I was definitely out of shape. I'd taken some heavy blows from my last two fights; and while my body had recovered, my self-esteem was yet to return. To make matters worse, at the beginning of 2017, I found out that the Olympic Boxing Association had added several new weight categories to the women's competitions, including 57kg. At first the news gave me a flicker of hope; where previously, for me to have been a proper member of the GB squad, I'd need to go down to 51kg – a weight that would have been virtually impossible for me to get to, let alone fight well at – or up to 60kg, which presented even more problems. Now with the new categories, the GB team would need to create new spaces; and yet, the call still didn't come. It was the final nail in the coffin. On my days off work, I'd stay in bed as long as I could, putting off starting the morning.

When the date came around for me to meet Samm, I'd completely forgotten about it. I'd erased boxing from my mind to the extent that I'd forgotten to cancel our session. When he called to ask if I was running late, it was sheer embarrassment that made me bundle myself onto the next train and head straight to the gym without a second thought. Thankfully, Samm didn't share the same passion for punctuality as Ricardo, and he met me with a welcoming smile and a forgiving shake of the head. 'I'm just glad you made it!' he said, as I apologised profusely for the delay. I put on my hand wraps while Samm showed me around. I felt like a ghost walking around that gym. It was a new space, and yet, seeing the bags gently swaying from the ceiling felt equally haunting and nostalgic. I stopped to watch two men sparring in the ring; their fists flashing at each other while sweat sprayed off them onto the cushioned blue floor. I'd forgotten what an incredible sport boxing is to witness live; the graceful movements amidst the violence of it all, the palpable fear, the precision of each punch; I was mesmerised.

Samm cut the tour short. 'How about we just get straight to it?' he suggested. I nodded. Samm slipped on a pair of pads while I put on my gloves. He led us to a quiet corner, and when I was ready, he started barking sequences at me. They started simple; a left jab followed by a right cross, finished with a left hook to the body. It felt good. I got a familiar thrill hearing the slam of my gloves as they pounded Samm's pads. For those first few rounds, I barely had to think; muscle memory was guiding every shot. We were dancing; arms extending, bodies twisting; moving to each other's rhythm. It felt so right. It had been over a month since I'd put on my gloves, and though it took me longer than normal to memorise the more complicated sequences, I was determined not to fail. 'Wow, you've got a lot of power!' Samm told me, stepping back and removing the pads. I didn't want to stop. I was dripping with sweat, but I could have gone for hours. I felt so alert, I was running on adrenaline. In this unfamiliar space, filled with strangers and run by a man I'd worked with for less than an hour, I was home.

ROUND SIX

Be resilient and resourceful

Finding myself with no club taught me resilience and resourcefulness. I didn't need a boxing gym; I could train in my normal gym, and I certainly didn't need my old coach. I knew enough about training, and Richard stepped up too. If I can train for a championship fight without any of the normal resources, then I promise you can work to make your goals a reality – without the tools you think you need.

Curb the comparisons

I'm not going to say stop comparing yourself to others, because if I'm honest, I still do it and sometimes we just can't help it. That said, you will never be the person you compare yourself to, and they will never be you. We are unique, moving through the world at different paces with different goals and priorities. It's fine to look at what other people are doing, but at the end of the day, you're the only one making decisions about your own life, so don't get so wrapped up in watching others that you forget to think about yourself.

Find a mentor

Sometimes we all need a helping hand, someone to guide us or bounce ideas with. Often when we're looking for a 'mentor' we imagine this formal relationship with a teacher-like person, but actually, having someone who supports you can be much less official. Sometimes it's worth asking yourself, Do I already have one? If the answer is no, go out and find one; never be afraid of asking for help. If the answer is yes, then you're one of the lucky ones. Make sure you let the person or people helping you know that you value them. The strongest relationships are ones which work on both sides.

Community is key

When I suddenly found myself without a club, I thought I had lost my community. In reality, it was never that black and white. I was part of something much bigger than LCB; I was still a boxer, and there were plenty of people I could have reached out to if I had let myself. Being part of a group can be such a special feeling. I've grown up belonging to a close-knit Somali community, and through boxing, I've always loved having other fighters around me. Finding your community is as simple as knowing that there are other people out there who share your values and have similar goals. Even strangers can be part of the same community, and to me that's the strongest reminder that we are never alone.

Be kind to yourself

Things might not have gone the way you hoped, but don't let your goals slip away from you. It's when you're feeling the worst that you owe it to yourself to be the kindest. I used to really punish myself whenever something didn't go to plan. As I grew older, I learned that I would get back on track much quicker if I accepted the situation and allowed myself to take the time I needed, before picking myself up and carrying on.

BE BRAVE

'The biggest adventure you can ever take is to live the life of your dreams.'
— Oprah Winfrey

Bravery is a quality that hasn't always come naturally to me. When I was at school, it took me a long time to stand up for myself because I was afraid of others. To be brave meant standing out from the crowd, when all I wanted to was fit in. Gradually, I would learn that I had to be brave. It didn't mean hitting back at anyone who wronged me, and it didn't mean going into the ring being completely unafraid of the dangers. Being brave can simply mean being open to try new challenges, being able to take risks and not always picking the easiest or the most comfortable option. Sometimes it takes a tremendous amount of courage – I can't think of anything braver than my parents' decision to leave Somalia – other times it's the small steps we take to make sure we're on the right path. Take my best friend, Danika – so much has happened to her in the past, but every day, she gets up and carries on. I knew that I had been brave for turning up to Nemesis. That might sound silly – on paper there's nothing heroic about an amateur boxer going to a boxing gym, but where I was mentally and physically, with my confidence and self-esteem at an all-time low, it took a lot not to give up. Sometimes simply walking into an unfamiliar room, choosing the uncomfortable option, is bravery in its purest form. Starting again at Nemesis signalled that, and on that occasion it paid off. The sense of relief was overwhelming, a renewed confidence in my abilities and an electric feeling from still having the fight in me.

That day I made a solitary pact that I was never going to quit again. I realised more than anything I had to make a promise to myself, before others, whenever I felt like quitting: a commitment that I would continue to try, to remember that I could do this, and to remember the rush of adrenaline the sport gave me. Training with Samm restored a balance back into my life and I was grateful to Amanda and the other England coach, Mick, for connecting us, and grateful to him for welcoming me into the club. Samm suggested I do a week's trial at Nemesis to see if it was a good fit, but I knew straight away I wanted to join. It made sense that Mick was old friends with Samm; they shared exactly the same sense of humour, one that I learned to embrace too. I'd often find myself laughing during training which was surreal and surprising, but it felt good. Our sessions were just as exhausting as working with Ricardo, but they felt fun, something I hadn't experienced in a long time. Samm was a gentle and caring coach, and because he trusted me to push myself, he'd never shout at me or accuse me of not being enough. When he did offer feedback or criticism, it always felt fair.

It didn't take long for us to establish a great working relationship, the kind it felt like I'd been waiting years to find.

Every Friday Samm and I travelled to Crayford, and I looked forward to those days like nothing else. I could feel my fitness improving, and Samm would often introduce me to new girls who I could take on in the ring. I knew I had a long way to go to fully get back on my feet, but it was an exciting time. It was January; a new year full of promise and opportunity. Richard and I were saving up a deposit to buy a place of our own, and I was finally part of a boxing club where I felt supported and valued, not bullied or pitted against others. I hadn't competed for a long time and I was desperate to get another fight in. 'We need to take our time,' Samm would say. 'I don't want to rush, we need to get your fitness up, you've got a lot more sparring to do, and then we can start to think about competitions.' I was constantly in his ear with fights I wanted to enter, but Samm was resolute. He'd laugh at how persistent I was, but he'd never give in. 'Soon,' he would promise. 'Just be patient.'

After the constant sunshine and open roads of LA, the busy bite of London in January felt particularly sharp. When I finished work in the evenings, I'd shuffle my way through the rush-hour crowd at Cannon Street and squeeze onto a Circle or District Line train to Victoria. By the time I changed lines and exited at Vauxhall station to go to Nemesis, the sky would already be growing dark – but I loved arriving at the gym and feeling like I was working through the night. Training was quickly intensifying, and it felt good. I knew I had made the right decision; I looked forward to it and worked as hard as I could. Every evening I'd leave Nemesis soaked in sweat. Every bit of my body would feel so exhausted that I'd often head home in a strange half-asleep state. The Jubilee Line to North Greenwich – the final leg of my journey – was always deserted at that time; sometimes I was completely alone, it was my ghost train home.

By early February, Samm had good news for me. He had decided I was ready for a fight, and he was going to set one up for the following month. I would be competing in a club show, a small event where other members of Nemesis and I would fight boxers from other gyms. Though the stakes would be lower, and the size of the event would be much smaller compared to my recent bouts, I didn't mind. I was just happy to be competing again. I punched the air in excitement when Samm told me the news, but that was only the start of it. He'd also received a letter from Amanda; I had been invited to another training camp – things really were getting back on track. That news was everything to me. I was still on the GB radar; they hadn't dismissed me and I was determined to give my everything and get onto the team. Life is so full of ups and downs; I had been haunted by a series of lows, so I wanted to make sure I was celebrating the highs and not being too hard on myself. It's so easy to worry about the future, but often things have a habit of just working themselves out.

This time we were staying in Aldershot, a small military town in Hampshire. My old teammate Raven was at the training camp too, and I was excited to be reunited with my partner in crime. When nobody was looking, the two of us switched our names around on the whiteboard in the lobby so that we would both get to stay in the same room. That first night, we caught up on everything. We laughed about how we'd managed to pull off my illicit meeting with Richard in Bulgaria (no one else in the team knew he had flown out to cheer me up), and like schoolgirls reunited after the summer holidays, we chatted late into the night. When you're doing something competitive like boxing, it's crucial that you take time to have fun. Spending time with friends is a great way to diffuse the pressure that comes with competing.

The next day, it was time to work, but we went in feeling calm and ready. The morning kicked off with an intense day of track, weights and circuits before a quick lunch break and then on to sparring sessions in the afternoon. I didn't eat much. With my club show fight just a few weeks away, I had already begun to start slimming down to my 54kg fighting weight, which wasn't easy. I hadn't had any nutritional advice about how to lose weight gradually and healthily, and so I wasn't doing it in a sensible way. I was completely cutting out carbs, which I needed for energy, and even reducing my water intake. It meant that I'd started feeling constantly tired. That afternoon I had to spar with Raven, and although I wasn't feeling a hundred per cent, I gave it my all. It's a real testament to our friendship how easily we can switch between close friends, whispering late into the night and putting the world to rights – to fighters, ready to destroy each other in the ring. My friend is an incredible boxer, and whenever we spar, there's never a dull moment. With a bit of a weight advantage on me, Raven always makes for a tough opponent. We love sparring, it's tough and unpredictable, forcing us both not just to push our bodies to the limit, but to be creative and strategic too.

As we were heading to dinner after the afternoon session, I started to feel a little nauseous. I made my excuses, and left the others to go back to the room, but by the time I'd reached my bed I felt a lot worse. I had this thundering headache which made it difficult to keep my eyes open. I put my hands on my forehead trying to contain the throbbing sensation and found that my face felt cold and damp with sweat, while the rest of my body was radiating heat. I started to feel anxious; I didn't understand what was happening to my body, or what to do to feel better. I felt unsteady on my feet, but when I tried to lie down I was overcome by dizziness. Instead, I stumbled to the bathroom and poured myself a glass of water. I knew I must have been dehydrated; I hadn't been drinking enough, which was stupid considering I'd been sparring. Raven and I had both taken a lot of blows that session – that's normal – but severe headaches and blurred vision after a fight isn't. As a boxer, you hear a lot of horror stories about injuries occurring in the ring. It's possible to get a trauma to the head and feel fine in the aftermath, only to be left brain-damaged or paralysed, or even worse, in the hours that follow. That's why it's so important to listen to your body. Work with it, not against it, and understand its limits. There will be days you set an alarm and you sleep through it. It doesn't necessarily mean you're lazy, it means your body really *needed* that rest. It's important to notice fatigue or pain. Even today, if I don't feel good, I make sure I take the day off or do a recovery session; it can be frustrating, but I know it's always worth it in the long run.

That day was the first time I realised that I had overdone it, and as a result a sudden wave of sickness had passed over me. I began retching over the toilet bowl, praying that nobody else would walk in. I vomited, and for a brief window after, I felt a little better. I took deep breaths and small sips of water, and slipped into bed fully clothed, but the feeling didn't last long. I was sick again. I called Richard, and through worried tears tried to explain what was happening. I could tell from his voice on the other end of the phone that Richard was concerned. He told me to tell the others I didn't feel well, that I should go to Amanda and ask for help. As he talked, I heard the click of the door handle and knew somebody was coming in. I wiped my eyes with the back of my sleeve and told Richard I had to go. I promised I would talk to Amanda.

I didn't want to worry the others, and although I was still shaky on my feet, I felt a little better, so when Raven asked why I hadn't been at dinner, I made some excuse about fighting weight and feeling tired. She knew something was wrong, yet I continued to suffer in silence. That's always been a recurring hurdle for me – sharing a problem with someone. I find it difficult to open up to others, despite knowing how helpful it can be. It's never a reflection on anyone else; I thoroughly believe that a good friend will want to have your back, and be there for you out of love, not pity.

Instead of confiding in Raven or finding Amanda, I went to bed early hoping to sleep it off, but the next morning I still felt shaky. I was reluctant to speak to Amanda, but since I'd promised Richard, I made a bee-line for her as we were leaving the canteen. I explained to her that I hadn't been feeling great. I'm sure I was imagining it, but at that moment I thought there was something in her tone and the way she looked at me, as she asked whether I could carry on training. I was sure she felt disappointed. 'No, no, I can train,' I quickly countered. 'I'm sure it's nothing, I just wanted to give you a heads-up.'

It wasn't nothing. Training that day was almost impossible. My body felt slow and heavy, and all I wanted to do was curl up in bed. By the time it got to the afternoon, I was dreading the sparring session. Raven knew I wasn't myself, and a few times throughout the day, she urged me to rest, but I didn't want to disappoint Amanda. I told myself that I just had to get through the rest of the day. I couldn't let myself get noticed by the England coaches for the wrong reasons. I should never have got in the ring for the afternoon session, but my pride got the better of me. I was so worried about disappointing Amanda, but it's important to be honest with your coach. You shouldn't keep anything from them, because the relationship works best when you're working together. I thought I was being brave, but I was being stupid; my body was telling me to stop and Amanda would have helped me, but instead I soldiered on.

Everything was a blur and all I can remember is feeling so out of it that I eventually had to slip through the ropes and take myself away. I packed my bags and found Amanda. I apologised and told her I had to go home. This time the only look in her eyes was one of concern. She sent me off immediately and made me promise to update her once I'd seen a doctor.

The journey back to Greenwich was torturous. It can't have taken more than an hour and a half, but it felt like an eternity. As soon as I finally walked into the flat, I had to rush to the bathroom to be sick again. In the mirror I saw my bleary reflection; my eyes looked sad and sunken and a greyish hue seemed to have spread across my face. Richard was nowhere to be seen. I called him at work and told him that I'd come home. He was back within the hour and bundled me into a taxi straight away. The car pulled up at the Royal London Hospital where a huge glass expanse grew out of the redbrick front entrance, revealing a mountainous stretch of wards. We told the receptionist, and then a nurse what had happened, and then bedded down in reception; it was full, and we knew it was going to take a while. Two, four and then five hours passed. We filled the time by taking short walks to the vending machine, scrolling aimlessly on our phones and intermittently napping as best we could under the gaze of the waiting room's stark strip lighting. I had stopped being sick, but the dizziness hadn't subsided. In a daze I huddled next to Richard, unable to concentrate on anything for more than a few seconds. Finally, we were called into a small room, split into two with curtains for dividers. It was about 10 p.m. and I was delirious from the wait, but relieved to be face to face with a medical expert. I talked the doctor through everything that had happened, being careful not to omit any details. I explained the intensity of the training camps and admitted that I hadn't been drinking enough water, that I'd barely eaten a full meal since hearing the news of my next competition. I could sense Richard's frustration as he listened to me admitting how careless I'd been with my health, but I didn't take my gaze off the doctor. I was terrified of the prognosis, but the doctor was patient and calming. She told me it sounded like I was dehydrated, but that I would need an MRI scan as well, just to be cautious. It would show if I had any injuries sustained to my brain.

Being in hospital was a frightening wake-up call. I realised that as tough as my body was, it had its limits too. We headed back to the waiting room with an extensive questionnaire to fill in, and after another hour or so, a nurse arrived to whisk me off to a different room where a hospital gown was waiting for me. The radiographer gestured towards the scanner. Maybe it was his relaxed demeanour, or maybe it was because it was one o'clock in the morning and I hadn't slept properly in days, but I found myself starting to relax. I reasoned with myself that being strapped into the scanner, though terrifying, meant I at least got to lie down.

I took a deep breath as I felt myself slowly being

drawn into the large tubular machine. I thought of a suitcase on an airport conveyor belt, disappearing momentarily from view, but soon to be out the other side. The doctor had warned me to expect a noise; it was something to do with the magnetic forces turning on and off, but that's about as much as I'd been able to remember. When it started up, I felt like I was inside a printer; the sound was a startling combination of clicking and humming and tapping and whirring. I soon grew used to the strange, rhythmic noises. After about twenty minutes, I was ejected back out from the tube, and met by the doctor's smiling face leaning over me. It took another half an hour before we were called to go through the results. The doctor told me I'd probably suffered a concussion after sparring with Raven and that I was definitely dehydrated, judging by my symptoms. She pointed at a screen which had my scan, a black-and-white X-ray-like image of my head and everything inside it. My eyes darted across the screen, although I had no idea what I should be looking for. She quickly assured me there were no signs of any kind of damage around the brain area; there was, however, some nerve damage at the back of my neck. There wasn't much I could do to heal it other than rest.

I was so relieved I burst into tears. I had no permanent damage, and we were able to go home. It was the early hours of the morning by the time Richard and I flopped into the first taxi we could find. Once inside, it became apparent that we had taken the news very differently. I was over the moon; I was in the clear, there was no permanent damage, and I'd be able to fight in no time. But to Richard, needing to have a brain scan was way too much of a close shave. It had shaken him up so much; he thought I was unsafe, and wanted me to quit boxing altogether. There was no way I was doing that, I'd made a promise to myself that I would keep going – but I promised Richard I would rest. I didn't go to work the next day, and I told Samm I wouldn't be able to make training for the rest of the week. After much consideration, I even told him to cancel my fight in March, which he agreed was the right thing to do. I couldn't believe I wasn't boxing again. I'd been through this so many times; my family making me quit, my own rash decision that I wasn't good enough, and now I had to take even more time off, with Richard convinced that I should never go back. Once again, the days started to feel agonisingly long. Without boxing, I'd always felt like I had no purpose. Richard and I couldn't see eye to eye. He knew how unhappy I was when I wasn't boxing, but the fear of me injuring myself – or worse – was just too much for him.

I took another week off training, before my stubbornness prevailed. The headaches had gone and there was no sensitivity in my neck, so I messaged Samm and told him I'd be back on Monday. He agreed, but like Richard, he expressed his concerns and advised me to wait. When I look back on that time, I can't believe how irrational I was being, ignoring my husband, my coach, and the medical professionals who had advised me not to get straight back in the ring. It was as if I couldn't detach myself from boxing; I didn't know who I was if not a fighter. Samm was trying to go easy on me, but I pushed myself as hard as I could that first session back. I told him I wanted to compete in the nationals, and after much back and forth, he reluctantly agreed to enter me.

We had a few months to get back up to my peak fitness, and in the lead-up, making weight was harder than ever. In the final days before the competition I was barely eating, and I don't think anyone was surprised when I lost my first fight of the nationals. It was horrible; I was completely out of my depth to the point where it was almost dangerous and I had to beg Samm not to throw the towel in. That fight taught me that I could no longer ignore all of the alarm bells around me. Rest is just as important as training, and I should have never have entered in the first place, I was in no fit state to fight. I used to think being brave was about being fearless, but often the bravest decision is the one to step back. I realised I should have listened to everyone else who told me to put my well-being first. That night, I was finally ready to. I asked Richard what he thought I should do. 'If I'm being completely honest, I don't think you should go back to boxing,' he said. 'But I know you, and I know how upset it makes you when you stop. So listen, if you're going to go back, you at least need to be sensible. There's no way you should keep fighting at 54kg,' he continued. 'I need you to move up to 57kg.'

He was right. It no longer made sense for me to fight at the lower weight. I'd lose any kind of advantage of being at the heavy end of my weight category if I had to make myself ill just to get into the category in the first place. Agreeing to move up and fight at a heavier weight was one of the smartest decisions we ever made. When I fought at 54kg, I'd go through periods of barely eating, and then I'd often find myself at the other extreme, bingeing after a fight. Trying to be a weight that was unnatural had driven me to an eating disorder. When I could finally fight at my real natural weight, I could compete as a much stronger and healthier competitor. Whatever your discipline is, the fundamentals of getting enough rest and maintaining a healthy relationship with food and a nutritional diet are so important, for your mental and your physical health. It's taken me a long time to not just accept, but to love my body for what it is. When we treat our bodies right, they really are capable of amazing things. I didn't always feel that way about my own, and there were times that I really hated it; when I was at school I wished my body was thinner, and when I lost at competitions I wished it was stronger. A few years ago, I started writing down the things that I like about my body. Some days, there would be nothing to write down, but other times, as I grew in confidence, I'd start to fill up the pages. I might have a good sparring session where my footwork got me out of trouble, and then I'd love my legs because they moved so fast! Other times I'd braid my hair before a fight and it would make me feel so powerful, like I was putting on armour. It's helped a lot and I recommend it to everyone; if you have a day where you don't find anything you love, refer back to the day you felt good in your own skin, the day you loved your body, your eyes or your hairstyle – because they were yours! Boxing has taught me how amazing our bodies can be to endure pain and build stamina, but they are all completely unique and worthy of celebration.

Finally, I was starting to feel comfortable in my own skin, knowing that I didn't have to lose weight to fight well. When I told Samm about my decision to move up, he was fully on board, but there was an elephant in the room: he already worked with a 57kg fighter. Her name was Ellie, and she'd been training with him for years. I'd been in this situation before, only the shoe had been on the other foot. I remembered when Ricardo had worked with another girl in my weight category, entering her into the National Championships instead of me. That had really stung, and I didn't want to put someone else in the same position. I asked him if it could pose a problem – what if we both wanted to enter the same competitions? 'Let's cross that bridge when we come to it,' Samm said. 'Maybe I can find somebody else to coach you, but for now, there's no reason why we can't carry on working together.' I was glad we were both being transparent, though the thought of finding another coach certainly rang alarm bells. We carried on training over the next few weeks, and I felt like things were getting back on track. Moving up a weight category had been a stroke of genius; I felt stronger, fitter and, finally, I really was ready to fight.

By now I had been competing for the best part of ten years, and had become part of an amazing crew of girls across the country. We were slowly starting to grow in numbers; the WhatsApp group was our way of keeping in contact and if anyone reached out with a problem, one of the girls would always respond and have your back. I loved the sense of camaraderie between the women boxers I knew. They were my second family, and it felt like we were all part of the beginnings of a real movement in women's boxing. Having that connection and community meant so much. Before that the sport had welcomed me, but it wasn't exactly ready for my presence. When I started out at the Trinity Centre I was one of a handful of girls. At Fitzroy Lodge, Palmers and Double Jab, there wasn't even a women's changing room when I joined. I put on a brave face, kept showing up and tried to not let it faze me: I was there to box. Sometimes when you're the only one it can be unsettling, and there's an expectation that you have to be amazing at what you do in order to pave the way for the next generation coming after you. The weight of that responsibility is huge, and often unfair. No one should shoulder that burden. The community I was a part of was making history, in the same way women like Katie Taylor and Natasha Jonas had done before us. In 2012, Natasha was the first British woman to box at the Olympics; seeing her achieve that milestone sent a ripple of hope through us all and made us realise we too could dream big. I'm aware of the spotlight on me at times, and on the things I do to bring awareness to the sport, and the causes I believe in. It's my hope that what I do, and what we all do as women boxers, inspires future generations. That we become a positive representation for those who are looking to find their place in the sport, to believe that they too can achieve and that the door is open for them.

That applies to a lot of things besides boxing, having a role model in that respect is so important. It's a responsibility I don't take lightly as I know many of the things I do and say have impact. I use my platform to raise awareness, and to educate, because I have the privilege to do so. I will always be vocal about equality in the sport, and in the world, in empowering young women, and fighting for their right to education and safety. I do it because I hope that someone out there is inspired to keep going, or have more self-belief.

As I connected with more and more women, I realised there was a whole pool of us across the country as eager to spar as I was, and while I could only fight with Samm at Nemesis every Friday, I was starting to get invitations from women at other gyms all over the country. One of them was Kirsty Hill, a girl I'd met on one of the Sheffield training camps. She fought at 57kg and said she'd love to train with me. I was thrilled, but the only problem was that she lived in Grimsby – over four hours from London. It was our mutual friend Isra who helped us out. She was from Peterborough, roughly halfway between us both, and so she gave us a contact for the owner of her gym, who said we could spar there without having to pay. I loved it when we all came together to help one another out like that, and I still spar with Kirsty today. I love training with women alongside me, it gets competitive in a really good way, and we all bring out the best in each other.

With Isra sorting out the hard bit, I had just one person to convince: Richard. Samm worked at his father's plumbing company on the weekdays, and so I knew there was no way he'd be able to get the time off to take me all the way to Peterborough. Instead, I had the idea of getting Richard to be in my corner for the sparring session. I knew he'd be up to the job; anything he didn't know about boxing wasn't worth knowing, and though he hadn't coached before, I was confident he would adapt quickly. Richard was surprisingly easy to convince. Though he still worried about me getting in the ring, sparring was just training, and he'd be in control if we needed to stop for any reason. I found myself looking forward to that sparring session a lot more than usual. I was curious about what it would be like having Richard in my corner. He'd helped me a lot with training, but he was my husband, not my coach; I wondered how we'd both adapt to working together. It was a risk for sure, but one that we both wanted to try.

I'd only met Kirsty a handful of times, and when the day came for us to fight, I was surprised at just how tall she was. As soon as we started sparring, she was able to hit me from far back, long before I was even in reach of her. Since I was moving up a weight category, this was going to be a recurring problem when fighting taller women. I couldn't work out how to make contact and I was wasting a lot of energy trying. 'You need to work extra hard to get her in range,' Richard told me. 'Don't just go once, be brave and try and land a combination; I think the flurry will fluster her.' When we resumed sparring, I did exactly what he said, and it worked. I managed to catch Kirsty off guard, hitting her when she least expected it, and then making the most of it by raining down punches on her when I was in range. When it comes to sparring, not a lot of coaches truly understand their boxers. Often people assuming shouting and aggression is the way to have an impact, but Richard knew exactly how best to work with me. He was incredibly intuitive. He understood me both as a person and a boxer, and he seemed to be able to predict my every move before I did it. He knew what my strengths and weaknesses were, and he kept calm, which meant in turn, I was able to translate his words into my performance. Richard was so passionate and knowledgeable, I felt as if he was right there in the ring with me and not behind the ropes. Getting to work with him like that was magical. He wasn't a coach, but he was by far the best person I could have had in my corner.

On the way home, neither of us could stop talking about how well it had gone. 'You were so good back there!' I told him. 'It's because there's so much pressure,' he said. 'If I mess up, it's you who gets hurt, and I don't want to see my wife back in the hospital.' Richard's honesty and willingness to coach me was a brave decision for him too. He was choosing to take a huge risk, to step out of his comfort zone to help me, and in the end, it paid off for both of us. I arranged as many sparring sessions as I could, and whenever Samm couldn't make it, which was most of the time, Richard and I would go instead. We weren't doing things by the book, but I loved having him on my side; it seemed to give me the extra motivation I needed in the most crucial moments. One of my favourite sparring partners was my friend Valerian Spicer, a London-based Dominican boxer in her early thirties. I loved being around her because Valerian was so inspiring. At that time, she'd recently given birth but it wasn't long until she was straight back in the ring. She's that full of energy, and as she is British Dominican, we'd often share stories about growing up with first-generation immigrant parents who kept us connected to the countries they had left. Valerian grew up in London, but in her heart, home was always Dominica. Like me, Valerian had flirted with being on the GB team, joining them for the odd tournament, but never being called up to trials. 'They think I'm too old to fight,' she'd tell me, with an exaggerated roll of her eyes, 'but that's my decision!' By boxing standards, Valerian was on the older side, being in her thirties, but so what? She was athletic, experienced and fast as hell; she always made for an exhilarating session, and while I was at Nemesis we spent a lot of time sparring together. Her with her husband, Laird, who was also her coach, and me, mostly with Richard as mine.

'He's so good!' said Valerian, pointing at Richard after one of our sessions. 'Why don't you make it official?' I didn't know what she was talking about. 'We are!' I said, defensively. 'We've been married for almost a year now.'

'No!' she said, smiling and shaking her head. 'You guys make the best team – you should bring Richard on as your proper coach.' I laughed it off, but Valerian wasn't the first to plant that idea in my head. It was completely unrealistic – Richard had a full-time job that was a lot less flexible than mine – but I had definitely fantasised about how nice it would be to have Richard as my coach. Nobody understood me like he did.

Valerian and I talked a lot about the politics of the GB team. She understood exactly how I felt; she'd been in a similar position just a few years earlier. Eventually, Valerian had chosen to stop waiting for the call-up, and had decided to fight for Dominica instead. As a great fighter for a smaller country, she was naturally embraced with open arms. 'It's the best decision I ever made!' she would say. 'You can pick the fights you want, and you don't have to compete against an oversubscribed team for a place. You can travel the world fighting – just you and your coach – and you don't have to deal with any of GB's politics. There's no restraints, no favouritism; plus, you get to represent the country you're from . . . that's something you could do too, you know, Ramla. You could fight for Somalia.'

The freedom and the agency the move had brought her sounded amazing; Valerian was training for the Commonwealth Games, the kind of competition I could only dream of fighting in. But though Valerian made it sound incredible, I was set in my ways about biding my time, patiently waiting for my GB call. I didn't know anything about the Somali team, or even if there was one. To switch allegiances to a different country felt like too much of a risk.

Valerian certainly made me feel more motivated to get back on the international circuit, and we agreed that in the autumn we would both enter the Golden Girl

Championship in Sweden, where I'd fought with my brother by my side all those years ago. During my next session sat Nemesis, I suggested it to Samm, but he shook his head apologetically, he wouldn't be able to get the time off to go with me.

Later that evening, I found myself pacing around the flat waiting for Richard's return; since Samm couldn't be my coach, I'd decided to ask Richard. To me, it was a no-brainer, but while getting him in my corner for sparring had been easy, I knew he wouldn't take a competition lightly. He wasn't trained, he wouldn't know the opponent – and if I got hurt, he would hold himself responsible. Still, I had to try. He was so brilliant as my coach. As a team we were unstoppable, and I was sure part of him would at least want to see what it was like in a proper fight. His first answer was no, but I was determined. We went back and forth over the risks, over his lack of qualifications, but then we started to discuss the positives – how natural it felt to be in a team together, how exciting the possibilities could be. I had no reservations about his coaching abilities; I trusted him completely. Eventually – and reluctantly – he agreed. Just for one fight. I was so grateful. In that moment I wouldn't have swapped him for the most qualified coach in the world. I know it was a risk, but I trusted my gut and it felt right to have him in my corner. I've been around so many coaches in my career and feel a lot of them are in it for themselves; there have been occasions where I've seen coaches push boxers into fights when they've not been ready, and there have been occasions when a coach goes above and beyond to be supportive. Richard's advantage was that he instinctively knew what I was feeling, and my style. I thought back to our first series of meetings when he was intent on watching me do pad work. I know he hadn't been taking exact notes since then and waiting for the opportunity to be my coach but his suggestions were valid, and he saw the potential in me. I knew we'd enter this experience open to learning from each other and growing together by taking on this fight as a team.

My first fight at the tournament was against a German girl called Monica. We didn't find out till the evening before the fight that I would be competing, and Richard went into overdrive trying to find information on her, but it was as if she didn't exist – at least online. He scoured the internet for hours but couldn't find a single video of her, or even confirmation of where she might be from, what other tournaments she'd fought at. A real coach with international experience would be more likely to know the competition, or have contacts who could find out, but I didn't care. I kept telling him not to worry, that I would go into the fight blind and he'd be able to get a sense of her in the first round, but Richard was adamant we went into it prepared. I love boxing for its immediacy. I knew that the training and the hard work and preparation was vital to have any success in the ring, but for me, competing is the reason I fight. Richard is the opposite; he knows that every minute of preparation is equally important to every minute of the fight. He doesn't just watch live boxing; he spends hours watching videos or reading books to try and broaden his understanding of our sport. Before I went into that fight, he needed to know who Monica was. A couple of hours later, he had got what he needed by using his secret weapon, his best friend, Charlie. I've never understood how, or why, but one of Charlie's hidden talents has always been the internet. He's fluent in all things technology, and he's exceptionally good at searching for things online – including an under-the-radar amateur boxer. There wasn't a lot to be found on Monica, but Charlie did manage to discover a key fact. Monica was a southpaw: someone who is normally a left-handed boxer who stands with their right foot forward. A southpaw is a nightmare for an orthodox boxer like me. It becomes much harder to find a good range, it involves a lot of technical precision, and often it can just feel off. It was going to be an uncomfortable fight for sure; I had to unlearn my usual footwork, but Richard told me exactly what I needed to do.

To him, the fact that Monica was a southpaw opponent never posed any threat. He'd already planned exactly what I needed to do and he calmly talked me through the ways I'd need to change up my footwork to ensure I got a good range. Most southpaws tend to be counter-boxers; I am too, which means it can be a bit of a waiting game. He told me to be patient. If she wanted to play chess, I would play chess too. Even if we had to wait twenty, thirty seconds before anyone threw a shot; it was crucial that I waited for her to come to me.

Inside the ropes, we stared at each other intensely, neither one of our facial expressions giving anything away. The fight started, and though Monica was harder to reach, with Richard's advice I managed to land my shots every time. It was such an exhilarating fight, and I felt like I was using my head much more than I was using my fists. The first round may have been slightly shaky, but by the second and third, with Richard's help, I knew exactly what I was doing. Waiting, drawing her in, turning her attempts into my attack. There were moments when I almost panicked; the referee kept telling me off for small things and I was worried he'd deduct points, but having Richard calm me down in between rounds helped me remain confident each time I got back in the ring. I could hear Valerian and Laird in the audience too, screaming and cheering along. It just felt so right. That day Richard and I won our first fight. Together, we had done it. We had been brave, taken a risk, and it had paid off. That made the reward feel even sweeter. We flew back to London the same evening.

Since there was no time to celebrate, when Valerian got back to London a few days later, she invited Richard and me out for a celebratory dinner before training kicked back in. Valerian had won her fight too, so as coaches and fighters, we all had something to celebrate. With my new weight category, I could eat what I wanted without worrying. It felt good; there's no better way to celebrate a win than with a curry – and we ate vegetable biryanis and fish with jasmine rice and rich buttery garlic bread. I love Indian food. I'm lucky to have grown up in close proximity to Asian communities and have the cuisine be in arm's reach whenever I fancied it. We toasted our victories in Sweden, before Valerian turned the conversation to what we would do next in our coaching relationship, but more so if I'd considered fighting for Somalia instead of waiting on a call from Team GB. This time, I didn't dismiss her. I was happy and relaxed and I felt open enough to at least entertain the idea more seriously. I knew the situation with GB wasn't working in my favour. For the last few years I had been constantly chasing shadows, vying for a spot, which, even if I got, I'd have no guarantee of keeping. If I was ever injured or I had one bad season, that would be it, my dream would be snatched away from me and I'd be gone. However, if I competed for Somalia, it wouldn't be plain sailing but the win would be greater – a chance to make history, even, and to compete with a flag on my back. Although I hadn't set foot back in Somalia since infancy, I had always known where I was from and my adult life was spent truly embracing my Somali identity. I wore it with pride. To compete for Somalia was more than making a bold statement. In that moment, I couldn't think of a better way to cement that pride and allegiance to my first home. I looked over at Richard, who had been silent while Valerian spoke, and I chewed the thought over in my head. For the first time I spoke it into existence; with confidence in my voice I said out loud, 'I would love to compete for Somalia.' I didn't intend to be brave with that statement, however I was bold in my assertion that I could do this. In certain situations, you don't overthink the logistics or all the reasons not do something. The decision stems from your gut and makes your heart beat faster – it's confirmation that this is the right thing you should be doing and pursuing. What made me feel more assured was the fact that the coach to help me achieve my new dream was sat next to me. We were both swept up in the win from Sweden, happy our bet on ourselves had paid off. The next step in our partnership wouldn't be easy but we had both shown we could work together harmoniously, and that was half the battle. I sprung the idea on Richard: what if we did it together? If I fought for Somalia and he became my coach in an official capacity? Richard was stunned; this would be a huge risk and a massive undertaking for both of us, but he told me he was very open to the idea. The other big issue was the financial risk and toll it would take. Valerian had planted the idea in my head to fight for Somalia, but I knew it hadn't been a smooth road for her to fight for Dominica, and she admitted she'd had to re-mortgage her flat to pay for the competitions. There were so many costs involved in competing for your home country – entry to competitions, international travel and accommodation being just the minimum. To take it seriously we'd have to pay for a nutritionist and a strength and conditioning coach like the other international teams, which would pile on the costs.

When Richard and I got home that night, practicality kicked in and the first thing we discussed was whether we would even be able to do it financially. We worked out the estimated costs, plus a small allowance for us to live on. We'd been saving up to buy our own flat for a while, both putting aside money each month into a shared account. We finally had a serious amount saved, which would eventually be the deposit on a small flat we could call our own. Those savings were everything we had. The results of our quick maths brought us crashing down to earth. To give it a fair shot, we would have to completely give up our dreams of owning a home. We would need to spend everything we had saved, and then some. The worst part was that even after all that, it would only last for seven months max – and by the end of the year, everything would be gone; if we hadn't managed to secure some kind of sponsorship or funding, we'd no longer be able to support ourselves. That was a massive reality check. I hated the idea of gambling away the entirety of our savings on my goal. We'd be risking everything we had on a fearless decision and a dream. I started to have doubts that I couldn't do it, and most of all that I couldn't do it to Richard, but he disagreed. He said it wasn't just my dream, it had become his too, and together we could make it a reality, if we continued to be brave and were both willing to take the risk no matter the outcome. He wanted to go for it. That night was a whirlwind; we stayed up all night trying to come up with a solution, trying to think of a way where we could tentatively try it out without fully committing, but that was impossible.

The second roadblock we encountered was a big one: there was no Somali boxing team – none. It didn't exist. If I wanted to fight for Somalia, we would have to set up our own boxing federation from scratch, and then get it approved by the International Boxing Association, which was no easy feat. Secondly, we would have to publicly declare our plans, which would mean severing my relationship with Team GB. The implications of the decision grew larger – this had to be a carefully planned risk, it would be a long, costly process with no guarantee that it would even work. By the time night had bled into morning and the first bars of sunlight were streaming through the window, we had made the decision. I left Somalia before I could talk, but I am Somali as much as I am British. There are over seven billion people on the planet, and somehow, I had survived war and poverty to get to where I was. I had found boxing, and Richard and I had found each other. A butterfly effect of actions and reactions had led to that moment. In the end, there was no way I could say no, I had to be brave. And so, just like that, we were doing it.

ROUND SEVEN

Be creative

There isn't a rule book on how to achieve your goals, because they are individual to you. Sometimes it might feel like all the doors are closed; and if that's the case, then go through the windows, make new doors! When I realised I wasn't going to progress in boxing by waiting for the GB team to call me up for a trial, I had to think creatively about other ways I could succeed.

Take risks . . .

Sometimes we have to take a chance on our goals. We have to be open to trying new things, even if they don't work out. Don't be afraid of putting yourself out there. The very act of trying something out tells yourself and the world that you are brave, you are ambitious and you are a force to be reckoned with.

. . . but take care

Recognise the difference between taking risks and being reckless. I wanted to succeed so badly that I stopped listening to the signs that my body was suffering. That was dangerous; in boxing your body is your instrument, the only physical tool you have. It doesn't work if it isn't properly looked after. No goal should negatively impact your physical or mental health. Work hard, but make sure you're taking care of yourself at the same time. Be kind to yourself, practise self-care, and make time to reflect on all you have achieved, all you are proud of.

Embrace change

In deciding to try and fight for Somalia, I knew that I would have to sever my relationship with the GB squad, a team I'd been dreaming of joining for years. It meant instead of the status quo, training camps and the odd competition as part of a wider team, everything would be different; I'd be making my own team and starting again from scratch. I knew it was going to be a massive change, but the alternative could have meant I was left constantly waiting for the approval of others. Sometimes, drastic change is the only way to ensure your goals happen on your own terms.

FOLLOW YOUR DREAMS

'Hold fast to dreams
For if dreams die
Life is a broken-winged bird
That cannot fly.'
     – Langston Hughes

It's easy to have a dream and then talk yourself out of it because it sounds too ambitious. You worry you won't be able to pull it off, or convince yourself nobody else has done it before, so you talk yourself into scaling it back and dulling its fire. Just remember, the first step is always the most terrifying. Deciding to compete for Somalia was the hardest decision I had ever made, and once I allowed my fears to subside and embraced the commitment and history I was going to create, the possibilities began to feel endless. I realised how much I was in control of my future, I wasn't waiting to be called up, I didn't have to follow convention – I could do it all my own way. That was such a liberating and intoxicating feeling that propelled me forward in times of doubt.

Choosing to do it was hard, but actually beginning the process of creating a federation that didn't exist was near impossible. To fight under the Somali flag, we were going to have to completely reinstate boxing in a country where it had been banned since 1976. Back then, Somalia was governed by a dictator, Mohamed Siad Barre, and he had deemed boxing an 'unwanted' sport after a competitor had been knocked down and had vomited during a fight. Barre was long out of the picture (he was exiled shortly after my family left Somalia), but the country remained unable to enter any official international competitions. The first thing we needed to do to be able to fight was to set up a federation, but each initial step seemed to present a stack of new hurdles. There's a stark difference between theory and practice. We had obviously never set up an organisation of this magnitude before, so we began by trying to get some advice. We spent hours trawling the internet and trying to find government bodies and existing federations who might be able to help us. We tried the Ministry of Youth and Sports and the Somali Olympic Committee. We called, emailed and sent letters to any official addresses we could find, but received no replies. When we realised none of the official government bodies were going to respond to us, we started targeting specific people – diplomats, journalists, politicians – but still, we were getting nowhere.

Then we took to social media, trawling Somali Twitter and Instagram looking for anyone who might be able to help us. A few hours into this, Richard wondered if he'd found a lead, a Canadian Somali man named Hassan Abukar. We didn't know what he did, but he seemed well connected. I scrolled through his account. Hassan was clearly a proud Somali. His Instagram page was a colourful mosaic of the country's rich green forests and panoramic sunsets filmed at Liido, Mogadishu's biggest beach. I felt a pang of pride seeing the way he presented Somalia; despite my parents' stories of their beloved country, I was still so used to seeing it as this war-torn and desolate landscape, a place full of corruption that could not support life. But here was Hassan showing a new perspective, one that looked peaceful and vibrant in a land full of hope. He shared pictures of fellow Somali people, their faces stretched with smiles. He documented building sites under construction which would soon become new schools or hotels. I found myself scrolling back through years, and discovering Hassan had even written a book, titled *Mogadishu Memoir*, his own intimate coming-of-age story set against the backdrop of a rapidly changing country. I wish I'd read Hassan's book when I was at school. The ways in which you see your country or heritage represented is so critical in informing the way you see yourself. I always used to be embarrassed to admit I was Somali, because I saw it as this inhospitable country and one which we'd needed to escape to survive. Growing up in the UK in the nineties and noughties, African countries were so regularly depicted as completely underdeveloped places full of war and drought and famine, and in turn, a lot of diasporic youth internalised those negative perspectives of home. Seeing Hassan portray Somalia in another way and hearing him speak online about it with such heart was so moving. He'd done the work of showing the world another side to our country, one that made Somalia look fresh, exciting, hopeful and so empowering. Instantly it made me feel proud of what we were trying to do. Even if he couldn't help us, I was inspired by his work, so I decided to follow him. Within the space of a few minutes, Hassan had followed me back and a message from him had appeared in my inbox. 'Hi Ramla, it's great to connect with you,' he wrote. I thanked him for following me back, complimenting him on his work and asking him more about what he did. Much to mine and Richard's excitement, he explained that he was a government official. We learned that Hassan was an aid coordinator for Benadir, a south-eastern region of Somalia that includes Mogadishu. He spent his time between Toronto and Mogadishu, and the more we spoke, the more I realised that he clearly held some serious clout.

Hassan was a stranger to me. We had no connection other than a shared heritage, but when I explained that I wanted to box for Somalia, he jumped on it and quickly promised to do everything he could to help me. I think that was the first time I've ever 'networked'. Hassan and I couldn't be more different across age, location and our lived experience. We never would have crossed paths in the physical world, but we're living in a time where it's easier to do your research and make connections online. I reached out because it was amazing to 'know' someone in Somalia who was connected to the community, and was promoting our culture in such a positive light. I also reached out because I thought Hassan might be able help me. Networking has such a bad connotation at times – it can be unnerving to put yourself out there, but similar to getting a mentor when you need a cheer-leader, and a team of support behind you, you also need someone you can share your ideas with, someone who you can work with to make those ideas grow and become real. I realise it's daunting, but don't be afraid to reach out to other people in your field, to share your dreams and crucially to ask for help. Even if it doesn't work out the first time, or how you intended, 'no' isn't such a scary word to hear. It's not a reflection on your idea, rather, that person may not have the capacity or time to dedi-cate to you. And it works both ways – in turn, you have to be open to people who approach you, and what advice you can give and opportunities you can create. One of the main reasons I set up the Sisters Club was to create a safe network for women where they could come together free of judgement and men, learning to box and build community as one. Hassan and I shared many of the same philosophies on paper, and I just knew I had to connect with him on a deeper level.

Within minutes of connecting, he was offering me amazing words of encouragement. 'What you're doing, I think it's incredible,' he typed. 'For yourself and for Somalia. Let me make some enquiries for you. In the meantime, you should try and generate some press. What you're doing, it's a huge story, let's try and create a moment – hopefully the right people will see it.' 'Press?!' I replied hesitantly, confused at the idea of anyone want-ing to read about me, Richard and all our desperate antics. That wasn't worth writing about at all in my eyes, and despite how far I had come I was still wary of attracting any media attention that Mum might see. 'Of course!' replied Hassan. 'Listen to what you've just told me. You're a former refugee who came to the UK with nothing and you've fought your way to becoming one of the best boxers in the country. Now, you're about to embark on another fight – to put your home country on the map for all the right reasons, to show the world what Somalia is capable of and to inspire future generations.'

I was glad our conversation was happening over Instagram, as I needed to take a minute to fully process what Hassan was saying. I didn't feel right being depicted in such a heroic light. I had always boxed simply because I loved it. I did it for myself, I even did it against the wishes of my family; if anything, committing to being a boxer was selfish. Even going about creating a federation was because I wanted to box, full stop. How could this man make me out to be doing it for Somalia? I went back to Hassan. I told him more of my story. How boxing had started as a means of me getting fit, which had turned into a passion, before becoming something altogether more complicated. It was a huge part of my life, and I loved it too much to contemplate quitting again. Competing for Somalia was the only logical way I could progress. Inspiring the future generation? Putting my country on the map? That wasn't what I was doing at all; I didn't deserve those descriptions. 'But Ramla, that *is* what will happen – whether you like it or not,' Hassan explained. 'You might not understand it yet, but if Somali people across the world get to hear your story, they will feel inspired. You may not have set out to become a role model for others, but it is a by-product of what you are doing here.' His words stirred something in me. Up until that point, I hadn't thought about how anyone else might perceive our actions. We were doing it for ourselves; I wanted to follow my dreams and, together, Richard and I wanted to become a team, but I realised we were being naive.

There is a reason Somalia hasn't had a boxing federation since a dictator banned it in the mid-seventies: it barely has a functioning government. There's a lot of civil unrest and it's still considered one of the most corrupt countries in the world. I knew too well that Somali news stories are dominated by war and terrorism. What we were doing was newsworthy too; only this time, Somalia could make the news for positive reasons. It was at that moment I began to realise the significance of our goal; if we were successful, this thing we were trying to pull off would be much bigger than the two of us and that meant a lot. Just flicking through Hassan's Instagram had made me feel a renewed sense of national pride, it had made me want to visit Somalia; that's a powerful feeling to invoke in a person. All it takes is one person to change the way you see a place, the way you see yourself. I realised that my story could resonate with other young Black girls; I could help them to grow up knowing they had so much to be proud of, and that no dream could ever be too big. I could be the kind of role model I wished that I'd had. That was an amazing feeling, but one that scared me too. I wasn't working towards my goal with a big team, I was on my own, with Richard as my coach. I felt a lot of pressure. I wanted to succeed, so that I could show future generations that anyone could follow their dreams, but I knew there would be so many obstacles in my path. I had to be strong, not just for myself, but for others after me as well. It made me think about my own role models, like Serena Williams. I've always loved her because she is so true to herself. She has always fought for what is right. If she's ever short-changed by a referee, she always speaks up about it, even if it's to the detriment of the final score. I've always been drawn to women like that – powerful and passionate – the kind of women who don't back down without a fight. And so, I thought about the idea of having more eyes on me, and I promised myself I would always act with integrity. I didn't have anywhere near the platform Serena has – I still don't – but if I can inspire just one person in the same way she has inspired me, I will be happy.

Hassan messaged a few hours later; he told me he'd spoken to his friend Jamal Osman, a journalist whose work had appeared across several Somali stations as well as in the UK on the BBC, Channel 4 and in the *Guardian* newspaper. Overwhelmed, I thanked Hassan, said goodnight and handed my phone to Richard to read the exchange. I glanced at the clock and realised it was almost midnight; I'd been on my phone for hours and I had to get away from the blue light of my screen. I got up from the kitchen table and went to lie down on the sofa, thinking again about what Hassan had said. I knew he was right; getting our message broadcast on

Somali TV stations was definitely worth a try, but I couldn't believe I was considering opening up to a journalist and putting myself on screen. That was the kind of opportunity I would have done anything to avoid. I had spent years forensically trying to hide boxing from my parents; now I was preparing to parade it in front of their faces by getting my own on Somali TV. Mum especially would spend hours watching TV while she went about the housework or hosted family for coffee. If we were successful in getting an interview broadcast, I had to accept that there was a strong likelihood of her seeing it, but I couldn't even begin to contemplate what that would mean for our relationship.

Richard slid alongside me on the sofa. I offered him a tired smile and shuffled over to make space, resting my head against his shoulder. 'For what it's worth . . . I think he's right,' he told me. 'I know what you're thinking. Your parents, what it could do to your relationship . . . I just want you to know that I'll back your decision whatever the outcome.'

I closed my eyes and felt the steady rise and fall of Richard's chest. I slowed my own breath so that we were perfectly in sync, and for a few minutes I thought about nothing else but the slow rhythm of each inhalation.

'I'll try and get an interview,' I told him, breaking the silence. I knew that if I wanted to represent Somalia, I would have to stand up and speak out; I couldn't do it with one foot in and one foot out, I had to go the whole way. That night I realised that my decision was bigger than just me; I just hoped my family would understand too. Completely wiped out with exhaustion, Richard and I spent that night in the living room, knotted together on the sofa like twisted tree roots.

An email from Jamal was already waiting in my inbox the next day. I learned that like me, he had travelled to the United Kingdom as a young refugee, and having built a career and a home here, he was in a position to use his platform and connections as a journalist to celebrate the achievements of fellow Somalis. Jamal said he was inspired by my goal and that he would love to be of assistance in any way possible; he worked for a number of outlets and he'd recently set up his own digital media company called Dalsoor. He thought targeting the Somali community would be perfect for getting the message out. He'd left his number and told me to call him to set up an interview. I was stunned. A huge part of me wanted to delete the email and pretend it never happened; I didn't have to be at work until 10 a.m. that day, and I worried that if I didn't get back to Jamal straight away, that I might never, and so I called him there and then, standing outside the gym and listening to the drone of the dial tone, while secretly hoping he wouldn't pick up.

'Hello?' A man with a deep voice and a strong Somali accent answered the phone.

'Hi,' I said. 'This is Ramla, I just got your email. Is now a good time?'

'Ah, Ramla! That was quick. Yes, hi, I can talk.' His tone was warm and familiar; I could have easily been talking to an uncle. We chatted a little about our shared background, and Jamal told me he'd love to work together. When he asked if he could come down to one of my training sessions with his videographer Sayeed, I took a leap of faith and enthusiastically agreed. The plan was to film Richard and me working together, before Jamal and I would sit down to do the interview. I kept imagining Mum's reaction; how crushing it would be for her to not just hear me talk about boxing, but actually see me do it. She would feel so betrayed. Then I thought of Hassan and everything he had said. I needed to step up and become a role model. I had to embrace the discomfort of being interviewed, knowing what it could bring in the long run.

'I have a session next week with my friend Valerian and her coach Laird,' I told him. 'That would be perfect, it's at Times ABC in King's Cross . . . Why don't you come along? I'll email you the details.' Hassan agreed, and I hung up and stuffed my phone into my pocket. I rushed into the staff room, bundled my belongings into a locker and went to relieve the receptionist on the early shift. It was really happening.

I could do my old job at Virgin Active with my eyes closed. During those frantic and uncertain weeks when Richard and I were scrambling to train wherever we could, spending late nights trying to progress with the Somali federation while being constantly met by false starts and dead ends, I started to find a new appreciation for my job. The stillness of being sat at a desk all day used to frustrate me, but now it provided me the bit of calm that I craved among all of the chaos. Plus, at quiet times I could use the reception computer to fire out emails and research tournaments. Slowly we were progressing, and with Hassan and Jamal on board, I felt hopeful. Although I had no birth certificate (with the war and leaving the country, my parents had never had a chance to register my birth), within a month of deciding to compete for Somalia, I'd got my Somali passport (which required a day trip to Brussels and a long wait at the Somali embassy), we had our first media opportunity lined up, and Richard was working on getting his coaching licence so that he could become the official coach to the Somalia team. That last part of the puzzle proved especially difficult. To do anything on an international level, you have to go through AIBA, the International Boxing Association. Richard had been in touch countless times to discuss how he could go about becoming my coach. He had managed to get his national level coaching licence – which allowed him to coach in the UK – but in order to do it for Somalia, he would need his Olympic licence. That's where things started to get complicated. To get an Olympic licence, Richard would need to do a ten-day AIBA-backed course, but to be eligible for the course, he'd need the backing of a boxing federation. The Somali boxing federation didn't exist yet, we were still figuring out how to get it off the ground, and to make matters even worse, one of the criteria for setting up a boxing federation was that the application would need to be supported by an Olympic-licensed coach. It was a complete catch-22; the federation needed a coach, the coach needed the federation, and we had neither. It's hard not to give up when you're met with what feels like an impossible situation, but we vowed not to take no for an answer. I knew I wanted to box internationally and I knew I wanted to get the federation set up. I'd made a promise to myself and to Richard, and once you choose to follow your dream, you have to give it one hundred per cent. You have to believe it will pay off; it requires a lot of faith, and a lot of hustle.

We knew we had to get Richard on the course, but even if we had the right paperwork, it was going to prove difficult. The spaces were highly sought after, and from what I knew from the GB coaches, the process of being nominated involved playing a real political game; applicants had to be highly regarded by both the existing coaches and the GB squad, and even then, it usually takes years before the GB board would finally select a new Olympic coach. This would be Richard's first real stab at coaching, and our team didn't even exist yet. If we did strike gold and somehow got him on the course, we'd only have a choice of two or three countries where he could do it, depending on how many applicants there were in any given year, and where their applications were coming from. The courses are long and arduous. They take place over ten days, and they're expensive and intense; if they're taking place in a foreign-language country there's not even a guarantee that you'll be taught in English. The assessment happens over the final few days, and you get your result just before you leave: you pass or fail, simple as that, and most people tend to fail.

Nobody on our side could put Richard forward for the course, because Somalia was not yet an active boxing country, so we decided to approach England Boxing. I had contacts, and so I emailed asking whether they would consider nominating Richard for the course. I explained that we obviously had no expectation of England Boxing ever giving him a contract; it would purely be a favour. We would pay all of the costs ourselves; all we needed was for them to send an email on our behalf. We knew they'd turn us down, but seeing the rejection in my inbox still hurt. We were back to square one, or minus one. By the time my interview with Jamal came around, I was starting to worry. Our savings had already slowly started to diminish after paying to use boxing gyms and travelling across the country to spar, and we hadn't even put anything towards the federation yet. When Jamal called me one Saturday afternoon to say that he and Sayeed were outside, I worried that I had completely wasted his time. But I forced myself to think positively. Sometimes in the early weeks when all you have is a dream, you have to let it carry you until it starts to turn into a reality.

Jamal was a tall, broad-shouldered man who commanded respect; he spoke with confidence and authority, and it felt strange that a man like that would want to interview me. He was joined by the videographer, Sayeed, a quiet man who occupied himself by setting up endless pieces of camera equipment. As I led them up the stairs, I suddenly saw Times ABC in the way an uninitiated stranger must see it; it was a dank sweaty space filled with worn-out equipment, with yellowed paint curling off the walls. What was I thinking bringing these highly regarded media professionals into a windowless boxing gym to chat about my far-fetched dream? My imposter syndrome reared its ugly head and that feeling of inadequacy and self-doubt returned, but I reminded myself that I deserved this opportunity. Nobody had forced Jamal to come, he hadn't come as a favour to Hassan, he came because he was interested in my story. That thought helped me grow in confidence, and as I nervously introduced the two men to Richard, Valerian and Laird, I started to feel more myself. We all so badly wanted the day to go well, I had to prove to Jamal, and myself, that my dream was worth taking seriously. Jamal must have sensed how nervous I was as he told me not to worry, to forget about the camera pointed in my direction. I've never liked being filmed. Cameras were my silent enemy. Growing up, I was also so conscious about my weight that I hated seeing myself on screen. Once I'd started boxing, cameras had become something I had learned to avoid.

Now, I had to unlearn all of those habits, and let myself be filmed and broadcast. I needed someone to see the video and help us, because we urgently needed guidance with setting up the federation. I knew it would take commitment, dedication and a lot of hard work. I had to put my fears aside and give it my all, and so I took Jamal's advice, and imagined it was any other training session. To warm up, Valerian and I skipped and shadow-boxed, while Laird and Richard looked on. Next, they had us put on our gloves and run through various different sequences with our respective coaches wearing the pads. After a while, I really did forget I was being filmed. Laird worked with me and Valerian on a check hook: a highly technical manoeuvre that a boxer can use to prevent a particularly aggressive opponent from lunging in at you. It was difficult, and involved my full concentration. The process sounds relatively simple: you throw a hook to the head of the person coming towards you. But, at the same time, you have to simultaneously pivot on your lead foot while swinging your back foot a whole 180 degrees. It's hard to get your head around, and it's even harder to execute, but if you can pull it off, the opponent who is hurtling towards you not only sails straight past you, but you will have also knocked them off balance; now all that's left is to finish them off. Or at least, that's the idea. No matter how well Laird explained it, demonstrated it, corrected my mistakes, I could not master the movement. 'Don't worry, take it easy,' he kept saying, sensing my frustration. 'There's a reason check hooks are rare in boxing; they're very difficult to get right.' Valerian struggled too, but watching her and Laird, I could see she was improving. Meanwhile, I just couldn't seem to grasp check hooks. I was flailing. I concentrated on his every word, Richard's too; I had to get this right. By the time we moved on to sparring, I had completely forgotten about Jamal and Sayeed. Just as they promised, they did a great job of being invisible, and I'd been concentrating so hard on my check hooks that their presence was no longer a distraction. When our session came to an end, I was about to collect my things from the changing room and head home like any other day, until Richard reminded me I had the interview to do.

Full of endorphins from training, I felt pretty powerful and wasn't nervous. All the self-doubt and embarrassment, the sense of being a complete fraud was gone. Instead, I was ready, excited even, to talk about my journey without hiding. I stood opposite Jamal in the ring, but he was not an opponent I had to fight, he was simply there to listen to my story. The interview lasted about twenty minutes, and Jamal left no stone unturned. We covered how my family fled Somalia when I was still a baby, how I had discovered boxing after years of bullying, and how insecurity had led me to that very first boxing class. We talked about my first National Championships, the tournaments I'd competed in abroad, training with the GB team, and finally, my decision to fight for Somalia. I told him how proud I was to be Somali; how I loved everything from the music to the way Somali strangers are always so welcoming wherever you are. Afterwards, he congratulated me and said I spoke with passion and conviction. A few years prior, I could never have spoken so openly, but by the time I did the interview, I realised I was ready to tell my story, and to add more chapters to the narrative of my life so far.

After the interview I filled Jamal in on all the difficulties we were facing and he gave me some sound advice. 'In my opinion, you don't need to wait for permission. You already have the contacts for the competitions; you should just start competing in them. Keep doing more press, and that will get the government on board. With your fights and the media exposure, they will have to respond.' Jamal reminded me of a popular saying: sometimes it is easier to ask for forgiveness rather than permission. Looking back, if I'd waited for others' approval and permission for what I wanted to achieve, I would have been waiting forever.

Off the back of the interview, Richard and I persevered with the Olympic boxing coach courses. We figured if we could find out when and where they were being held, that we'd at least know how long we had to try and get him onto one of the programmes. The information was relatively easy to uncover: they were due to take place in Mongolia, Namibia and Malta, within the next two months. Richard contacted each country's governing body straight away, explaining our situation and asking if there was any way he could attend a course. The Namibia representative never replied, but the Mongolia team said they would put him forward as a Mongolian coach as a favour; Malta came back a few days later with a similar response. We went with the earliest course and the cheapest flight: Malta. Four weeks later, we'd paid £2,000 for the course, and a few hundred more for flights, and Richard was on the first plane out of London, headed to Valletta. For ten days, he would be subject to gruelling training and theoretical exams, while I stayed at home with my own checklist to get through. Number one was parting ways with Samm Mullins, a task I'd been putting off for a few weeks now.

There's nothing I hate more than a potentially uncomfortable exchange with a coach. I think we both knew that I was going to leave Nemesis; I'd been training there less and less, and Samm knew I wanted to compete internationally. Part of me wanted to just stop showing up – I knew he'd get the message – but ultimately, I had to tell him face to face, I needed to do it the right way. Samm had always been so kind to me, and he was incredibly understanding. We'd already spoken about time commitments to each other and what I needed if he was to be in my corner. He may well have already seen it coming, but as I approached the gym after work one evening, I felt a heaviness in the pit of my stomach. I couldn't help thinking about Ricardo; how he used to talk to me, the shouting, the anger. I imagined how badly he would have taken something like this, and feared that Samm would react the same way, but I knew I had to act with integrity, I owed it to Samm to tell him. It turned out I didn't need to worry. While Samm seemed sad that we were parting ways, he was understanding about my reasons for leaving, and he seemed genuinely impressed with my goal to fight for Somalia. We both knew he couldn't keep coaching two women in the same weight category.

'Ramla,' he said, patting me on the back after we both knew our brief conversation had come to an end. 'Best of luck. Me and everyone else at Nemesis, we'll always be rooting for you.' With one final hug, we parted ways for the last time.

*

Ten days after Richard had left, I got the call that he had passed all of the assessments: he was now qualified to be the official coach of Somalia. I screamed at him down the phone, while welling up with excitement. I was so proud of him, of our team and all that we had achieved so far. With Richard back in the UK, neither one of us could wait to get back on our journey. There were smaller competitions that weren't governed by AIBA, which would technically accept me competing for Somalia without needing to see paperwork, but I was torn. From the very beginning, we had always said we wanted to do this properly. We had committed to going through the official channels and doing it the right way, but there were no official channels; we'd still had no response from the Somali government, and it seemed we may have had no other option than to just start fighting. Jamal's video was about to come out. I knew we needed a fight to keep the momentum going.

The day the interview went live on Dalsoor's You-Tube channel, my life changed forever. It turned out Dalsoor had a huge following, and versions of the video began to spread across several other Somali and British sites. When I received a call from my uncle out of the blue, I knew straight away that he must have seen it. My uncle is my mum's older brother; she's always looked up to him for advice so I wondered if it was her who'd seen the video first. Maybe it's because he's older, but of all the siblings, my uncle always struck me as the most integrated into Western culture. He can speak fluent English, and he's pretty laid-back compared to Mum. I think he's always understood the clash between African and Western cultures that my brothers and sisters and I faced. Still, I braced myself for bad news. 'Hi, Uncle,' I said.

'Ramla, you've been on the TV,' he said, with what I hoped was a laugh. 'I've just watched your interview! Now tell me, your mother really has no idea?'

I took a deep breath, and began to explain our difficult history when it came to boxing. Mum hadn't even shared my boxing with her own siblings out of fear it would bring shame to the community. I was relieved when he eventually cut me off. 'It brings *pride* to the community!' he said. He said that I was showing to our community how positive boxing – or any sport – can be for our health and well-being. To my uncle, my public project was shining a positive light on Somalia, he was saddened that I felt I had to hide it from my mum. I was completely overcome with relief. He told me he was going to speak to my mother, that he would do everything in his power to make sure she was on board, and that all I had to do was focus on boxing; he would make sure my family were proud. I was speechless. My uncle was a very persuasive man. While my mum had always worried what the Somali community would think of me, my uncle made a good point. So many people in my family suffer from diabetes, high blood pressure and high cholesterol; if he could present me as a positive role model for the community, then perhaps she might be able to see the positives and slowly change her opinion. I trusted him, and when he called me back a few days later and told me he'd done it, I felt both relieved and suspicious. It was a strange conversation. I felt as though we were both talking in riddles; my uncle telling me that he had told Mum and that she accepted our situation, me thanking him profusely, but knowing deep down that when it came to my mum and what she thought about boxing, there was still a long way to go. I wasn't sure what to do with the information I had just been handed. Should I call her? Send her the video? Thank her? In the end I left it. When you're dealing with another person's emotions, we have to act with patience. I knew she had a lot to process; she was frightened of me getting hurt, worried about other people judging me; I needed to give her time.

My uncle wasn't the only one to reach out to me after seeing the video. A month later a man called Fabian contacted me on Instagram. He was a retired sprinter who, like me, had competed for the Great British team, before switching alliance to his home country of Barbados. He congratulated me on what Richard and I were doing, offering himself if I ever needed advice, since speed is an immensely important skill in boxing. I told him I'd love to sprint properly, and he offered to take me on the track one day where he could talk me through techniques. Those months were some of the scrappiest months of my career. I'd train with whoever I could, whenever I could, and after a great first session with Fabian, he joined our renegade little team as the strength and conditioning coach. Though he was a sprinter by practice, he followed boxing religiously, and so he knew how to adapt a runner's skills for inside the ring; I learned a lot from him about speed and agility. Having no af-filiation to any gym or club definitely had its downsides, but it was also incredibly freeing. I was learning a lot, and though it may not have been from experienced boxing coaches, I valued the insight from Richard and Fabian. They brought different perspectives to my training.

With so many people reaching out to help me, I felt a duty to do the same. In so many ways I was relying on the kindness of others who believed in me. When Adam, one of the old coaches from Fitzroy Lodge, asked if I wanted to volunteer to teach some young people, I enthusiastically agreed. The very first session I taught was all kinds of madness. Adam had brought a bunch of sixteen-year-olds to the gym, and they were so excited to put on gloves and punch each other that they clearly had no interest in listening to me. I had to shout over them to have my voice heard; and it frustrated me that the ones who did want to listen were being drowned out by a group of loud boys at the back. I'll be honest, it didn't go great. Don't get me wrong; I love young people. I loved the passion that every boy and girl brought to that class, and I have so much respect for teachers and coaches and youth workers who dedicate themselves to working with young people, but I didn't have the skills to manage a big group like that, it was impossible to teach them. I really wanted to help people learn new skills, so I kept going back and teaching more sessions, before I pulled Adam aside and told him it wasn't working. 'I want to keep volunteering,' I promised, 'but not like this.' It's important to recognise your strengths – and your weaknesses too. I realised I could be much more helpful teaching a different group – then I told him my idea.

Ever since I started competing, I've always wanted to see more women in boxing, especially more Muslim women who might not have the same access to the sport. For decades, it's always been seen as a men's game, but some of the best boxers I've ever seen fight are women. In teaching boxing, you're teaching an invaluable set of skills. Even if someone doesn't ever want to compete, they're still learning about focus and self-defence, while becoming fitter and stronger. That's why I wanted to run a free women's class, a safe space where women could learn to fight, surrounded by other women. Adam gave me his blessing, and so instead of kids' classes, the Sisters Club was born. We advertised in local mosques, and with no men in the room, some women would come and feel comfortable enough to take their hijabs off to train. Others trained with their hijabs on – it never mattered – everyone was welcome. Exercise is so important for not just your physical health, but your mental health too, and if it weren't for those weekly sessions, many of the women wouldn't have had another space they would have felt comfortable using.

As word spread, the numbers grew and grew, and women started attending from all sorts of different backgrounds. Though it had been aimed at Muslim women, I realised that many women need a safe space and a sisterhood to be part of. Some of the attendees opened up to me about how they had suffered domestic abuse and didn't feel safe around men; there were many women who came because they wanted to learn how to defend themselves so they could feel more confident, and others who simply wanted to get fit. It's the same today – everyone is welcome – and nothing fills me with joy more than watching women learning how to box together. It's an amazing community where everybody has each other's backs.

I started the Sisters Club during a big period of change in my life, and it helped to ground me. With Mum aware of my boxing, I'd begun posting videos on Instagram from the sessions, as well as from my own training. I noticed my profile steadily growing. Every day I was getting twenty or so new followers; most of them were women, and many were Somali. I was receiving a lot of messages too. Strangers from all over the world were telling me how they were moved by my story. It was so surreal; boxing had always been my secret, now people I'd never met were backing me, telling me they knew that I could bring home gold medals for Somalia, or that they wanted to take up boxing too. Despite everything I'd been through with my family, it gave me a real fire in my belly. For the first time ever, people were rooting for me to succeed; I had to make them proud.

Six months passed, and I began to get noticed by the sporting world too. In February 2018, I was invited by Nike to do a panel talk as part of their new campaign, Nothing Beats a LDNR. The event – which was encouraging young people to embrace sporting opportunities – was taking place at St Martin-in-the-Fields High School, an all-girls comprehensive in south London that wasn't too different to my own secondary school. It wasn't until the week before the event that I found out who else would be part of the talk: Emelia Gorecka, a professional long-distance track and field athlete, and three-time winner of the London Marathon, Paula Radcliffe. I'd never done any kind of public speaking before. Sitting next to a medalled long-distance runner and one of the most iconic women in sport was a real pinch-me moment, but once I got speaking to Paula I realised that she was so down to earth. She was friendly and unassuming, and yet her achievements were completely out of this world. I was so lost in her stories that I almost forgot I had to speak too. The night before, I'd been terrified I wouldn't be able to get my words out. I'd written paragraphs of notes, but seeing the other panellists speak so naturally, I decided to do the same. I looked out into the audience and saw myself in many of them. Young girls full of potential, waiting for their adult lives to start.

I introduced myself and told my story, how I came to the UK as a child refugee fleeing civil war in Somalia, and how as a Muslim woman, I had faced opposition and stigmatisation for pursuing boxing. I talked about how I'd persevered, how I wanted to become a champion, and how I wanted to be the first boxer, man or woman, to compete for Somalia. 'Hopefully – Insha'Allah – I will represent Somalia in the 2020 Olympics,' I told them. It was the first time I had said it aloud to anyone else but Richard. The Olympics had become my target, and I trained with ferocity and believed in it. Even though the world shut down in 2020, when the pandemic hit and

Covid-19 derailed my ambitions, I don't look back on that day and feel humiliated for speaking my truths, for saying my goals out loud so that I could be held accountable for them. I still plan to fight in the Olympics, and continue to add a new chapter to my story.

After the event, I didn't want to rush off, but I had to get back to work. Despite the apparent stature of who I was or what I was doing, I was still grounded in reality and had to work. I made my way to the exit, and was approached by a man with mousy-brown hair and a well-groomed beard. 'I was hoping to grab you before you ran off,' he said. 'I'm Dan Smith, the head of sports marketing at Nike.' I'd been given some clothes to wear for the talk, and I realised I was about to leave still wearing them.

'I'm so sorry – do I have to give you these back?' I said.

He laughed and shook his head. 'No, no, of course not, we'd love you to keep them. I was actually just wondering if you'd be able to come into the office next week? We thought you were brilliant today, and we'd love to discuss ways in which Nike might be able to support you as an athlete.' I was stunned. Ever since we had agreed to fight for Somalia, Richard had emailed every sports brand under the sun trying to forge some kind of relationship. The few replies we had got were all rejections. I was a nobody in the boxing world. I hadn't gone to the Olympics, I hadn't fought in the World Championships; compared to a lot of fighters, I still didn't have a lot on my CV. But I did have a dream, and once I'd said it out loud, people were slowly coming on board with my vision, placing their faith in me, determined to help me bring it to life.

This moment was promising; however, it was not without its reality check. It's one thing to dream, but to make a dream come true, there's often a whole lot of arduous admin that goes on behind the scenes. Richard had thrown himself into the calculations and had created a detailed breakdown of how much financial support we needed for the rest of the year, making sure every penny was justified and accounted for down to the decimal point. Considering budgeting and time management, and making financial plans can be very boring, but learning these crucial skills reminded me that it was always important to plan, to have evidence for your 'argument', and to be prepared to have answers for someone's questions. There's also another common saying: 'Fail to prepare and prepare to fail.' We had to be ready. Richard and I knew Nike would never give us anywhere near the full amount straight away, but we wanted to show what we were up against. Compared with the other boxing federations, we were in a real David-and-Goliath situation.

Armed with our spreadsheets printed off and proudly housed in a thin red plastic folder, I headed to the Nike office a few weeks later wondering how on earth I would go about asking them to fund me. For a fledgling athlete like me, walking into the headquarters of a global sports brand was like a kid entering a theme park. From my employment history, I understood offices to be grey, soulless spaces sound tracked by the low humming of a printer and the near-permanent ringing of several phones at once. At Nike, every wall was covered with either sprawling illustrations of athletes or glossy expensive-looking campaign shots. As I was led to a meeting room, I took in the pictures of sprinters, fighters, footballers, basketball players, each athlete sharing the same look of sheer determination and absolute focus. Dan shook my hand and introduced me to the wider team, a few of whom I remembered from the school event. After introductions, they told me they recognised what I was doing and that they wanted to support me. Then it was up to me to tell them how we might be able to work together. I'd never been in a meeting like that before, and as friendly as everyone was, I couldn't help but feel out of place. I found myself constantly fidgeting with the folder I'd brought with me, curling back its edges and then using my hand like an iron to straighten it back out. I took a deep breath, and calmly began. I told them I needed some kit because I was sweating and burning through everything so quickly, and it was costing us a lot of our diminishing savings. Everyone nodded along, and Dan instantly agreed to this.

I paused. 'To be totally honest, what I need most is money,' I told them. 'This athlete life is very expensive, and we're doing it completely on our own without the support of a club or a federation. We both work full-time but it's not enough to cover the costs . . .' I slid the folder across the table and explained the breakdown. Keeping their game faces, they flipped through the pages of the budget, Dan still nodding.

'Well, we can definitely help you with the kit,' he said, still leafing through the rest of the folder. 'Let me get back to you on the money front.' I was proud of myself for stating what I needed.

Talking about money can be frightening and awkward – quite simply we don't talk about it often and openly enough and we should – especially as women. Knowing and claiming your financial worth is important for so many reasons – personal confidence being one, and the gender pay gap being the other. We all have to get through uncomfortable conversations: job interviews, pitches and presentations. Remember, you are a powerful and valued voice in those rooms and you deserve to be there. Be prepared, and be yourself; the work will speak for itself.

A few weeks after the meeting, I still hadn't heard back from Nike. The weather had been awful for a few days, with constant rain, and one afternoon after returning to the flat completely soaked from a run, I felt a real longing to be in the ring. I was feeling restless, and propped my forehead against the window, closing my eyes to block out the foggy grey expanse that lay beyond the cold pane of glass. I missed real boxing; the uncertainty of when I would compete next was getting to me, more than any of the answers we were waiting on. I needed to fight. I'd quit Nemesis so that Richard and I could enter all the tournaments we wanted, yet we'd not entered anything. I knew deep down I had to be patient, remind myself of what we had achieved, and take great pride in that. In the year since making the biggest decision of our lives, there had been some wins. Richard had qualified as a fully trained coach and together we'd made huge progress with the federation. We'd forged a relationship with Nike and we even had a man helping us on the ground in Somalia, in Mogadishu; a man called Abdirahman Ali Mire, the Somali uncle of a Norwegian boxer, who'd been in touch after seeing the video. His nephew wanted to compete for Somalia too, and since he regularly travelled back and forth, he had promised to get the documents we needed signed. It had been a year of hard work, but our dream was slowly starting to resemble a reality. In a lot of ways, I was over the moon, but I felt like we had a million things going on *to do with* boxing, but still no *actual* boxing. I hadn't competed since Richard and I had gone to Sweden over a year ago. The paperwork and the press and the training all needed to be done, but without a single fight on the horizon, I was starting to feel impatient. I didn't become a boxer to just attract more followers on Instagram, I was here to fight. Time unfortunately, wasn't on my side. I was in my mid-twenties – twenty-five at best, I guessed – and most women boxers I knew retired in their early thirties. That's the nature of the sport – for some you peak at that age, and you've amassed a significant number of bouts and championship wins to bow out. I thought back to what Jamal had said, about how I shouldn't wait for permission or approval from others. I decided he was right. Yes, it was a risk to start competing for Somalia before the federation was up and running as things could easily backfire, but on the other hand, the right person could see me in the ring, and then they would simply have to take notice. I talked to Richard and he agreed; it was time to get back on the road, and with that we entered the Hvidovre Box Cup in Denmark, a small international competition that wasn't governed by AIBA. They accepted our entry without any questions, and I was finally going to fight for Somalia.

The day we left for Denmark, Mum called me while we were at the airport. Ever since I had moved out, our relationship had felt a lot more relaxed. She was no longer there to constantly question where I was going for the weekend or why I had a bruise on my face, but in moments like this, I'd see her name flash up on my phone screen and still feel blind panic. Why now? Did she know I was on my way to do a boxing tournament? I picked up, and I was relieved when she began giving me an update on her sister's health and the dates for her next Somalia trip. I thought the conversation had come to an end, when suddenly, her voice lowered.

'My brother told me that you are still fighting.' I stopped walking towards the gate and let the crowd of the airport engulf me. I didn't know what to say, so I said nothing. 'I've always known.'

'I tried to quit,' I told her. 'I really did, but I . . . I can't . . .' I was grateful when she cut me off.

'I know,' she said quietly. There was a big pause before she spoke again. To my surprise, she asked me when I was next fighting. I told her we were at the airport travelling to Denmark to compete for Somalia for the first time.

'For Somalia?' she repeated. 'Call me afterwards. Good luck, Ramla.' And with that she hung up.

I had waited so long to hear those words; I kept replaying the conversation over and over for most of the flight. After years of secrecy and confrontations, it seemed she had finally made her peace with it, even if she didn't wholly approve of my boxing. The fact that she'd wished me good luck really meant something. I had my mum's acceptance, and if nothing else it was a start.

By that point in my career, I'd learned that the accommodation for boxers during tournaments is rarely glamorous. This time round we weren't staying in a hotel but the national training centre for the Denmark team, in a soulless dorm-like room they put me and Richard in. It didn't matter. Nothing could distract me from my first fight for Somalia; I felt on top of the world. The hard work and the long wait to get to this point only made everything feel more exciting. My opponent was Natalija Cincarevic, a Swedish fighter, though she had the nickname 'the Serbian Viking'. Natalija was one of the most intense opponents I'd faced in a while. From the moment we locked eyes, I could tell she was ruthless. She fought with a menacing frown, and when the first bell went, she charged straight towards me with what felt like more than our shared 57kg body weight. Natalija was strong, and she kept crashing towards me like it was a bullfight; she was barely landing any hits, just charging and charging. And then I remembered: check hook. Everything I'd been working on in the session with Laird and Valerian – the one filmed by Jamal and Sayeed – suddenly came back to me. Hook and pivot. The next time Natalija charged at me, I threw a shot to her side and slid away, leaving her charging into the ropes.

The bell rang, signalling the end of the first round. Richard was ecstatic. We were both breathless as he calmly talked me through the next round. 'Right at the end there, you confused her. She's strong, but you have the upper hand on technique; use your skills, you've got this.' The manoeuvre that had taken me months to master finally felt effortless, and it was worth the wait. Again and again, I used Natalija's own strength against her with check hooks and slips that she could never have expected. By the end of the second round, I was in control of the fight and I was enjoying it; she could rarely land a shot before I'd ducked under it or slipped away to the side. In the final round, Natalija seemed angry. She came at me with a desperate amount of force, charging and hammering away in my direction; but it was no use. Though she landed a few extra shots in the final round, when the bell rang, I knew I had won.

I was through to the finals, and my second fight was two days later, this time against a Danish girl named Bettina Dahl. She was very tall for her weight, which meant she could often land a punch while I still wasn't close enough to hit her. I stayed calm and forced myself to think on the spot; I'd been in situations like this before, so what if she was taller? In the second round, I learned to be stricter with myself. I went in there and focused on what I had to do. I didn't let myself think that there was a chance I could lose, I believed I was smarter and sneakier. I delivered fake throws, pretending to hit her in order to anticipate her reaction. I made her duck and slip away from invisible punches, before coming at her with my own attack as she was trying to centre herself. I'm not usually an offensive fighter – I win my bouts by knowing how to evade shots and fight defensively – but this time I had to step up and out of my comfort zone. Though she was tall and strong, I made an impact with clever combinations that she wasn't expecting. For years I had sparred with men because there weren't enough women for me to fight. It had been frustrating and at times even dangerous, but I realised I had learned so much determination and fearlessness from all those uneven pairings. The bell rang, and when the judges unanimously awarded me the win, I didn't realise I was crying until the hot tears completely clouded my vision. Richard and I aren't tactile at competitions, we keep things professional, but after the fight I couldn't help but throw myself into his arms. We had done it. After a year of doubt and debt and uncertainty, we were taking home our first gold medal for Somalia.

When I saw Bettina post-fight in the warm-up area, I went over to thank her for the fight. 'You are deceptively strong,' she snapped. 'Your arms look like twigs, but you hit like a hammer.' I watched her face wrinkle into a smile and instinctively hugged her. It turned out we got on well when we weren't trying to knock the other one out. Bettina introduced me to her wife, and we exchanged details and promised to keep in touch.

I was already on cloud nine in a taxi back to the training centre when Mum called and I finally got to say the words I'd longed to share with her for years.

'Mum, I won.'

She sounded tense. 'You did?' she gasped. There was this incredible shift in mood as she began crying down the phone. She told me that she hadn't been able to sleep, that she'd been up all night praying for me and that she was so glad I won. 'I'm proud of you,' she told me, and I had to pinch myself. It was the moment I'd been dreaming of, but it wasn't a dream.

I thought back to where I'd been a year earlier. I could have sat at home, sulking and waiting and feeling sorry for myself because I never got that call from the GB squad. I could have kept waiting for them to invite me to trials, but instead, I took my future into my own hands. I pursued a dream that nobody else had turned into a reality before. I didn't know if it would work – it was still early days – but at least I'd gone in with a hundred per cent conviction and a hundred per cent passion. I would accept whatever happened, knowing that even if I failed, I had done everything in my power to follow my dreams.

ROUND EIGHT

Dream big

Don't be afraid of aiming high. Having a dream is something that nobody can take away from you; it's yours. Let it drive you. My goals are what make me work hard, and as I progress and grow closer towards them, I love the feeling of confidence it brings me. I still have so many dreams I haven't met – some that I might never meet, but in allowing myself to dream big, and letting those ambitions guide me, I know I'm living the fullest version of my life that I can.

Be loud

Whatever your dream is, say it aloud, admit that it exists. That's the very first step of working towards your goal: letting yourself and others know that it's what you want. Write it down, tell someone you trust and ask them to hold you accountable, and contact the people who might be able to help you; the more people on your side, the more likely it is that your ambitions will become a reality. When I first started doing press, I felt so self-conscious. I worried that people would read about my story and think, There's no way she's going to be able to fight for Somalia. The messages I got couldn't have been more different. Once I put my dreams out there into the world, so many people reached out and wanted to support me.

257

Put in the work

Following your goals can take a lot of hard work, with no guarantee that you'll be able to pull it off. But even if you don't – by working hard you will still achieve so much in the process. Whatever it is you want, if you keep at it, stay committed and seek help when you need it, you will be moving forward. It might not be at the pace you wanted, and there may be hundreds of setbacks along the way, but keep going, keep working. If I had tried to fight for Somalia and it had proved impossible, I knew that when I was older and retired from boxing, I would still feel proud of myself for doing everything I could to make my dreams come true. I can't imagine anything worse than regretting the fact that I was too scared to even try.

Learn the boring bits

Getting to fight with a Somalia flag on my back for the first time was the most incredible feeling, but getting to that point took a lot of work behind the scenes. I had to budget, I had to spend hours and hours emailing people, I had to research federations and funding; there was so much admin that went into making that moment. Your goals might be glamorous; but be prepared for a whole lot of tedium on the way. It will be hard, but it's necessary and it's worth it.

Don't ask for permission

I'm an introvert, I hate drawing attention to myself and I find it much easier following the rules instead of making my own, but when it came to following my dreams, I realised there was no rule book. I had a support network, but nobody was going to hold my hand and talk me through the processes and make it easy for me. I had to do it on my own, or not at all. Remember, you are in control of your own destiny: if you wait for the approval or the encouragement of others, you could be waiting forever.

KEEP GOING, KEEP GROWING

*'The success of every woman should be the inspiration to
another. We should raise each other up. Make sure you're
very courageous: be strong, be extremely kind, and above
all be humble.'*

— Serena Williams

By the spring of 2018, I felt unstoppable. The competition in Hvidovre may have been a small one that flew under the radar in the eyes of AIBA, but I had won it for Somalia, with nobody else but Richard and Fabian on my team. I didn't have to hide boxing from Mum anymore, and we achieved another win – an email from Nike offering me sponsorship. It wasn't a huge amount, but it would definitely help us get by. Beyond that, it did something massively important: it helped me to understand that I was valued as an athlete – they had taken a chance on me and that meant something. In a way it was a confirmation for the path I was on, and it also made me assess how much my thoughts used to be dominated by fear and failure. I had conveyed confidence in that meeting, the cousin of fearlessness. I had executed courage in my fight.

Despite all the setbacks I've faced, ultimately, I have

always chosen to keep going. I'm sure people I'd encountered on the way thought I would disappear, but I respectfully declined. I kept going, and when I was met with an obstacle, I found a new way to progress. There's something incredibly freeing about ripping up the rule book and choosing to do things your own way. I remember one evening Richard and I decided to plan what competitions we wanted to enter that year. As we jotted down ideas and checked entry deadlines, we were filled with a bubbling excitement; both of us were in it for the fight, but we were also going to see the world with each other. We could really celebrate where we had got to, and use hindsight to assess how and why we'd ended up here. I never let myself forget the inappropriate behaviour of my early coaches, my family's refusal to accept my boxing, and the years of longing and waiting to fight internationally – all of those experiences could have led to me quitting – not because it was the easiest route out, but in challenging times it seemed like it was the only option to solve my problems. Somehow, I dug in, somehow I knew I should keep going, and every time I was faced with a difficult decision, or a crossroads that might have led to me quitting again, I realised I had grown a little more since the last time – until I grew into the person I am today.

We let ourselves celebrate with a few days off after Denmark, but then it was back to work. While we were waiting for our fate to be decided by the international governing board, we could continue to enter smaller tournaments that weren't run by AIBA. We entered the

Sparkasse Open, a competition taking place in a small town in south-west Germany called Bensheim. In the autumn, we hoped we'd be AIBA-approved, and pencilled in the Ahmet Cömert boxing tournament in Istanbul to be the first time I'd officially wear the Somali vest. We still had work to do on the Somali boxing federation; we needed to liaise with Nike to work out our new relationship; there were more competitions to contemplate entering; and, of course, training. The one competition that I desperately wanted to enter more than anything was the World Championships. It's the pinnacle of an amateur boxer's career and one of the reasons we chose to set up the federation and go it alone. In 2018 the competition was taking place in New Delhi, India. AIBA had our application, but while they were deciding whether to approve the federation, we were up against another problem: there's a rule in amateur boxing that states a fighter cannot compete for two different countries within two years. The last time I had competed for England was in the Bulgaria tournament in November 2016; the World Championships would fall just short of two years later. That meant we were engaged in a complicated back and forth with AIBA, urging them to both recognise Somalia as a competing country, and to allow us to enter the 2018 World Championships. I had no idea if we'd pull it off, but we certainly put in a strong bid. In countless emails, we explained how important this was; how I would be the first person to ever compete for my country, that this was exactly why people compete, and that the sport I loved – indeed, any sport – should stand for progress, inclusion and equality. Our larger mission, the one written between the lines in the letter, was to show young girls all over the world that no dream is too big, that it doesn't matter where you're from, and that you can succeed on your own terms. Sometimes, you really have to go the extra mile to prove you're serious and that you won't take no for an answer. I hoped a personal letter would remind them of the human being behind the request. I was more than a classification weight; I was a real person with heart and I was adamant to find a way forward. It reminded me that I had to use my voice, and that when I did, it was a testament to how far I had come. At any given time you have to learn how to be louder than the voice telling you that you can't do something. You have to make someone connect with you on an emotional level. You have to put the passion into your voice, and make it undeniable for someone to tell you 'no'. I don't necessarily mean that the loudest voice in the room wins – there's a power in silence, too – however, having that conversation and conveying your commitment goes an incredibly long way.

Since becoming a Nike-sponsored athlete, I've been asked to be involved in the occasional photoshoot. It was a definite overhang from my youth – the humiliation that burned through me when Mum showed the video of me at Faiza's wedding, combined with the years of hiding boxing from my family – that meant I disliked nothing more than being in front of the camera. My first shoot with Nike was in collaboration with a US designer called Matthew M. Williams, featuring ten athletes. I was terrified they'd try and put me in a skimpy pair of shorts or ask me to pose like a 'real model', but I already knew if that was the case I would have to use my voice and stand my ground. Believe it or not, my wardrobe is probably seventy-five per cent sportswear; I'm most comfortable in a tracksuit, I only own sports bras, and I prefer to wear sliders everywhere I go. Growing up, I wore Luul and Faiza's hand-me-downs until they no longer fit, and fashion often felt like this exclusive party that only the rich and the well-connected could participate in. I had experienced the transformative power of clothes, and knew that on the rare occasions I dressed up, I did actually enjoy it. There was something fun about stepping out of my comfort zone in glamorous pieces, yet at the time I felt most at home in my new Somalia tracksuits.

The first photoshoot was like nothing I had ever experienced before. It was in a large studio in east London, with endless people – some with clipboards, others with headsets or walkie-talkies – rushing around, while the sounds of house music filtered into every corner of the huge space through a network of speakers. Dan from Nike was there to talk me through everything and chaperone me from one room to the next. He ushered me into a smaller room where lightbulbs lined the mirrors, and quickly introduced me to the hair and make-up artists before swiftly disappearing. A man did my make-up, while a woman worked away at expertly braiding my hair. After an hour, I was led back into the main studio space and introduced to the stylist: a young woman with bright green hair dressed in streetwear. As she talked me through the looks, I'd be wearing – a thick black neoprene top and leggings that weren't too dissimilar to what I'd wear to train – I started to relax, knowing I would be comfortable in the clothes. Throughout my entire life, I have never worn anything too tight or too revealing. It's partly my faith and the way I was raised – I think about my mum a lot and I know if I wore something that exposed too much of my body it would upset her – but it's also just my personal preference. We all have a certain set of morals and beliefs that are unique to us. It's crucial to stand your ground if anybody ever asks you to compromise them. Some women feel empowered when they wear clothes that show off their figure, whereas I prefer to be covered up, especially if it's in a photoshoot where I don't have control over who sees it. It's a personal choice, and walking into the studio that day, I knew I had to be myself. If I had always bent over backwards trying to please every brand, every photographer or stylist, then I don't think people would understand who the authentic me really was. But by going in, and wearing the pieces I felt comfortable in, sticking to what felt right, I was uncompromised, and confident that I was taking part as my real self.

The person being photographed before me was a high jumper. She was tall and slender, with a beautiful face and big brown eyes. She was so natural in front of the camera. I worried I was going to embarrass myself in comparison, but I realise now, it made no sense to compare myself to the other women, and other athletes. We'd all been invited there, we had earned our place, and while she certainly benefitted from having long legs and a slender physique in her sport, mine required a specific weight and strong muscles; of course we looked completely different, that's exactly what made the shoot so special.

As I was preparing to go on set, I met another of the athletes, a man who looked about my age, with short bleached hair and tattoos up one arm. He walked up to me and introduced himself in an American accent as Miles Chamley-Watson. He asked what I did, and when I said I was a boxer, he seemed genuinely impressed. Talking about boxing made me forget all about the pressure to look a certain way. I was in my element, telling him about the Somalia team and the World Championships. It felt like the shoot covered every sport going, but when I asked Miles what he did, I did not expect his reply. He said, 'I'm a fencer.' 'A fencer?!' I repeated, trying to hide my surprise while imagining him wearing bright white armour and wielding a long thin blade. I'd never met anyone in fencing before, and I was excited that the shoot had brought together so many different disciplines. Miles nodded before doing his best to answer all of my questions. I'd been surprised by his answer, however it affirmed the beauty of difference to me – and as I spoke to him I realised that having a sport you connect with so much, despite what it may seem like to the outside world, or your peers, is like your superhero power.

I liked Miles a lot. He told me he was a mix of Jamaican, Irish, British and Malawian, and had spent the first eight years of his life in the UK before moving to America. It was there he discovered fencing, while living in New York. He did a lot of modelling too – it was something he enjoyed – so when I admitted I was so nervous I wanted to be sick, he responded with a big smile, and in his eager transatlantic accent he told me that I had nothing to worry about. Miles had been the perfect distraction, and he had reminded me that all I had to do was be myself. Now it was my turn in front of the camera.

It was such a small gesture, but hearing a stranger tell me I belonged there gave me the confidence I needed to get in front of the camera, when every bone in my body was telling me to make a dash for it. Our meeting was a reminder of why we should always be kind to others. We rarely know the full extent of what someone else is going through, and showing them kindness in a quick moment can help someone struggling feel at ease. It takes a lot less energy to be friendly to someone, than to be the opposite. With a confidence boost, I got through my first shoot – I even enjoyed it. I enjoyed the creativity that comes with modelling. It felt strange to shadow-box in front of a fashion photographer with hair and make-up artists ready to jump in and adjust my hair or add a touch of powder to my face, but everyone was so enthusiastic that I soon forgot why I'd been so nervous in the first place. Luckily, I knew nothing about the photographer who was asking me to throw a shot towards the camera or change my facial expression. It was only later that evening when Richard was asking me about the day that I learned the man behind the camera was widely recognised as one of the most famous fashion photographers in the world. I had never heard of Nick Knight, but Richard showed me that he had shot Naomi Campbell and Kate Moss and had directed music videos for Lady Gaga and Kanye West. I couldn't believe it. When I finally saw the pictures I was in shock. I'd never seen myself looking like *that* before. I looked strong, I looked powerful, I looked beautiful. I hadn't gone into the shoot thinking I would love it, or even that I'd be good. However, looking at the photos, I realised the importance of trying new things. Also, that I wouldn't mind doing this again.

Around the time of the shoot, a management company approached me, asking if I'd be willing to meet with them to discuss representation. When it came to my career outside of the fights, Richard and I were very green, and so our approach tended to be: say 'yes' to everything. It was a small London-based agency that looked after a handful of athletes, booking them campaigns and endorsements and helping them get press. We figured that if they did end up signing me, they might be able to bring in some paid work. I went alone to the agency's nondescript central London office to meet with one of the founders. I instantly got a bad vibe off him. He spoke with an alarming amount of confidence and had a really intense stare, and I felt as if my entire body was under the scrutiny of his gaze. I showed him some pictures from the Nike shoot, telling him it was the first bit of branded work I'd done. He nodded, before flicking open a laptop and showing me a picture of a woman in a bikini. 'You'd be great for something like this,' he told me, with a grin.

I felt my face form a frown. 'Let me be clear,' I said. 'There's no way I would do a swimwear campaign or anything like that . . .'

He scoffed at me. 'Let *me* be clear,' he said. 'You have to show a bit of skin if you want to make it in the commercial world. If you're not willing to get your kit off, I don't really know what we can do with you.'

I pointed out that none of the men his agency represented seemed to have done any swimwear shoots, and he scoffed at my words again. Needless to say, I got my things and left his office. Never before had I been asked something so compromising, something that completely ignored my morals. It was alarming that putting my foot down and saying no was offensive to him. That was all it took to decide I didn't need a manager, and more importantly to decide I never wanted to work with someone whose values didn't align with my own and what I was trying to achieve. I didn't waste much time thinking about the meeting; after months of waiting on tenterhooks, the AIBA had finally reached a verdict – we had been approved, and the Somali Boxing Federation had been approved. We were now free to enter official international tournaments.

By the time my next fight in Istanbul rolled round, the few hiccups that had occurred in between seemed like a distant memory. Fabian left as my strength and conditioning coach, as he'd had ambitions to become my manager and we couldn't afford to keep him on. I was down a coach, but Richard and I made it work; we were so excited to be competing again that nothing else seemed to matter. The taxi journey from the airport to the hotel was a brief one, but I spent it with my eyes glued to the windows. There was something so enchanting about the city, and as it sped by, I tried desperately to take in all of the glittering mosques and bustling markets, the slick modern hotels slotted in between cobbled streets and ancient spires. The only city in the world to be located on two continents, it seemed Istanbul was the perfect melting pot of Asian and European cultures – and of new and old worlds.

Once we arrived and unpacked, I laid my brand-new Nike kit on the bed. Matching black tracksuits for Richard and me, and the two full fight kits – identical apart from the colour, depending on which corner I would be in. I thought about the teamwork that had gone into making the garments. One person sketching out designs, another stitching on the Somali flag – a single white star against the light, bright sky-blue background. I thought of my mum, fleeing her beloved Somalia straight after having me, and now here I was, wearing the country's flag on my back. Though we didn't speak much about my boxing, I sensed that deep down the reason she had accepted my choices was because I was doing it for Somalia. I felt so optimistic. This was a special fight and I was doing it for my family and the country I was born in. It was my destiny, I told myself. I had to win.

We don't always get to write our own destiny, and a few days later when I found myself alone in the ring with Skye Nicolson, a very experienced Australian fighter, I realised I couldn't rely on *wanting* to win, I had to *fight* to win, and that wasn't going to be easy. I had waited forever for that fight, but as soon as the bell rang, I had to let everything that led up to that moment go. Once a fight begins, you have to be in the here and now, every bit of focus needs to be on you and your opponent. Skye was a real slick fighter. Her first shot caught me out of nowhere, and she boxed with this pared-back style where she managed to make every shot look effortless. If she got tired, she certainly never showed it. Skye was another southpaw. Maybe because a lot of orthodox fighters aren't used to facing an opponent whose stance mirrors their own, it gives the southpaw an advantage, allows her to be slower and more calculated; they never see her attack coming. But not me. I knew where I needed to be. This was my fight and there was no way I was going to let her take it from me. I knew to step up my counter-attack and be ready with my defence. I knew what side she'd attack me from before she did it.

It was a tough fight. By the final bell my head was throbbing and I could feel the sting from the sweat that had seeped into my eyes. I wanted to collapse onto the ground but I stayed standing. I locked eyes with a girl in the audience who looked the same age as me, and wondered who she thought had won. I shut my eyes and waited for the final decision, but it never came; the judges called a split decision. It had to be me, I thought as I waited again for the results. I'd waited so long and worked so hard, but it's not the judge's job to look at our backstories, to know what it took to get in the ring, the hurdles, the doubt, the trying. They are there to pick the boxer they think fought best, and on that day it was Skye.

I was devastated. A loss always hurts, and it was made worse by the fact it was my first fight so I was knocked straight out of the competition, just like in Bulgaria. Though it hurt to congratulate her that day, in the years that followed, Skye and I have become friends. Every fighter has a whole life that exists outside of the ring, and I've learned valuable lessons from making friends with the people I'm competing against rather than always seeing them as my adversaries. Skye is always full of positivity and I love seeing her at international competitions. Women are so often pitted against each other, no more so than in a boxing ring, but in supporting the people you compete with, you're forging a relationship that lasts way beyond the fight. Losing doesn't always have to be a bad thing either. While nobody wants to go out in the first round, someone has to. In fact, a lot of people do, and for me it meant I suddenly had all these brilliant girls to train with. After I lost to Skye, I got to spar with women from Croatia and Turkey, I even sparred with Skye again after she lost her second fight. I relished the opportunity to train with these women from all corners of the world. At home, I still didn't have enough opportunities to fight women in my weight category at my level, I often had to resort to sparring with men who were much heavier than me. That's why I seized the chance to spar with a woman, and if it had taken a loss to get me there, then so be it.

When I heard that Alessia Mesiano, an Italian boxer, had also been knocked out of the competition, I was desperate to set up a session with her. I'd been watching her from afar for a while, and like many of the Italian fighters I'd come across, she was incredible. The Italian team was made up of some of the most composed, skilful fighters on the amateur circuit, full of slick combinations and accomplished defence strategies. I knew I'd learn something from working with Alessia, and I hoped Richard and I had a lot to offer too. I sent Richard to look for Alessia's coach while I headed back to the hotel, happy. I may have lost, but I wasn't defeated. Growth happens when you least expect it; in the difficult moments when things haven't gone your way. In forcing yourself to hold your head up high and make the most of a bad situation, you become the strongest version of yourself. There's a Nelson Mandela quote that a lot of people in boxing say – 'I never lose. I either win or learn' – and that's how I accept the losses; I know there's always a way I can grow from it.

After a fight, you sometimes get this strange sensation of being whiplashed, and I was ready to give in to my post-fight fatigue and sleep it off when I heard the click of the keycard in the hotel door. 'I've got interesting news,' said Richard with a weary smile. I propped myself up on the bed as he told me about his conversation with the Italian team. Alessia didn't want to spar. She was exhausted and wanted to take a few days off after the fight, but our two coaches had got talking. Richard said he explained our situation to Maurizio, the lead Italian coach. Richard had told him that as a newly established boxing federation for a small country, we didn't have access to training camps and sparring opportunities. Maurizio wanted to help, and so he'd invited me to the next Italian training camp a few weeks later; naturally Richard had accepted.

I was thrilled. Not only would I get to spar with some of my favourite fighters, but I would be totally immersed in the coaching of the Italian team. I'd never heard of a country opening up their training camp like that. It was going to be an amazing opportunity; maybe my fate had always been to lose.

On the last day of the tournament, we spent the day exploring the city. We visited the Grand Bazaar, a maze of thousands of small shops selling rugs, lamps, ceramics, sweets and spices, and gold jewellery that dazzled in the dark. I thought of my parents' shop in Somalia; it must have been every bit as magical. In the afternoon we headed to Beyazit Mosque, one of the oldest places of worship in the city. We didn't go in; the never-ending queue of tourists waiting to get inside curved down side streets and didn't seem to move, but seeing it from the outside was enough. Known as the White Mosque, the looming towers and massive domes of Beyazit made me feel so small and so lucky to be standing there, not just in its shadows, but a part of its community. People will often write that I'm the first Muslim to win a boxing title for England. That's not something I ever set out to do, but I'm proud of the achievement. Islam is a huge part of who I am, and my faith has definitely helped me become the fighter I am today. When I'm sad or stressed, I often think back to that day at the White Mosque; a still, silent place of prayer right in the beating heart of a city that never stops.

We weren't back in London for long before the Italian training camp was due to start, so I vowed to make the most of it. I'd take runs around Greenwich Park, invite Danika over for movie nights and help Mum with her food shopping at Whitechapel market. The rest of the time, Richard and I were training. AIBA had confirmed that we could participate in the World Championships; it was a huge milestone, and the biggest fight of my career by a long way. I hadn't got much sparring practice in since we'd been in Turkey, so I felt relieved when we landed in Italy a few weeks later for what I knew would be an intensive few days of work. The training camp was in Assisi, a small walled town at the top of miles and miles of wooded hills. Assisi was the type of place that belonged on a postcard. The Roman ruins, the cobbled streets and miles of endless forests . . . Four weeks ago, I'd never even heard of the little Italian town; now I was staying there with some of the country's most accomplished boxers.

Maurizio Stecca was the coach Richard had met in Turkey. He had amazing credentials; an ex-professional boxer, Maurizio had won the gold medal at the 1984 Olympics when he was just twenty-one, before winning three World Championships. I was determined to learn everything I could from him, which wasn't always the easiest, being a non-Italian speaker. Luckily, the girls on the Italian team took me under their wing in a way I could never have imagined. Alessia, the World Championship gold medallist I had hoped to spar with in Turkey, made sure to translate Maurizio's instructions, as did a few of the other girls: Roberta, Irma and Valentina. Although we couldn't chat much in the sessions, through smiles, gestures and broken English, they all made me feel so welcome. That training camp taught me a lot about how I might one day lead my own team. It made me consider what kind of community our Somali federation could become once we got to a point where we could take on more fighters. I hope one day it will be like Italy: inclusive and welcoming to any outsiders. I want our team to be one that people are proud to be on. Maurizio taking me in was inspiring; when smaller teams work together, it's like forming one big global squad.

Maurizio's emphasis was on technical precision, and you could see it in the girls' impeccable footwork. At times I felt completely out of my league while I watched them. I was unable to land the tricky shots Maurizio was teaching, but when it came to fitness, it was my turn to excel. I was the last woman standing on the beep test, an exercise where we had to run 20m in increasingly quick intervals. Every boxer has their strengths and weaknesses, and I was getting a window into the worlds of other fighters, as well as my own. As the World Championships grew closer, I felt a huge pressure resting on my shoulders. I wasn't just boxing for myself anymore; messages of support from strangers had started to flood my inbox. I was fighting for myself, for Somalia, and for every woman who had ever been told that she wasn't enough. I received a lot of hate too; and I still do. Complete strangers hiding behind the anonymity of fake accounts will send me heinous abuse every day. Most of it is racist, often it's Islamophobic or sexist, sometimes it's all three. When I first started to read these sorts of messages, I found them sad and shocking. Nobody had ever warned me that as you become more public-facing, you become the target of trolls, especially as a woman of colour – and it was a hard reality for me to get used to. Now, I don't even read those messages. I don't give them the validation by responding. I don't let the hate get to me because I refuse to even acknowledge it. Hateful people will always spew evil words, it's not my job to retaliate, and often the most powerful move is to walk away.

November 2nd, 2018, we were flying to India.

In our flat in Greenwich, I sat bolt upright to the sound of a beeping alarm and Richard's voice calling my name from the bathroom. 'Are you up yet?' His face appeared from around the corner, 'We should leave pretty soon.' I got out of bed, showered, and packed the remainder of my things. I was operating on autopilot. My body was methodically folding clothes and winding up phone chargers, while my mind was at East Ham Leisure Centre, 2003, my first ever boxing class. The memory was so vivid I felt like I was watching myself on a cinema screen. A teenage girl looking scared and confused as she tries to navigate her first pair of hand wraps. Ten years later she's about to fly halfway across the world to compete in the boxing World Championships. I winced at how easily it could have all come crashing down. If Mum had never bought me that gym membership, if Danika hadn't been by my side supporting me, if Yahya hadn't covered for me when I had to sneak out of the house, if Amanda hadn't looked out for me, if Valerian hadn't pushed me to realise my own potential. If Richard hadn't—

'Ramla! We have to leave in five minutes – are you ready?!'

I was ready. I slung my bag over my shoulder and we left for the airport.

That year, the World Championships happened to fall at the same time as Diwali, the Hindu festival of lights. We expected to see the celebrations when we arrived in India, but we didn't expect the party to have already started at Heathrow airport; the terminal had been filled with a flash mob of Indian dancers and drummers while airport staff in bright clothing handed out sweets and small plastic lanterns: a tiny taste of the India we would experience seven hours later. Sometimes I think my whole life can be broken down into a series of surreal moments where I've felt the kind of extreme happiness that comes around so rarely you have to grab it with both hands and never let go. Stepping into a ring for the first time, winning my first National Championships, falling in love, earning the support of my parents, then walking into New Delhi airport to fight for the World

Championships and seeing a smiling man brandishing a sign that read 'TEAM SOMALIA' – that was definitely one of those moments. I couldn't run over to him quick enough. The man already knew my name, and explained to us that he had been hired by AIBA to take us to the hotel. I'd never had a private driver before, I was still trying to make sense of it as we walked out of the airport and were hit by a wall of heat, twenty-eight degrees in November. The air felt thick and smoky from the Diwali fireworks and the awaiting sea of cars crowding the entrance. 'WELCOME TO DELHI' read a massive flower arrangement of orange and yellow blooms.

When we arrived at the hotel, the atmosphere was tense. Loads of athletic-looking women were walking around the lobby, subtly trying to size each other up and work out who was in the same weight category. I could feel their gaze on me. I smiled at the onlookers, but nobody smiled back. This was the World Championships, and some of these women weren't out here to make friends, which I get, but I've never understood the need to be cold. It costs nothing to be kind.

We'd arrived in India eight days before the tournament started, which gave me time to acclimatise, train, and fall in love with the country. The orange sunsets, the beautiful women in intricate saris, the smell of fresh rotis; it was magical. I'd been warned about how foreign travellers would often fall prey to upset stomachs after eating Indian food, so in the beginning I was cautious, mostly eating protein shakes and the cereal bars I'd brought with me – but after a while it didn't feel right being welcomed to India without trying the country's incredible cuisine, the food that I had grown up eating. I'm glad I did. It was delicious, and the spicy vegetable curries gave me all the protein I needed to train through the jet lag and exhaustion.

The tournament was taking place in an arena called the KD Jadhav stadium, which hosted a large gym that each team had limited access to. On the days when we couldn't use the gym, Richard and I would train in the hotel's garden. It wasn't much more than a scrap of grass, kept green and hydrated by sprinklers, but it became our spot, a quiet oasis at the back of the hotel, away from the dust of the main roads. Of course, it wasn't our spot for long. While the bigger federations must have all hired spaces, the Panama team soon started using our garden. Like us, they were small, consisting of just two fighters and one coach, and after a few days one of the girls approached us asking if we all wanted to train together. Her name was Athena, and she introduced us to the other entry on the team, a girl called Alessia. Both were highly revered fighters in their native Panama. After a few sessions of training together, I was glad that Athena, especially, wasn't in my weight category. At 75kg, she was a heavyweight fighter – and after experiencing the sheer force of every punch when we worked together with pads, I didn't envy her opponent. Her ferociousness forced me to work extra hard on my defence slips and rolls; I did not want to take the full impact of her shots just before the World Championships. We got talking one evening, and it turned out Athena was good friends with Valerian; boxing, it seemed, was a small world for those who chose to embrace the competition.

With the hotel completely full with fighters, it had become a hub for all things related to the World Championships. There seemed to be a camera crew almost permanently set up in the lobby, interviewing the stars of the competition and the previous year's winners. One evening when Richard and I had just finished a long session in our garden, we walked through the lobby as the camera crew were packing up their equipment for the day. As we passed by, I overheard a producer whisper to her colleague before we locked eyes, and she enthusiastically beckoned me over with an outstretched hand.

'It's Ramla, right?!' she asked. I nodded shyly as she began introducing me to the rest of her team. 'We're from the Indian Boxing Federation and we're covering the World Championships. If you have a minute, I'd love you to do a quick interview?' I worried about messing up or saying the wrong thing, but I knew it was a good opportunity, so I agreed to do a short piece for the camera. Like when I was with Jamal, the presenter proceeded to ask me about everything – my upbringing, my boxing career, my family, my faith – they'd clearly done their research.

The video went up that evening, and I didn't think much of it, until the next morning when I received three more requests. Two were from Indian newspapers wanting to interview me and take pictures while I trained, while the other came once again from the Indian Boxing Federation: I'd been invited to have a role at the opening ceremony, along with Mary Kom, one of India's biggest boxing stars and one of my own personal heroes. The world of amateur boxing is full of inspiring stories and breakout stars, especially in the women's categories. Mary Kom was India's. She grew up poor, in a rural village in the north-eastern district of Manipur. She tried boxing when she was still at school, and loved it so much that at fifteen she moved alone to attend a sports academy in the state's capital. Like me, she kept boxing a secret from her family – she feared they would worry about an injury to the face, which would ruin her chances of marriage. Against all the odds, she kept going – fighting, competing and progressing until she became a world champion. To see her in the ring is to watch poetry in motion; she's fast and slick and graceful, she fights with such beauty, but don't be fooled, she can easily knock out a woman twice her size with one quick backhand. Not only is she the only woman to become World Amateur Boxing champion for a record six times, but Mary was also a new mother, a member of parliament, and an absolute poster girl for women in boxing.

While I didn't have any World Championship wins or political roles under my belt, somehow, my story must have resonated in India, too, because I was suddenly finding myself being treated like a celebrity. I did the newspaper interviews, and once they came out I started getting recognised outside the hotel. I didn't know how to process the sudden interest in me, but I was definitely appreciative of the Indian support.

The evening of the opening ceremony, we were called

to a brief rehearsal in the Indira Gandhi Arena, where the tournament was taking place. I was introduced to Mary, who was so sweet and constantly had a reassuring smile on her face. We were both given the statement we'd be reading; just a couple of lines each wishing everyone luck and reminding all fighters to be fair and to treat each other with respect. We went through it a couple of times, me helping Mary out with the English pronunciation before we were called to go on stage. I got so nervous about the speech that once it was over, I forgot to be nervous about the next day's fight. Instead I lost myself in the excitement of the ceremony. It was an amazing event to be part of; Richard and I got to meet the Indian president, Ram Nath Kovind, who shook my hand and wished me luck. The audience were cheering from the top of their lungs as each team entered the arena, and every country was joined by a volunteer who held their flag for them. I didn't even get a chance to catch the name of the young man who waved ours so proudly, because he was so full of questions about Somalia. He was a natural entertainer, loud and playful, and when I told him about how Somalis celebrate with a high-pitched 'Lilililili' noise we make at weddings and parties, his eyes widened before he did it right back to me perfectly. When our team was called into the arena, he did it again, jumping up and down, shouting, 'Team Somalia! Lilililili' I laughed about it all the way back to the hotel, before fear of the next day's fight finally did set in.

*

By 2018, I had a strong sense of what typical boxing audiences were like: mostly men, very rowdy, and often just there in the hope of seeing someone get hurt. It was different with international fights, but the UK tournaments I entered usually attracted a very white audience; though slowly, the boxing scene was growing more diverse. Occasionally I could win an audience round by my music choice or performance in the ring, but usually I got the sense they didn't really care who won; they just wanted to see a gnarly fight. They were there for a knockout, though they'd accept a nice blow to the head too. That's why, the following afternoon, when it was finally time for me to step into the ring in India, and I was greeted by an ocean of smiling brown and black faces, some wearing the Somali flag, others brandishing home-made posters reading 'Go Ramla!' or 'Somalia is with you' – I felt tears flood my eyes. The noise was like nothing I'd experienced before either; it was as if everyone in the arena was cheering and shouting at the top of their voices, willing me to win.

The show of support continued until I was in the middle of the ring looking my opponent, Doaa Toujani from Morocco, straight in the eye. Only then, just before we began, the lights seemed to dim and the arena fell silent for a few intense seconds. I heard the bell, and almost instantaneously Doaa began charging towards me with a bloodthirsty look in her eye. She was fierce and bullish in the way she fought, and at times her power was frightening to combat, but what she boasted in strength, she lacked in precision. She was heavy on her feet, charging towards me with a flurry of punches, but

I knew when to retreat and how to seize the right moments to land my own shots. The first round was impossible to call. As we each went back to our separate corners, desperately trying to catch our breath before round two, Richard slipped through the ropes and got down on one knee in front of me, just like that summer in Peckham when my whole life began to change. Calmly, he mopped my head with a towel as he talked me through tactics; stay calm, watch out for her hook, confuse her, never let her know what you're thinking. From the opposite corner I could hear Doaa shouting at the two coaches beside her. I turned back to Richard, sipping water and listening intently to his every word. Those moments with your coach go so quickly they feel like a dream. Though in some ways it's a short break from the fight, it's not the time to lose focus, matches can be won or lost in those twenty-second intervals.

When the fight resumed, I successfully landed several throws to the head while Doaa scrambled to keep her balance. In a bid to confuse her, I dropped my hands, daring Doaa to try and land a shot to my own head. She tried, but I trusted my intuition, ducking and slipping before her outstretched arm could touch me. By the final round, I could sense her rage. At one point we ended up locked in a hold so intense we both fell crashing down to the floor with an audible thud. Once we'd got back onto our feet, I could tell she was exhausted, and though my arms were heavy and sore too, I seized the chance to keep at her with quick repetitive shots to the body. She returned with a slew of blows aimed at my head, but I was able to swiftly move backwards and avoid the worst of it. I had definitely landed more clean shots, and when the bell rang moments later to end the fight, all I could think about was calling my mum to tell her I was going through to the next round. But I never got to. The verdict went to a split decision. Finally, the judges called Doaa's name instead of mine and inside I plummeted to the ground like a bird shot out of the sky. I was heartbroken. It hurt so much; I've watched the video back and seen the pain as it spreads across my face. I pulled myself together, hugged Doaa, and went to shake hands with her coaches. It was over.

For a few days after the World Championships result, I felt numb. My mind went into a kind of lockdown state, refusing to allow any thoughts concerning the fight, which at least allowed me to make the most of my remaining time in India. I wasn't going to be able to understand or process the score, and it was in the past anyway. All I could do was move on. I had been here before, and no longer was I going to let a loss break me. It's been the moments when I suffer that I have learned the most. Suffering has taught me so much about strength; you work through the pain, and then you carry on, you keep going.

The day after the fight I got a call from a friend of Hassan's called Ahmed who worked at the Somali Embassy in Delhi. He told me he'd watched the bout among hundreds of Somalis. 'You should have won!' he told me, but it was the other part of what he said that struck me. 'Hundreds of Somalis?' I asked. In India, had they really turned up to see me? That in itself was enough of a win for me; knowing I was connected to fellow Somalis all over the world. I thanked him, and to my surprise, he offered to drive Richard and me to the Taj Mahal the next day. 'A little something to cheer you up!' he said. I was moved by his generosity, but I instantly said no. We'd already looked into going ourselves, and it was at least a six-hour drive away. I couldn't ask him to take a whole day out to chauffeur us. But Ahmed was persuasive. He wouldn't take no for an answer, he said it was the least he could do, and that Hassan would be disappointed if we didn't meet, and so, the next day, the three of us set off for the city of Agra. Ahmed was in his late thirties and he showed up wearing a linen shirt and a huge grin. It was a strange feeling, having this new base of supporters to cheer me on, both online, and those who showed up in real life. I was so grateful that they believed in me, even when I didn't. I couldn't let them down, I so badly wanted to win for them; but as I watched my platform grow in the aftermath of the World Championships, I slowly realised that beyond boxing, people were interested in me because my story resonated with them, not just because of how I performed in competitions. When I looked at the new people following me, many were young Black girls, refugees, Muslims, or all three. They saw themselves in me, as I did in them. They didn't care if I won or lost a fight, because I was out here representing them on a global stage, and that is more valuable than any trophy.

I couldn't thank Ahmed enough for taking us out that day. The city of Agra was a long drive away and I slipped in and out of sleep as we weaved through shortcuts and side streets. It felt luxurious to be sitting down in the back seat of an air-conditioned car, while outside the Delhi traffic raged on, hot and loud. When I woke up, the crowded city had given way to a much wilder landscape. Either side of the road, green hills stretched for miles and miles, while the road ahead seemed equally endless. I had no real idea where I was and it was perfect; I loved the unexpected adventures that boxing brought me. We arrived at the Taj Mahal around lunchtime, and as the vast structure came into view, I realised it was every bit as beautiful as I'd imagined. It was so massive and grand, but the closer you got the more you realised how intricate the details were; the Arabic calligraphy around the doors, the geometric patterns on the marbled floor. I tried to imagine it being built sometime in the 1600s before lorries or cranes or any form of technology – just the sheer strength and determination of an army of humans, working together for years to build something completely unimaginable. That day was refreshing and revitalising. Taking time out to see more of the country is one of my favourite parts of an international trip; it's such a privilege to be able to travel and to see the world and meet new people. Through boxing I've got to immerse myself in so many different cultures and meet the most inspiring individuals. It's shown me how big the world really is, and it's taught me how to be more open, more tolerant and more understanding of people who are different to me. Getting out of your own bubble from time to time is so valuable. You don't have to travel across the world to learn about other cultures. Sometimes just walking down my local high street I hear so many different languages, I witness fashion from all over the world, and smell so many different types of food; it's one of the things I love the most about living in London.

Before we flew home from the World Championships, Richard managed to set up a sparring session with one of the Japanese fighters as well as a girl from Trinidad and Tobago, and with the tournament still going, I went to watch the Panama team in their fights, as well as Amy Broadhurst, a friend of mine who fought for Ireland. I felt proud to be cheering them all on; I know how difficult it can be for women to make it in boxing – considering the sexism, the lack of funding and support. To be fighting at the same tournament as these women and the rest of the world's greatest amateur boxers is a constant uphill struggle, but one that fills me with pride. We might have been competing against each other, but we were all connected; and as women in boxing, we were part of the same team. That's why I didn't leave India feeling disappointed, and shortly after I returned to London, I was asked to take part in another Nike campaign, as well as my first photoshoot and interview for a magazine called *Twin*. I said yes straight away, not because I was in any rush to be in front of the camera again, but because I felt a huge sense of responsibility.

When I was young, dark-skinned, with big curly hair and a chubby face that I resented, I never saw anyone who looked like me in magazines or sports campaigns – not remotely. The same went with the film and television I grew up watching, at least until Mum would overrule and switch to the Somali channels. I don't think I understood the effects that lack of representation in the media had on me until years later. I used to lie about my ethnicity because it somehow felt almost wrong to be Somali when so many of the images of beauty I was fed were of a very white kind of beauty. I remember how desperately I used to wish my hair was lighter and straighter, and no wonder, when it was so rare for me to see women who looked like me in the spotlight. I look at the role models young people have today and it fills me with joy. I love seeing Somali women in the public eye: women like Maya Jama, who presents prime-time TV and radio shows – and the model Sabrina Elba, who appears on the pages of *Vogue* and the runways of Paris. When I was a kid, I felt so different to everybody else; I can't even begin to imagine how much more comfortable I would have felt in my own skin if I'd have had women like Maya and Sabrina to look up to. Of course, I know it's not as simple as saying that young people today have it easier. I didn't grow up with social media, and we all know how much pressure there is to look fun, perfect, popular and accomplished on Instagram. I have to take regular breaks from it or I start to lose perspective of what's real and what's important. But the one thing I love about it is seeing so much diversity. I didn't have an outlet like that when I was growing up, there wasn't this app I could open up to see a whole world of women who shared my looks or my faith or my passions. That's the side of Instagram I love, the side where

I get to see Black women, strong athletes, proud Muslims, anyone out there working hard and killing it in their fields – it's such an inspiration to me. So as nervous as I was for that first magazine shoot, the very fact that I'd been asked to do it did a lot for my self-esteem, in showing me that you don't have to be skinny or light-skinned or six foot to appear in the pages of a magazine. Not anymore, those days are long gone. The week after, I did my next shoot with Nike, this time for a campaign called Fight For Your Dream, which profiled four different athletes who were using sport to break boundaries. We filmed at Miguel's, a boxing gym in Brixton, which I was thrilled about; I felt at home. It was just a small crew that day, and after having my hair and make-up done, the director – a girl called Emily – got Richard and I to train while they filmed us. By now, I knew the drill, and when Emily asked me questions about the campaign, and how I personally was fighting for my dreams, we talked about the role model I was learning to become. That video was the first time I talked openly and publicly about my dream without fear of failure. 'I want to fight for Somalia at the Olympics,' I told her. 'I want to be the first person ever to do it.'

ROUND NINE

Celebrate the successes

When you work hard, it's important to take a moment to celebrate the achievements that come along the way. They might not be the end goal, but they're a sign you're on the right path. After years of feeling like the underdog, when I first started fighting for Somalia, even unofficially, I felt like I was finally free. We still had a long way to go, but reflecting on all we had achieved gave us the fuel to keep fighting.

Be thankful

There are so many people I am grateful for. I wouldn't be where I am today without my family and my closest friends, the people on my team. But beyond that, even the kindness of strangers has helped motivate me so much during the hardest of times. When Hassan's friend took me and Richard to see the Taj Mahal, it was a reminder of how a small gesture can go a long way in making somebody feel better. I receive so many messages of gratitude and support from people all over the world who I have never met; I appreciate them so much and I don't take a single one for granted.

If it scares you, try it

Entering the world of fashion was terrifying for me. Photoshoots gave me imposter syndrome, and I always used to worry that I was trying to make my way in a world where I didn't belong. And yet, on the other hand, I knew that it was bigger than me. In taking up space in the fashion industry, I was showing people that we belong – Black girls, Muslim girls, girls who exist in traditionally male-dominated spheres – we belong, and we deserve to be represented in the media.

Stand your ground

We all experience times when people ask something of us that we don't feel comfortable with. There's a difference between taking risks for ourselves and being pressured to do something for the benefit of others. If you feel uncomfortable, trust your gut, take a step back and think about your decision. It's important to learn how to say no.

BE YOUR OWN CHAMPION

*'Everyone has the fire, but the champions know
when to ignite the spark.'*

— Amit Ray

Growing up, I didn't really have role models that I looked up to. There were people I admired; mostly my mum – the ultimate champion – and my sisters. Later, I found myself drawn to a wide variety of women in sport too – Serena Williams, Lucia Rijker – but their backgrounds and their trajectories always felt so different to mine. There wasn't one individual who I looked at and thought, I want to be just like her. When I was coming up on the scene, there were so few British women who managed to make a career out of boxing that I never imagined I could take it as far as I have today. I thought that my dreams were unrealistic and that I needed to get a 'real job'. I'm glad that over time and with much reflection my perception of myself changed, and I allowed myself to believe I could. I embraced being a dreamer, and I learned to be a fighter. I realised that if there wasn't a role model you could look up to and follow, that's OK – sometimes you have to just do it your own way – you have to be the first and become your own champion. My path required that I had to be and do so many firsts; I was the first woman member in a handful of London boxing gyms, the first Muslim woman to win an English boxing title, the first person to box professionally for Somalia. I hope that I get to add more 'firsts' to my life CV. I hope my story shows people that if nobody is championing you, do it for yourself. I hope that by doing so in my career, I will make it easier for the next generation – who can look to me as that role model, and see what I've done to leave the door open for them, because there are still many 'firsts' out there to be claimed.

It wasn't until 2019, eight years after my first boxing fight and sixteen since I first donned a pair of boxing gloves, that I found myself in a position where I could quit my job at Virgin Active, and focus on boxing full-time. It was a scary decision – sending my resignation email felt so surreal – but it was finally time for me to embrace boxing as my career. Nike were asking me to do more campaigns and had slightly increased my sponsorship, and since I wasn't earning much more than minimum wage at Virgin, both Richard and I decided it would free me up to train, and that would be worth whatever we might end up losing in income. We hoped the small media spotlight that I had gained by doing my first few interviews might somehow lead to endorsements and funding.

Another boost was that shortly after the World Championships, I signed to Anthony Joshua's management company, 258 Management, where I still am today. I am one of just five boxers on the roster, and the only woman. I'm in good company, with my friend Joshua Buatsi, along with Lawrence Okolie, a heavyweight fighter, who like me, got into boxing after being bullied at school for being overweight. We're a small team, but what we lack in size we make up for in noise; we're always there for each other. When anyone has a fight coming up, you can trust that the messages of support are flying in the WhatsApp group. I'm so proud to have made it onto that team. As I was signing the contract, I thought back to the awful company I'd met with before; in sticking to my morals and refusing to be manipulated by them, I had ultimately found a much, much better management team. And then I had my other team: Team Somalia. We must have been the smallest squad in amateur boxing, but Richard and I had a global network of supporters who wanted to see us succeed. When I fight, I fight for all of them, and for every person who's ever been told their dreams are bigger than their circumstances. I knew we might not pull a win off every time, but why should anyone stop us from trying? Competing for an African country with no funding or boxing history took a lot of sacrifice. Not only was it costly, but we had no skin in the game when it came to corrupt boxing boards who tend to favour larger federations. I still wouldn't have it any other way. When they come, the wins feel that much sweeter.

Our next competition that year was going to be the Africa Zone Championships. It wasn't a competition I was familiar with, but when we got the invite, I felt this pang of excitement; I had never fought in Africa before, it was a huge competition and it meant I would be fighting some of the continent's best boxers.

It wasn't long after quitting my job that I received an email from a woman named Daniella Muñoz, a scout at IMG Models, one of the most prolific model agencies in the world. Their roster includes global catwalk stars such as Kate Moss, Halima Aden and Gigi Hadid. She had seen my Nike campaigns and read about my story, and wanted to discuss signing me. I felt completely shocked that a glamorous agency like that would be interested in someone like me, but a week later I found myself in central London waiting to meet with Daniella along with Emma Quelch, the vice president and managing director, and Christine Fortune, the head of the talent department. The IMG office is located at 180 The Strand, a huge brutalist building in central London which is almost entirely dedicated to fashion. There's Dazed Media and Fact Magazine, an event space and IMG Models. Waiting in reception, I found it impossible to understand the hierarchy of positions people held, or who worked for who; everyone who wandered in and out seemed equally and effortlessly stylish. I watched as a girl walked past wearing long dangly earrings that touched her shoulders, and trousers so wide they completely engulfed the heels that were clicking across the floor underneath. I was a long way from the boxing gym, and I felt slightly out of place in my jeans and trainers when I met the IMG team. However, I reminded myself that I'd been invited to be there. I was interested in what they had to say. It was another example of how far I had come. All three were lovely and charming, and instantly put me at ease by congratulating me on the work of establishing a national Somali team. They spoke with a certain frankness as they explained to me how the talent department worked. They represented clients who didn't come from traditional modelling backgrounds; actors, influencers or athletes like me. Their job, they said, would be to find me the right brand endorsements and editorial coverage. They stressed that it certainly wasn't about saying yes to every single opportunity, but only agreeing to offers I felt comfortable with, and working with people who shared the same values. When I told them that wearing revealing clothes would be a non-negotiable for me, nobody batted an eyelid. I explained what had happened at my last meeting, and the insistence from the agent that I'd need to show a bit of skin if I wanted to make it in the commercial world. As I spoke, all three of them stared back at me in shock before piping up in anger; Emma said I should have never been spoken to like that. And in fact, my stipulation was the case for a lot of their clients; it didn't present any problems. They assured me that whether I signed with them or somebody else, pressuring clients to look a certain way or take on a job they weren't comfortable with was completely unacceptable. I signed with IMG that same day.

True to their promise, the first job they got me felt like a great match. It was a campaign with a brand called Amanda Wakeley for International Women's Day, shot by the incredible photographer and contributing editor of *Vogue*, Laura Bailey. I couldn't believe that just like that, I was booking fashion shoots. Being in front of the camera was still a new experience for me, but Laura helped me to feel myself, reminding me that there was no pressure to pose or act a certain way, I just needed to relax and be me. Being in her presence and in her gaze was extremely calming. As she clicked away, she told me about her children, and distracted me with questions about boxing. The campaign also included a video, and I got to tell the story of how boxing had changed my life, as well as discussing the importance of young people's access to sport. I always used to think fashion was just about big flashing lights and glamorous clothes, but the early campaigns I was a part of showed me how fashion can be used as a tool to spread awareness and create change. When I decide to collaborate with magazines and fashion brands, I'm connecting with a new audience who isn't necessarily familiar with my story. It's given me another platform to talk about the things I care about, advocate for and am creating. From that very first campaign, I vowed to myself that I would utilise those opportunities to talk more, to become a voice for my community. To champion diversity and inclusivity and fight injustice.

In 2020, following the murders of George Floyd, Ahmaud Arbery, Breonna Taylor, and so many other Black people senselessly killed by law enforcement, I had a significant platform. I attended protests in London and I spoke up online. The Black Lives Matter movement has always been important to me. I'm a proud

Black woman first and foremost, and the issues which affect my community affect me deeply too. I care about our lives, our access to equal opportunities and our rights to feel safe and be treated with dignity. I care about the narrative of Somalia, and want to speak proudly about all its changes. I will continue to build, elevate and support other Black men and women on my platform as well as using my time and finances to promote justice and equality – that's non-negotiable. In the moment I didn't view these things as 'radical' or worthy of praise, but I realised many of the brand and media opportunities I have been given come from the way I have used my voice. I don't take for granted how lucky I am to be featured in glossy magazines, which is why I've made sure to never compromise my values, and to educate people about the true power of young Black girls, Muslims and refugees.

Just before the Africa Zone Championships, I booked another Nike campaign due to be shot in Los Angeles, which meant taking a flight from LA to Switzerland, Switzerland to Johannesburg, and then the final leg, Johannesburg to Botswana. The journey took around thirty-five hours and we were in complete bits when we landed, but we had two full weeks to acclimatise before the tournament began. I had no idea what time zone we were in and I could barely remember getting off the plane and checking into our hotel. When I finally emerged the next morning, I was ready to see the capital city of Gaborone by daylight. In the two weeks before the competition started, Richard and I fell head over heels in love with Botswana. Everyone we met was so welcoming in a way I'd never experienced before. My fellow competitors were so proud of the African nations they represented, and so was I. The city itself was a mall-filled urban sprawl, but despite being a capital, Gaborone had a tranquil feel. Far beyond the city limits lies the wilderness that Botswana is famed for: the Okavango Delta where big cats and herds of elephants roam free, and the Kalahari Desert, the largest unbroken stretch of sand on the entire planet.

I'd been wanting to visit Botswana since the summer of 2018, when Valerian had been training for the Commonwealth Games. She'd invited Richard and me out to one of her training camps on the Gold Coast in Australia, and the head coach for the Botswana women's team – Lechedzani Luza, or 'Master' as everyone seemed to call him – had also been there. Contrary to the nickname, Master was a soft-hearted coach, an ex-Olympic boxer whose goal was to see more women get into the ring. He'd told us to visit Botswana and to train with the team; and now, maybe we could. I really hoped I could get at least one sparring session in before my first bout. Luckily Master welcomed us with open arms, and within a few days I was training with Team Botswana. They were an incredibly close-knit group. They always seemed to look out for each other and everyone on the team was constantly cheering one another on, even in training. They were tough too. No matter how tired they were, they just kept going. It was galvanising to be around and I felt grateful that they'd taken me under their wing, just like the

Italian team had before them. The fighter in my weight category, Kenosi, was very confident from our very first meeting – and when I heard she was one of Botswana's prize boxers, I wasn't surprised. When Master suggested we get in the ring and spar each other, I was apprehensive; there was a chance we would fight each other in the tournament, and if we sparred now it meant she'd get to see how I fought. Of course, it would also be useful for me to experience fighting her, and since I needed the sparring practice, I agreed. It was an intense session. We'd been training together for a few days but I didn't feel like I knew her. Kenosi was quiet – never rude – but it was impossible to tell what she was thinking. I didn't know what to expect, but when we began sparring, I discovered she was an explosive boxer, fast and scrappy, with an exceptionally powerful hook. I left the session hoping I wouldn't have to face her in the competition.

A few days later it was time to move out of our hotel and into the athlete housing. After two weeks of our light spacious surroundings, comfortable bed and delicious room service, I moved into a crowded convent across the road from the University of Botswana, where the competition would be taking place. That definitely brought me crashing back to reality. It was so hot, there was no air conditioning, and with competitors constantly coming in and out from training and queuing to use the showers, there was a smell of sweat that clung to the air. I slept badly that first night, but in the morning, I couldn't help but remember how lucky I was to be there. When I started out, I used to think the European boxing tournaments were the be-all and end-all. America's golden era of tournaments finished in the nineties, and even then, it didn't fully include women fighters. Australia had some great women boxers too, but ultimately when it came down to agility and skill, it was Europe hands down. However, being in Botswana for the Africa Zone Championships made me think differently. Many of these countries didn't have a quarter of the resources afforded to European fighters. A lot of the competitors would have come from families like my own, where boxing was not seen as an appropriate career for a young woman. And yet the African teams still managed to produce the most incredible boxers: women like Kenosi who were like fire in the ring, quick and combustible, a danger to any opposition.

As was my luck, Kenosi was going to be my first fight. It was well known that she was one of the best boxers in the entire competition. Not only was Kenosi already the favourite to win gold, but she was also the home competitor, and if a fight is really close, the home favourite often gets the decision. It isn't fair, but that's boxing. I knew I was going to have to work really hard to stand a chance of winning, and after being in a ring with her before, I knew the fight was not going to be pretty. As we walked into the venue, Richard reiterated exactly what I needed to do if I was to win. Kenosi was tall, and to fight a taller opponent, you basically have to have exceptional footwork – but even great footwork will only get you so far. As those three-minute rounds crawl on, you grow more and more tired – even the fittest of boxers. As a result, by the end you're usually so much slower on the feet, and that's when they'll tear back their advantage. That morning, Richard drilled into me the importance of staying alert throughout the whole fight, never letting my guard down – not even for a second. Both in the gym and in the ring, real champions are made in those toughest of moments when exhaustion threatens to take over, but when we choose not to give up. When your physical body is completely drained, it is your mental strength that will carry you through – will encourage you to keep going – will remind you, you are stronger and more resilient than you realise.

I made sure to keep telling myself that over and over again as Richard and I entered the arena. The modern sports facilities were the gem of the University of Botswana and the massive circular stadium was filled with a sea of blue lights that made it resemble the inside of a spaceship. On walking in we were met by so much noise and energy. In one corner, the South Africa team were huddled together in a circle, both the men and women fighters. They were all chanting, quietly at first, until their voices grew louder and louder before eventually they erupted into a spectacle of hugging and shouting. It was beautiful to witness; they seemed so united as a team. I knew Richard had already introduced himself – earlier in the day he'd asked a South African coach to be his second coach during my fight. A 'second' assists a fighter during a bout. Rather than instruct, they slip into the ring in the breaks to give their fighter water and wipe the sweat off their face. I decided to go over and say hello. I got to talk to some of the men's competitors. They seemed shocked that I was the only fighter on my team, and promised to come and cheer for me ... unless I had to fight South Africa of course. I thanked them and went to get ready. I found a changing room, put on my kit, and found a space to warm up with Richard. We worked through my mobility, before I started shadow-boxing around the space. I could sense someone else close to me – and glancing over the room, I realised it was Kenosi. We caught eyes, and then quickly looked away from each other. Thankfully we didn't have to endure too much of the awkwardness; our second coaches called us both into the ring: it was time to fight.

The South African coach in my corner went by the name of 'Baby'. I've never watched *Dirty Dancing*, but I was familiar with the infamous quote, 'Nobody puts Baby in a corner.' I loved nothing more than having him in my corner. Baby was my ultimate cheerleader, seizing every opportunity to shake me by the shoulders and promise me I was going to win; I needed that kind of belief and support. Kenosi towered above me. Even before the fight had started, I noticed I had to look up to her in order to stare her down. Whatever alliance we might have formed by training together was gone. In the ring, we stared at each other in a frosty silence. I was relieved when the bell went; no more training, no more sparring, the fight was on. Kenosi hit hard. I'd experienced it during our spar, but I realised she had definitely been holding back. I felt relief with every clean shot I managed to land, while desperately trying to avoid her blows. Every time Kenosi landed a shot, the stadium erupted as Botswana cheered her on, but she wasn't the only one drawing the applause; each time I felt the impact of my own punches, a huge wall of noise came from a distant section of the stadium. I didn't know where it was coming from but it meant a lot to me in those crucial first moments of round one.

I read somewhere that Kenosi was a bully at school. She's said it herself, she was always picking fights, and that's how she got noticed by one of her earliest coaches. I thought of my own school days. The tormenting wasn't physical, but the words used to knock me back like a powerful blow to the face. Now here we were, a decade later, the bully and the bullied alone in the ring. We both went back to our corners and Richard assured me it had gone well. Baby chanted my name while pulling out my mouthguard and shoving a straw into my mouth. 'You can do it! You can do it!' he screamed.

In the second round, Kenosi kept holding me. Holding or clinching is a tactic where a boxer wraps her arms around the opponent instead of fighting. It gives them a moment to rest and recover; you do it when you're getting exhausted. Kenosi's arms were heavily locked around mine, and I had to use all the force I had in me to keep working, keep hitting while she tried her best to restrain me. Richard had warned me that this might happen – I stayed calm, hitting her again and again with shots to the body until she released me from her grip. I knew it was a close fight; we were both landing a lot of shots, but what might win it for me would be the fact that I kept working, kept hitting her, even when she was excessively holding.

Back in my corner for a second time, I was exhausted

from her intense grip. I clung on to every second I had to catch my breath, urgently trying to recover for the third and final round. When the bell rang again, it felt like no time had passed at all. That's the magical thing about boxing; inside the ring, time does all sorts of things, it stands still, it slows down, but in those breaks, minutes turn to milliseconds.

I have only one standout memory from the final round, and that is Kenosi lurching forward and hitting me with the most force I've ever experienced in any fight. Immediately it set off a ringing in my ears, a blurring of my eyesight and a sharp, searing pain all across my face. I felt dizzy and frightened, and I imagined myself collapsing to the ground, but I couldn't give her a knockout, not in the final round, and definitely not like that. I tucked my chin to my chest and kept my arms high; if she hit me in the head again, I could lose consciousness. I still couldn't see properly. I kept blinking, desperately trying to regain my sight. I had no idea how much longer I had to endure. A few more shots were exchanged from us both and when I finally heard that bell, I was completely over the moon. At that moment, I didn't care if I won or lost, I was just happy to be alive and for the fight to be over.

'I am so proud of you,' Richard said. I looked into his eyes as he gently removed my headguard. I thanked him and smiled.

'I think they'll give it to her,' I told him.

'Maybe they will, but hold your head up high, you fought incredibly.'

'Excuse me?!' Suddenly Baby's face was centimetres

from my own, shouting at me. 'You won that fight! Stop talking in this way,' he tutted in disapproval as Richard and I laughed at him.

'OK, Baby,' I said. 'Maybe we've got this.'

Back in the ring waiting for the results, I looked around and realised exactly where the noise of support had been coming from during the fight; of course, Team South Africa had my back! Once again, they were smiling and shouting my name, leaping up and down and willing me to win. I locked eyes with one of them, who mouthed: 'You won!'

Did I? I looked over at Kenosi. Her hand was in the air, she was expecting to be crowned the winner. I put mine up too. I believed in myself. I shut my eyes to try and block out the rush of my own thoughts and the roar from the crowd, until the sound of the announcer cut through everything.

'And by a four-to-one decision, the winner is . . .'

That pause, time elongating once more . . .

'RAMLA AAALIIIIII!'

I leapt skyward before I realised what I was doing, and when I landed, I jumped up and down again and again. I swear I jumped up so high. The audience were jumping with me, I clocked people standing on their seats, beaming with pride. I couldn't believe how loudly I was being cheered on as a foreign fighter. Just thinking about it now gives me goosebumps. I won the two fights that followed, but neither of my opponents put up as much of a fight as Kenosi. I faced a Zambian boxer for the semi-finals and then a South African competitor for the finals – which meant I lost a lot of support in the audience.

Winning both those bouts meant I had finally done it; I got to take home my first major gold medal for Somalia. It wasn't until the medal ceremony that I heard the Somalia national anthem for the very first time, and I couldn't stop crying. I couldn't believe I'd never thought to play it: that proud, jubilant song. My win marked Somalia's first ever medal in an international boxing tournament. It was a huge milestone for the country; and for me, my wildest of dreams had just become a reality.

The atmosphere was amazing, there were so many festivities after the competition; they had dancers and live music. It wasn't like anything I'd ever experienced in the European competitions; it was a thousand times more fun. I felt so proud and relieved that I'd switched my allegiances to Somalia.

The first thing I did when we got back to the hotel was call Mum. Being able to speak freely to her about boxing felt more amazing than any win. I'd waited years for her acceptance, and now I was finally making her proud, because I was doing it for the country she loved so much, the country I loved too. Though I was thousands of miles away, I had never felt so connected to Somalia, and to my mum. I had challenged her views on what was acceptable as a Muslim and as a woman. She could have completely shut me down – for years she did – but the fact that she was eventually willing to compromise and understand that I could become a positive role model for our community shows how much empathy she has as a mother. That night, I celebrated her.

*

When we got back from Botswana, victorious, my work with IMG really began as I learned the strange skill of switching from being a boxer one minute to a model the next. I adapted to a world of brand campaigns and interviews quicker than I expected. It was made easier because brands wanted to work with me not just as a model, but as an individual. I realised that if I was authentic, if I took my agent's advice and only worked on projects that made sense, then I could be myself on a photoshoot just as much as I could be myself in the ring.

When they told me I had an offer to work with Pantene, I couldn't have been happier. In my first ever meeting with IMG, I had told them my ambition of wanting to do a hair campaign. It may have taken me the best part of thirty years to get there, but I really love my hair. I have a lot of it, and when I wear it down – thick and natural and curly – it's so big that I can't help but get noticed when I walk into a room. It's so versatile. When I'm in the ring, I always wear it braided; it's part of my ritual preparing for a fight. In my adult life, my hair has become this huge part of my identity, but I didn't always feel that way. I grew up in a school where most of the girls were Indian or Bangladeshi, with long, dark shiny hair that dazzled in the sunshine and billowed behind them in the wind. I hated my own, without ever really understanding why; all I knew was that it didn't look the same as the other girls', it didn't feel the same. I wanted the long soft waves that everyone else seemed to have. Outside of the school gates, the media didn't help my case either. In the nineties and noughties if you picked up a mainstream women's magazine, chances are you'd see a white cover star gazing back at you, her face framed with yet more hair that looked the complete opposite of mine. For the longest time it made me feel like an outsider, like everyone else's hair was right and so mine must be wrong. It was too thick, too coarse, too curly. I used to beg my sister Luul to straighten it, but since we couldn't afford straighteners, she would lie me down on the floor and do it with the iron, completely destroying my hair. Now when I look back at that period of my life, I realise that all I needed was to feel recognised. If I'd found more magazines with Black cover stars, watched more films and TV shows with Black characters, then I don't think I would have ever hated my own appearance like that – because my hair really is amazing. For way too long, I lived in a world that celebrated a far too limited notion of beauty, and so I was proud that my very first beauty campaign was one that showed off my thick, black African hair in all its glory.

The next few campaigns and magazine articles represented a surreal time in my life – the platforms grew bigger and bigger. I was in *Time* magazine, on Sky News, featured in Buzzfeed, and along with thirteen other athletes, I even got to be on the July 2019 cover of *ELLE* magazine. The amazing Serena Williams aside, it's still so rare to see an athlete on the cover of a fashion magazine, so to have all of us included – sprinters and high jumpers, football and basketball players – it felt really, really special. I felt like I was part of the beginning of a new movement where athletes and activists could be role models in a space traditionally reserved for pop stars or supermodels. When I was growing up, none of the girls at school cared about athletes because we weren't told about them. I love the fact that today, it's much easier for young people to connect with inspiring figures across so many different fields. In the Pantene commercial, I made friends with one of the other ambassadors, Paris Lees, a journalist and transgender activist. She was so smart and funny, I loved being in the same room as her, but it wasn't until after the shoot when I read her pieces that I learned so much more about her, and began to realise just how much she had gone through. I'm glad that amazing, positive role models like Paris exist to educate us all. She is a beacon of hope and positivity in the trans community and I'm honoured we get to work together.

I'd learned to take campaigns and magazine pieces in my stride by then, until one shoot changed that. To this day I class it as the shoot that changed my life, and it is one of the wildest moments in my career to date, both in and outside the ring. It all started when I got an email from Laura Bailey – the brilliant photographer who had made me feel at ease the second we met. She had mentioned my story to her editors at *Vogue*, and had managed to land me a small feature in an upcoming issue. I was stunned – *Vogue*. Actual *Vogue*. I read and reread the email over and over until the letters turn into symbols etched into the screen. It was supposed to be for a small column where I'd be profiled by a journalist and photographed by Laura, but a few weeks later she called me to say the feature had been bumped up. Along with fourteen other women, I had been selected to be part of a special issue: we were going to be on the cover of the magazine. I still have no words to describe the feeling of being asked to be on the cover of *Vogue*. I could never have foreseen this, and the fact that it was alongside fourteen others didn't take away from the achievement, it made it even more memorable. I arrived, a complete bag of nerves, and with a black eye from sparring the previous week. I was terrified the photographer would be angry and everyone would judge me, but after ten minutes meeting the likes of model and activist Adwoa Aboah and actress Gemma Chan, I found myself laughing and joking with them as if we were old friends. We couldn't get enough of each other. The theme of the magazine was 'Forces for Change', and each woman was in some way making a positive contribution to society.

As I heard their stories, I grew more and more excited by all that inspiration in one room. I got talking with disability activist Sinéad Burke about the Inclusive Fashion and Design Collective that she'd co-founded. Like me, Adut Akech was a former refugee who now used her modelling career to push for diversity in the fashion industry. All of us couldn't be more different – activists and actors, politicians and dancers – and yet there was a clear thread that united us all. We weren't just individuals excelling in our field; we were all fighting for change, for a future that looked fairer, for a future that looked just like us.

Just before I was called to go on set, I met Edward

Enninful. Two years prior to our shoot, he had made history by becoming the first Black editor-in-chief of the publication. I was so overwhelmed to meet him that our conversation was a short one. He thanked me for being in the issue, and I thanked him back, profusely, for putting this young Black boxer with a black eye on the cover of the most famous fashion publication in the world. The photographer shooting us that day was Peter Lindbergh, an infamous German artist, and an icon of contemporary photography. I was nervous about meeting him too, and even more nervous about getting in front of his camera, but I shouldn't have been. It turned out he was a massive boxing fan, not just one of the new fans who follow Anthony Joshua and Tyson Fury, but a real connoisseur. His knowledge was extensive, and we got into a great conversation about vintage boxing; talking about legendary promoters like Don King and Arturo Gatti, an Italian Canadian fighter who completely owned the circuit in the nineties. When I look at those pictures now, I can see that he completely captured the real me. Maybe it's because we were so engrossed in our conversation about the great champions, or maybe it was a by-product of being in the same room as all of those incredibly inspiring women, but he captured my soul in those images. Sadly, Peter passed away less than a year after our meeting in 2019. I'll forever be honoured that I got to sit in front of his lens.

I knew I was participating in a special-edition issue honouring women who were making real change in their fields. However, when one of my agents told me that there was a possibility that Meghan Markle was behind it all – I was stunned. Her involvement as guest editor of *Vogue* wasn't confirmed until days before the issue came out. I didn't know what to say when I found out, and I couldn't muster up many more words when we finally got a chance to speak. I was back training, in a sweaty windowless boxing gym, working on the bag when the call came through. My hair was damp with sweat and I couldn't contain the heavy panting of my breath through the receiver as I listened to her talk about what a special issue we had all been part of. I hung on to every word of her soft American accent. I didn't know what exactly to say for shortness of breath, and the shock of what was happening, so I just thanked her again and again for picking me and recognising me as a force for change. I really, really was thankful. Looking around me at the gym as we said goodbye, the reality of straddling two completely different worlds struck me, and yet it felt so natural. I knew I was exactly where I was supposed to be.

The opportunities I've been given in the last few years never cease to amaze me. In an incredibly short time I have found myself travelling the world to fight one day, and sitting on the front row of fashion shows or being invited to celebrity-filled parties in New York the next. But the truth is, the most important opportunities are *always* the ones where I can use the platform that I've grown to try and give back to my community. I almost always skip the parties, and though I have met so many influential people in the last few years, my closest friends are still the ones I made in boxing gyms. Muhammad Ali once said that 'Service to others is the rent you pay for your room here on earth,' and that's exactly how I feel. Growing up, we were the ones on the receiving end of other people's kindness and generosity. We didn't have a lot, but what we lacked in material wealth, we made up for in the richness of our close-knit family; and when we really needed help, there were so many people and organisations that supported us. Now that I'm older and more self-sufficient, I want to give back, just like the inspiring people who helped us out when times were hard. That's why the Sisters Club is one of the most important achievements in my life. I have experienced racism – online and offline – my whole life, and that's what drove me to create a safe space where any woman of any race, religion, from any community can come and work out, learn new skills and meet other people without fear of prejudice. Giving back to my community is what motivates me the most, and I do it in any way that I can. I became an ambassador for the brand Coach in 2019. Going to fancy fashion shows and wearing their clothes is the smallest part of our partnership; I'm even prouder to be part of their Dream It Real campaign, an initiative supporting young people as they decide what career to go into. I've gone into schools and given speeches about how I turned my dream into reality. I've talked about the failures along the way, I've talked about how I grew up on a council estate and achieved a life way beyond anything I was taught to imagine or could see was possible for a girl like me. It's amazing to be in a room full of kids; there's so much ambition and potential. My role was small – in encouraging them to think big, to follow their dreams and not be afraid, I was lighting a fire they already had in them.

In December 2019, I became a Unicef ambassador. I was invited to visit Za'atari refugee camp in Jordan, the world's largest camp for Syrian refugees, to see the organisation in action. At its peak (sometime in 2018), the camp had become Jordan's fourth biggest city, housing around 150,000 refugees. On arrival we were met by miles and miles of makeshift homes: clusters of UN agency branded white tents, corrugated iron structures and run-down caravans. There was one main market street that sold food and supplies, which was ironically referred to as the Champs-Elysées. To me it showed how hard it was to crush a human spirit; sometimes you can lose everything, but still manage to have a sense of humour, a sense of hope. No one should ever have to live the way the people I met were living. It was freezing. The camp was overcrowded, a lot of the tents leaked, and there was minimal access to electricity and running water. It was heartbreaking to see, but despite this, so many of the people I met carried with them a strong sense of hope. When I was younger I was embarrassed to admit I was a refugee, but when the kids I met that day excitedly asked me, 'Who are you? What are you doing here?' I couldn't have been prouder to explain that I'd been in the same boat as them once, that I admired their resilience and energy and that I knew they would make it through. This had been the reality of my life and my family's life for so long – all the makeshift and temporary places we had to make home in, the queues my parents stood in for hours every day to get rations from charities and NGOs, the places we passed through while waiting to make it to the UK. If it hadn't been for the work of incredible charities, NGOs and the kindness of strangers, there's no way I would be where I am today.

I spent most of my days there at the Makani ('My Space') centre, which provides education and psychosocial support to the camp's children. Sport is a big part of that; and the centre runs martial arts lessons; during my stay, I got to run my own boxing classes. When I'm training, everything else slips away. It doesn't matter whether I'm in the ring, sparring or just shadow-boxing alone; I don't need to be wearing kit or gloves to feel that sense of urgency. All my focus is on working my body, I think about nothing else but every slip and shot. I saw that in the children I worked with; the transcendental power of doing something you love. It may have been temporary, but for half an hour they could punch and play, they could get to be children again. I found myself particularly drawn to this one girl called Shahd. She was about twelve, and had emerald-green eyes and long brown hair which she always wore down, flying across her shoulders. She was a complete ball of energy with the most contagious giggle. We couldn't understand each other, but she was a natural at boxing, imitating my movements perfectly. I loved the way she struck at the pads with every last bit of energy she could muster. She reminded me of when I first started out; when I was given something to hit, I'd go at it until my arms were aching and my knuckles were stinging. That's the power and the hold boxing has always had on me. To some people, it looks violent, but for me, it's where I found peace. You might feel like your world is crumbling around you, but getting to do something you love is a small salvation that nobody can take away from you; you are your own champion. When I came home after that trip, I thanked God that I had found myself in sport, and I made a promise to myself that I would keep using my position to fight for others. The people I met in Za'atari deserved so much more, just like our family did when we too were fleeing hardship and violence.

As an athlete, you naturally want to be a champion. Winning a fight is the most unbeatable feeling, but it's one that will not last forever. Most women boxers retire in their thirties. In a few years, I too will have ended my fighting career. I am ready for my next adventure. That's why I put the same energy into the work I do outside of the ring with Unicef, with Coach, with the Sisters Club – because I know it's what really matters, and it matters so much more than any fight. I have fallen in love with boxing and it has changed my life. It's allowed me to gain an incredible platform where I can share what I have learned with others and offer support to my community. Sport has taught me all about hard work and perseverance and when it is no longer an everyday part of my life, I will still have those skills. I know deep down that I want to create a legacy that long outlasts my boxing career. I want to be remembered for using my platform to help others, I want to be remembered for putting in the work. I believe that we all have it within us to become a champion, both to ourselves and the people around us. I'm not talking about winning medals and being at the top of your game. To me, being a champion is about each of us using our unique position in the world to make it a better place. That comes from discovering your passions and finding your community, but it also comes from asking yourself what you have to offer others. I always dreamed of becoming the greatest boxer I could be, but when I look back on the moments I am most proud of, I realise that they rarely took place inside the ring. The older I have got, the more aware I have become of the prevalence of injustice and the responsibility we all have in fighting it. We all have a fighter within us – make time to bring that person out. Whether you use your words, your skills, your platform, your power or your influence, remember that to be a true champion, you must look out for others, you must leave a legacy.

My name is Ramla Said Ahmed Ali Bana Shooble Ahmed Hajji Sharif Ali. I am a fighter. I am a daughter, a wife, a sister, a friend. Sometimes I am a model, mostly I am a boxer. I am an activist and I am a champion. I strive to be a voice for people who have been silenced, I promise to never stop learning; I promise never to give up without a fight. This is not where my story ends – quite the opposite – this is just the beginning, for me and for you.

ROUND TEN

Champions are made in the toughest moments

During a difficult fight, my entire body is in pain. My knuckles sting, my ankles hurt from the constant movement, and the dull ache in my triceps from keeping my arms raised the whole time becomes almost unbearable. It's in these moments that a weaker fighter will give up; they will throw lazy shots that don't land because they don't have enough energy to hit with speed and force, or they will drop their arms, leaving themselves exposed. Learning to power through the toughest times is something I learned in boxing, and still apply to life outside the ring. It's easy to act with pride and integrity when everything's going well; but remember how to behave on the bad days, as that's when real champions are made.

Be authentic

When people I didn't know started taking an interest in my life, I felt a lot of pressure. I've always been a private person, but as my story resonated and my platform grew, I began to lose some of the anonymity I'd had my whole life. I realised the only way I could reconcile my private life with my public life was to act with authenticity at all times. I wanted to be liked, I wanted the opportunities I was getting to keep coming, but I never wanted to become something that I am not. You can't please everyone; so never change for someone else. Never lose sight of who you are in order to try and please others.

Create a legacy

I don't want to be remembered for winning boxing matches, I want to be remembered for the things I've done outside the ring. Our time on this planet isn't long; fight for change and stand up for what you believe in.

Fight for others

I have experienced sexism, I have experienced racism and I have experienced Islamophobia. I know how devastating it is to be on the receiving end of hate, how severe an impact it can have, and how victims carry it with them their whole lives. Maybe you have experienced it too, or perhaps you've been lucky enough not to have had hatred poured on you for the way you look, the place you're from, the things you believe or the person you're attracted to. Either way, we all have a duty to speak up and fight for the oppressed. I don't need to have directly experienced ableism, anti-Semitism, homophobia or transphobia to know that it is wrong. Learn about what others go through, and when you see prejudice, call it out. Never let yourself benefit from the discrimination of others. Learn how to be an ally to the best of your ability.

Never give up without a fight

Some fights are won in an hour; others take a whole life-time and then some. We might not always win straight away, but that shouldn't stop us from trying our best. We all have a fighter within us; think about the injustices you can fight and the communities you can fight for. Stand up for yourself and for your loved ones. Use your unique skills and your position in the world. You are not power-less. Believe in yourself. Be strong, be brave and never give up, not without a fight.

ACKNOWLEDGEMENTS

This book, like the rest of my achievements, would not have been possible without my parents. So Mum, Dad – thank you. You are my biggest role models, and the single strongest force that has shaped me into the person I am today. You were never afraid to be fearless in times of adversity. In the face of danger you always fought for what you believed in, and you instilled those qualities into me from a very young age; you are the ones who taught me how to become a fighter.

I am so grateful to Richard Moore. One partner, many different roles: he is my coach, my husband, my team. I'd already been boxing for the best part of a decade, but I never realised just how far I could take it until he entered my life and made me see my own potential. Together, we embarked on a task that often seemed impossible. His unwavering belief and constant support has got me to where I am today.

Thank you to Danika, my best friend and the woman who taught me how to be fearless. She has always led by example, and it's through watching the way Danika moves through the world that I have learned to stand up for myself.

When it comes to boxing, there are many people who have helped me become a skilled fighter. Terry Palmer took a chance on me at a time when a lot of people didn't care about women's boxing. He imparted so much wisdom and knowledge to me, and prepared me for the ring in a way that went far beyond training.

I have so much gratitude for my friends Laird and Valerian; they truly made me believe I could fly. They planted a seed in my head which started a ripple effect of everything that has followed. If it wasn't for them, so many of my proudest achievements would never have happened.

Hassan Abukar showed me so much generosity and kindness despite the fact I was a stranger to him. Thank you to Hassan for backing my dreams.

To Emma, Christine and Daniella at IMG Models – I never saw myself entering the world of fashion, and it would not have happened if it wasn't for all of you. I was so scared to go to our first meeting, but you made me feel valued and safe, as you have continued to do on all my shoots. I have grown to love modelling and my fashion work has proven instrumental in funding my boxing career; without signing to IMG I would not have been able to continue fighting.

Thank you to Shannon Mahanty, Lemara Lindsay-Prince and #Merky Books for giving me the platform and opportunity to share my story and, in doing so, not shy away from my story. #Merky Books were the perfect fit, they were less concerned about conforming to a specific format and more eager to ensure that young Black voices were being heard, which is a real testament to their approach in literature and everything they are trying to achieve as a publishing imprint.

Finally, I would like to thank anyone who has ever

stood in my way. To the people who doubted me, the ones who told me no; to anyone who has ever made me feel like I was not enough, I remember you. Your words and your actions hurt me, but I proved you wrong. Look at me now, you fuelled my fight. I have nothing but gratitude for you, from the bottom of my heart, thank you.